The Philosophy Scare

The Philosophy Scare

THE POLITICS OF REASON
IN THE EARLY COLD WAR

John McCumber

The University of Chicago Press CHICAGO & LONDON

The University of Chicago Press, Chicago 60637
The University of Chicago Press, Ltd., London
© 2016 by The University of Chicago
All rights reserved. Published 2016.

Printed in the United States of America

25 24 23 22 21 20 19 18 17 16   1 2 3 4 5

ISBN-13: 978-0-226-39638-5 (cloth)
ISBN-13: 978-0-226-39641-5 (e-book)
DOI: 10.7208/chicago/978-0-226-39641-5.001.0001

Library of Congress Cataloging-in-Publication Data
Names: McCumber, John, author.
Title: The philosophy scare : the politics of reason in the early Cold War / John McCumber.
Description: Chicago : The University of Chicago Press, 2016. |
Includes bibliographical references and index.
Identifiers: LCCN 2016005510 | ISBN 9780226396385 (cloth : alk. paper) |
ISBN 9780226396415 (e-book)
Subjects: LCSH: Philosophy—Study and teaching—Political aspects—California—
History—20th century. | Academic freedom—California—History—20th century. |
University of California, Los Angeles. Department of Philosophy—History—
20th century. | Philosophy—Political aspects—United States—History—
20th century. | Cold War. | Rational choice theory—Political aspects—
United States. | Naturalism—Political aspects—United States. |
United States—Intellectual life—20th century—Political aspects.
Classification: LCC B52.3.U6 M33 2016 | DDC 191—dc23 LC record available at
http://lccn.loc.gov/2016005510

♾ This paper meets the requirements of ANSI/NISO Z39.48-1992 (Permanence of Paper).

In memory of David L. Hull, colleague, friend, and teacher—
because philosophy is a process, too

CONTENTS

ABBREVIATIONS

AA: Kant, Akademie-Ausgabe (publisher of Kant's *Gesammelte Schriften*, 1902–).

CAF: Joseph Drumheller, *Communism and Academic Freedom* (1949).

CPR: Kant, *Critique of Pure Reason* (B edition, vol. 3 of AA).

CUAC: Annual Reports of the California State Senate Fact-Finding Subcommittee on Un-American Activities; cited by report number and year (1950–1970). UCLA Library.

HUAC: House Un-American Activities Committee.

MECO: Raymond B. Allen, *Medical Education and the Changing Order* (1946).

MOA: Max Otto Archives, Wisconsin Historical Society, Madison, WI.

RCT: rational choice theory.

RSP: Hans Reichenbach, *The Rise of Scientific Philosophy* (1951).

SCIV: Kenneth Arrow, *Social Choice and Individual Values* (1963; first published in 1951). References to the 1963 addendum "Notes on the Theory of Social Choice" included in the second edition are abbreviated *SCIV*(A).

SSR: Kuhn, *The Structure of Scientific Revolutions* (1962). References to the 1969 "Postscript" are abbreviated *SSR*(PS).

TD: John McCumber, *Time in the Ditch: American Philosophy and the McCarthy Era* (2000).

TL: Hans Meyerhoff, *Time in Literature* (1955).

UCLAA: UCLA Archives, Los Angeles. Unless otherwise noted, all letters cited in the following prologue are in UCLAA, series 410, box 3. Letters dated 11 March 1947 or before are in folder 2; letters dated 12 March 1947 and after are in folder 3.

"US": Paul Oppenheim and Hilary Putnam, "The Unity of Science as a Working Hypothesis" (1958).

Aristotle is cited from the Bekker edition; Plato, from the Stephanus edition.

On February 24, 1947, the *Los Angeles Examiner*, the city's Hearst newspaper, published an article bearing the headline "Otto, Center of Atheistic Row, to Teach at UCLA."[1] Prominently placed in the center of the local news page, the article reported the hiring of Max Otto, a well-known philosopher at the University of Wisconsin, to be UCLA's Flint Professor of Philosophy for the coming fall term.

The Flint Professorship was only a one-semester appointment, but hardly an ordinary one. University of California president Robert G. Sproul characterized it, in his formal offer letter to Otto, as "perhaps the most distinguished endowed chair on the Los Angeles campus," and, according to the UCLA *General Catalogue*, it was held in succession by such luminaries as C. D. Broad (1952–53), Alonzo Church (1960–61), H. L. A. Hart (1961–62), Alfred Tarski (1966–67), and Friedrich von Hayek (1968–69).[2]

Otto's "atheistic row," the *Examiner* explained, had been provoked years before by his contribution to the anthology, *Is There a God?* (Wieman 1932). Drawn in part from articles Otto had written for *The Christian Century*, in dialogue with theologians but advocating atheism, the book had attracted the attention of an unsuccessful political candidate for various offices, John B. Chapple. Chapple's efforts to enlist clergy against Otto's employment at the University of Wisconsin had had only mixed success, the *Examiner* reported, because other clerics, as well as the university administration, had strongly defended him. Otto not only kept his job but eventually became chair of the Wisconsin Philosophy Department and president of the Western (now Central) Division of the American Philosophical Association.

The *Examiner*'s revelations struck a chord in a southern California so deeply religious that two years later, Billy Graham's eight-week Crusade for Christ would attract three hundred and fifty thousand people to the corner of Washington and Hill Streets—from an overall civic population of less than two million.[3] Within a month of the *Examiner* article, the UCLA philosophy department had received slightly more than two hundred letters of protest from religious conservatives. One arrived on the letterhead of Aimee Semple McPherson's Foursquare Gospel Church, headed then by her son Rolf (as it was until his retirement in 1997);[4] another, on that of the Council of Catholic Women of the Archdiocese of Los Angeles. Most, however, were from concerned individuals.

The campaign was directed not only against Otto personally but against philosophy itself as an academic discipline. Philosophy's special place as a target of American antisubversives had been established on the East Coast in 1940, when Bertrand Russell was appointed to teach at City College, New York. The appointment was bitterly opposed by religious authorities because of Russell's well-known libertinism and atheism. One of the arguments used by Russell's defenders was that he had been appointed to teach logic and mathematics, not metaphysics or sexual morality; but the judge who decided the case, John E. McGeehan, ruled otherwise: "It has been argued that he is going to teach mathematics. His appointment, however, is to the department of philosophy at City College" (quoted in Monk 2001, 237).

Russell's appointment in philosophy was pronounced dangerous to the "public health, safety, and morals," and Russell, who at the time was basically a war refugee, had to withdraw his acceptance of the post.[5] The publicity concerning this case was nationwide: it inspired a lawsuit in Los Angeles that sought to strip Russell, who was at that point teaching at UCLA, of his appointment there. The case was thrown out of court. But Russell did not have tenure, and the university's president, Robert G. Sproul, sent him packing anyway.[6]

Otto, unlike Russell, appears to have led an exemplary personal life, even by the puritanical standards of mid-twentieth-century America; the complaints about his appointment were strictly motivated by his "atheism," and that meant by his philosophy. Thus, several of the anti-Otto letters pointed out that it was Otto's appointment in a *philosophy* department that gave him, in the words of one writer, "free course to propagate his atheistic doctrines."[7] This view was seconded by one Stanley Thatcher: "If you had engaged Professor Otto to teach any other subject, it would be very well for you to say, you or the University were neutral, but you have engaged him to teach Philosophy. May I

ask you 'what is *his* Philosophy?' Isn't it Atheism? Doesn't it follow therefore that he will actually be teaching atheism to the youth of UCLA? . . . A copy
of this letter is being sent to each member of the Board of Regents."[8] The letter of a Miss M. McEwan provides further evidence that this sort of widespread
and passionate response would not have been forthcoming if Otto had been
hired to teach, say, biology or French: "I am not writing this hoping that Prof.
Otto's appointment as a teacher at the University be cancelled, but I do hope
you will give him another subject to teach in place of Philosophy."[9]

What happened to Otto after that, as we will see in chapter 1, is a matter of
deep obscurity, some of it clearly intentional. One thing, however, is certain:
Max Otto never served as Flint Professor at UCLA.[10]

Introduction

The evidence seems to me overwhelming that there is a definite historical connection between the social movements of a period and its dominant metaphysical teachings.

SIDNEY HOOK, "Naturalism and Democracy"

On evidence to be presented in this book, the domestic tumult of the early Cold War favored the dominance of a "new and improved" philosophical paradigm, better adapted to the times than what was already on campus. I will call it "Cold War philosophy." Composed of heterogeneous elements that mainly had in common a mathematical veneer and their adaptability to Cold War political pressures, this "new and improved" version of philosophy valorized concepts of scientific objectivity and practices of market freedom, while prudently downplaying the anti-theistic implications of modern thought. Encouraged by "sticks" wielded by forces outside the university and by "carrots" proffered from within, this paradigm speedily came to underlie work in many disciplines. In some areas, it still does; in others, its rejection was not only definitive but, as we will see in the epilogue, explosive.

Cold War philosophy's role in postwar American intellectual life, though important, has gone largely unseen. One reason for this is that, as is usually the case, crucial developments in the early Cold War were overlain by multiple layers of chaos and confusion; the transitory was easily mistaken for the decisive and vice versa. Another reason is psychological. Modern governments generally pride themselves on the free rein they give to academia, while scholars pride themselves on their intellectual autonomy. Few administrators, and even fewer professors, would enjoy stating openly that their scholarly lives had responded to political forces.[1] Add to this the academic community's traditional penchant for confidentiality, which as Hannah Arendt pointed out can be traced back to the death of Socrates (Arendt 1958, 12), and one thing becomes clear: the full extent of political depredations on academic life will always be understated.

Yet another factor obscuring political pressures on academia is that they can arrive from disparate origins and operate in very different ways, which makes it hard to see whether and how they worked together. In the case of Cold War philosophy, some pressures arrived sporadically, like sudden blows from sticks wielded by the public at large (see chapter 1). Others came on steadily from well-funded heights of government and academic privilege, and worked on academics as carrots (see chapter 3). Still others originated within universities themselves, as their administrators were increasingly co-opted into the anti-Communist fight (see chapter five). The discourses on which they impinged, moreover, were of fundamentally different types. When philosophers talked about "objects" during the early Cold War, they could be smacked, if not into obedience, into systematic stealthiness (see chapter 2). But when philosophers were discoursing on the "subject" (i.e., the rational mind; i.e., themselves), they were also quite capable of succumbing to carrots (see chapter 4).

Finding our way through all these thickets poses serious methodological problems. Michel Foucault and Thomas Kuhn have blazed the conceptual pathways that I follow, and I begin with a short and selective discussion of their views.

FROM PARADIGMS TO DISPOSITIVES

For both Foucault and Kuhn, the claims of universal reason have been moderated in favor of a pluralism of local approaches.[2] Individual investigators can therefore be affected by things like cultural conditions without surrendering their rationality, and such is the case with these two. Where Kuhn, the American, is interested in how what he calls "paradigms" relate to the individual investigators who pursue them, Foucault, the Frenchman, is concerned with the way sociopolitical forces external to the academy constitute what he calls "dispositives." For present purposes, then, each thinker's approach fills a gap in the other's. Kuhn's discussion of the "internal" relations between an approach and its own adherents is both richer and more explicit than Foucault's, whose de-emphasis of the investigating individual ("Do not ask me who I am, and do not tell me to remain the same" [Foucault 1972, 17]) leads to aporias in his accounts of his own procedures (see McCumber 2000a, 110–40). It is Foucault, however, who opens up what most needs exploring here—the dark realm of sociopolitical pressures that influence academic discourse, so to speak, from below. I begin from above, with Kuhn.

Kuhn's 1962 *The Structure of Scientific Revolutions (SSR)* has, like the middle chapters of Hegel's *Phenomenology of Spirit*, a curiously dialectical title. Where Hegel gave us "the spiritual kingdom of animals," "pleasure and necessity," and "the law of the heart," Kuhn investigates the "structure of scientific revolutions," as if revolutions were not moments when structures fall to the ground. The reason for this unification of opposites is that Kuhn, like Hegel, is talking about processes that, being processes, do not end as they begin.[3] Scientific revolutions arise for Kuhn from "crises" fomented by the accumulation and recognition of anomalies in an accepted theory or set of theories (*SSR*, 67). At a certain point, a new approach occurs by accident to one or a few minds, usually young (*SSR*, 90, 144). Others then "convert" to it (*SSR*, 150–58). Inculcated by early scientific training (*SSR*, 136–37), it ramifies, rigidifies, and finally becomes subject to a crisis of its own (*SSR*, 64–67). The revolutionary process is thus structured, and what undergoes it is what Kuhn calls a "paradigm."

Kuhn's notion of a scientific paradigm is elusive, and the elusiveness is not merely a matter of his presentation.[4] Not only do paradigms exist and function differently at different stages of their life cycles, but, as guides to research, they are necessarily both open-ended (*SSR*, 10) and comprised of heterogeneous commitments—"conceptual, theoretical, instrumental, and methodological" (*SSR*, 41), as well as institutional (*SSR*, 11). Kuhn's best characterization of paradigms is perhaps his first: they are "universally recognized scientific achievements that for a time provide model problems and solutions to a community of practitioners" (*SSR*, viii). This brings problems of its own, however, for the very status of paradigms as models means that their service is not always fully explicit. Imitation is a matter of degree, and scientists can imitate a paradigm without knowing exactly which features of it they are imitating (*SSR*, 46).

Paradigms are therefore obscure, even to their own adherents. That they even exist was hardly obvious at the time of Kuhn's writing, and two of his arguments for that existence need attention here. First, since later scientific discoveries lead to theories that make different predictions than earlier ones, they are not logically compatible with their predecessors; scientific progress is not a cumulative matter of adding new truths and theories to old ones, but involves leaps—that is, revolutions (*SSR*, 97–99). What these leap from and to, then, are paradigms.

A second reason for thinking that there are such things as paradigms, emphasized in Kuhn's 1969 "Postscript," is the empirical fact that scientists form distinct communities: there is observable overlap among membership in certain societies, publication in certain journals, and citation by certain colleagues (*SSR*[PS]), 176–77). These networks of scientific collaboration are to some extent closed against outsiders. Their members share a variety of commitments about which problems are the most important, which methods and instruments are best for tackling them, what should count as a solution, and so on (see *SSR*[PS]), 182).

Thus, if we want to identify (for example) a philosophical paradigm, it often helps to descend from philosophy itself, as a set of doctrines and arguments, to the level of the people who do philosophy. On that level, we find that a paradigm is accepted and sustained by two complementary processes that Kuhn calls "conversion" and "inculcation." Conversion refers to the acceptance of a new paradigm by individuals already practicing in the wider field. Insofar as it is rational, it is inspired by the new paradigm's promise to resolve certain "puzzles," which are perceived as urgent, but with which the current paradigm cannot deal (*SSR* 23, 153, 169; *SSR*[PS]), 206). This promise, however, is rarely compelling at the outset, when the new paradigm is still too undeveloped to have adequately solved many such puzzles (*SSR*, 156–57). So conversion in science, as in religion, usually amounts to a sudden and mysterious shift in allegiance that comes about through what Kuhn calls "the individual's sense of the appropriate or the aesthetic" (*SSR*, 155).

A paradigm already in place is sustained through inculcation. Inculcation relies on authority (*SSR*, 80, 136), and its main vehicle is the textbook, which seeks to explain the field to young people who may subsequently become members of it (*SSR*, 20–21, 165). A textbook conveys a single paradigm, with little sense of its alternatives. There is no place in it for critical evaluation of the paradigm itself, and indeed the authority of textbooks helps inoculate the paradigm against such scrutiny (*SSR*, 136).

Given the elusive nature of paradigms, even to their own practitioners, one may wonder how accurate the portrait of a paradigm in a given textbook can actually be; in fact, Kuhn writes, textbooks tend to falsify the nature of science in general, and so of paradigms themselves. Concerned to convey the currently standing results of the paradigm they are inculcating, textbooks present science as a cumulative process in which new theories are presented as following old ones in progression—like bricks in a wall (*SSR*, 140), with each brick better than the last. Inculcation thus provides "a narrow and rigid education, probably more so than any other except perhaps in orthodox theology" (*SSR*, 166).

More than uncritical, scientific inculcation for Kuhn is in some respects actually unconscious, operating on a neural level. To "perceive" objects, Kuhn argues, is to group them by similarity; and while the general ability to do this is innate—no human would last long without it—the particular groupings themselves are acquired (*SSR*, 111–13; *SSR*[PS]), 189). These learned perceptions—which, I note, may be learned from textbooks—are epistemic bedrock: they constitute the "fundamental components of immediate experience" (*SSR*, 129). As a result of this unconscious rewiring of their perceptual capacities, the world "looks different" to scientists in different paradigms (*SSR*, 150), whose minds are different from the neural level up.

One thus belongs to a scientific community, for Kuhn, in a *bodily* way: adherence to a given paradigm is in part a matter of the neural circuits produced by one's inculcation (or, sometimes, by "conversion"). This makes adherence to a paradigm absolute, and gives the scientific community vast power over individual scientists, for the paradigm determines not only which puzzles its adherents seek to solve (*SSR*, 5, 24) but what they perceive as the facts of the case (*SSR*, 141). Since what determines an individual's place within the scientific community is her ability to solve puzzles (*SSR*, 80), the scientific community becomes the "exclusive arbiter of professional achievement" (*SSR*, 168): "What better criterion than the decision of scientific groups could there be?" (*SSR*, 170; also see *SSR*, 167).

The Kuhnian scientific community thus operates independently of outside authority. Empirically speaking, communication even from one group of scientists to another is "arduous" and often precarious (*SSR*[PS]), 177). Thus, there is in practice "no higher standard" than the assent of the relevant scientific community (*SSR*, 94). In a long passage that must be quoted *in extenso*, Kuhn tells us that the "mature" scientific community exists

in unparalleled isolation from the demands of the laity and of everyday life. . . . There are no other professional communities in which individual creative work is so exclusively addressed to and evaluated by other members of the profession. . . . Just because he is working only for an audience of colleagues, an audience that shares his own values and beliefs, the scientist can take a single set of standards for granted. He need not worry about what some other group or school will think and can therefore dispose of one problem and get on to the next more quickly than those who work for a more heterodox group. (*SSR*, 164)

The inefficacy of more general standards for scientific achievement means, via obvious parsimony, that there are no such standards: "There is no neutral algorithm for theory-choice, no systematic decision-procedure which, properly applied, must lead each individual in the group to the same decision. In this sense it is the community of specialists rather than its individual members that makes the effective decision" (*SSR*[PS], 206). The community of colleagues thus stands above the individual scientist, but nothing stands above it. It has displaced not only the individual scientist but universal reason itself. This leaves little unity over to science in general, which "seems to be a rather ramshackle structure with little coherence among its various parts" (*SSR*, 49). The Kuhnian scientific community, bounded against outsiders and governed only by the intellectual commitments conveyed by its paradigm, thus exercises what I have elsewhere called "dispositive" power over its members: it constitutes them *as* members in the first place, and then orders their activities (McCumber 1999, 14).

As directed against overall accounts of science and, indeed, of reason itself, Kuhn's work has been highly influential: few philosophers of science today profess the "brick-by-brick" orthodoxy he confronted in 1962. But when Kuhn's invocation of the autonomy of the scientific community is taken to mean its freedom from pressures emerging from society at large, it becomes less plausible. After all, the primary example of such autonomy at the time of Kuhn's writing was the Manhattan Project, sponsored by his own intellectual godfather James Bryant Conant (see *SSR*, xi). Research on the project may have been conducted in places of "unparalleled isolation," such as Alamogordo, New Mexico, and Oak Ridge, Tennessee, but it was organized and paid for by the American government in order to develop an atomic bomb.[5] That Kuhn recognizes that isolation from daily life and society hardly buys automatic independence from political factors becomes evident when he argues for his exclusion of them: "Explicit consideration of [external social, economic, and intellectual conditions] would not, I think, modify the main theses developed in this essay, but it would surely add an analytical dimension of first-rate importance for the understanding of scientific advance" (*SSR*, x). The exclusion is defended here, but not explained. In view of it, however, there is perhaps no surprise in learning that when Kuhn discusses his main example of the importance of such "external" factors, which is the Copernican Revolution, he lists social pressures for calendar reform, medieval criticisms of Aristotle, and Renaissance Neoplatonism—but not Christianity.[6]

The Kuhnian scientific community thus has autonomy vis-à-vis universal reason, but not as against the power and turbulence of sociopolitical developments. It would be nice if defenses against such turbulence were unneeded—if we could simply accept Kuhn's assurances that in "mature" scientific communities at least, sociopolitical currents never carry intellectual disciplines along with them. Such being obviously not the case, we must turn elsewhere—to Michel Foucault. Where Kuhn moved us from doctrines and arguments to the community of scientific practitioners, we can see Foucault as taking us down another level: from the scientific community to the darker realm of sociopolitical forces and of what Foucault calls "power."

Consider, for example, Foucault's discussion of an institution with "especially exemplary," or paradigmatic, status, one that functions like a Kuhnian paradigm within an isolated network of participants. As a "privileged place for experiments," it formulates its own heterogeneous set of commitments. One joins this institution, not through choice, but by conviction. Once within, one is subject to the institution's control over one's perceptions, a control that "induces a state of consciousness and permanent visibility that assures the automatic functioning of power."[7] The institution in question, to be sure, is not a scientific community. It is Jeremy Bentham's Panopticon, his plan for a prison in which an inward-facing ring of cells surrounds a central tower, occupied by guards, so that the guards can see into each cell at all times but no cell has an unobstructed view into another one.

The political dimension of the Panopticon opens up at that very center: any member of society has the right to enter the observation tower and observe the guards, to see if they are performing their jobs well (Foucault 1979, 207). For all its closure, the prison is thus regulated from outside in a way the Kuhnian scientific community is not. The regulation, moreover, is not performed by a designated group of experts, but merely by members of society at large, including both relatively organized political forces coming from government and relatively disorganized ones coming from such social sectors as "commerce" and "industry" (Foucault 1979, 308). It follows that regulatory initiatives vary widely in strength and origin. Where a paradigm for Kuhn already contains, as we saw, widely heterogeneous components, for Foucault the heterogeneity is greater still, comprising such things as "discourses, institutions, architectural forms, regulatory decisions" (Foucault 1980, 194), and the like. This sort of sociopolitically vulnerable paradigm is what Foucault calls a *dispositif*. The term is often translated as "apparatus" (see Agamben 2009) and sometimes as "deployment" (Foucault 1990, 75), but apparatuses are intentional, while deployments are applications of something else. In view of its connection to my own analysis of domination, noted earlier, I prefer "dispositive."

All this heterogeneity, for Foucault, is governed by a single basic distinction: that between the sociopolitical pressures on a dispositive, the strategic "relations of forces" which bring it into being or affect it; and the "types of knowledge," the discourses themselves that are founded on and in turn support these (Foucault 1980, 196). The former, just because they come from disparate regions, may be external, not only to science in general, but to all organized knowledge. They may count as "irrational" and even, as with Bentham's prison, as coercive.

The distinction between strategies of force and forms of knowledge is admittedly rough-and-ready; it is hard, for example, not to see rational choice theory, which I discuss in chapter 3, as both. Perhaps the best way to sharpen it would be functionally: a "strategy of force" can be defined for present purposes as a practice, discursive or not, that affects other discourses in ways independent of its own rational validity—where "rational validity" must itself be defined contextually.

On this level, what corresponds to Kuhn's relatively benign concepts of conversion and inculcation is an often rawer kind of process that can be called "subjectivation" because it produces minds, or "subjects," that adhere to the paradigm, and does so by "subjecting" those minds to various disciplinary imperatives through force of some kind. The nature of subjectivation, in abstract terms, is clear: it is the production, by the relations of force that form a dispositive, of the people who in one way or another adhere to that dispositive. As Giorgio Agamben puts it, a Foucaldian dispositive thus begins as something external to the knower, but is then internalized—a process that results in a new type of knower or knowing subject (Agamben 2009, 11). This account is general enough to include Kuhnian conversion and inculcation, with the changes they introduce in neural structure, and much else besides; as I use the term, *subjectivation* differs from conversion and inculcation in that it is exercised, not by a scientific community itself, but by diverse sociopolitical forces external to it. The diversity means that the abstract account of subjectivation just given cannot be filled in. Where Kuhn could discuss conversion and inculcation in some detail as general themes, subjectivation for Foucault can only be pursued locally, via "microhistorical" descriptions of individual cases.[8]

Kuhn and Foucault thus turn out to complement one another. Both claim that disciplinary communities are closed, each governed by a heterogeneous set of commitments unique to itself. For Foucault, these commitments are vulnerable to sociopolitical developments. Kuhn excludes such developments from his account, which highlights the intra-academic operations of textbooks. Though the emphasis here lies perforce on the Foucaldian level of subjectivation, examining how political pressures of the early Cold War turned people into certain kinds of philosophers, the roles of Kuhnian conversion and inculcation must not be understated. Indeed, a basic premise of this book is that Hans Reichenbach's 1951 *The Rise of Scientific Philosophy* played the inculcative role of a Kuhnian "textbook" during the early Cold War, and it played that role because of the clarity, rigor, and scope of Reichenbach's vision of philosophy. It is also true, however, that Reichenbach's views were far better adapted to the sociopolitical pressures then buffeting philosophy than were its rivals.

METHODOLOGY FOR THE CURRENT INVESTIGATION

The investigation for which Foucault and Kuhn prepare us is a complex one. For one thing, because the relations of force that impinged on intellectual life during the early Cold War came from very different regions and worked in very different ways, the evidence for them is of very different kinds. It includes, on the Kuhnian level, a classic work in economic theory (Kenneth Arrow's *Social Choice and Individual Values*), a well-known one in philosophy (Hans Reichenbach's *The Rise of Scientific Philosophy*), and various works by other philosophers. On the Foucaldian level, it encompasses a wider variety of documents: university catalogues and administrative records; reports of governmental committees; letters, both public and private; memoires; magazine and newspaper articles and editorials; and so on. Each of these diverse kinds of documents has its own degree of credibility, and each must be handled with its own kind of care.

The complexity increases further when we recognize that American philosophy at the onset of the early Cold War was a genuinely pluralistic field in which several forms of knowledge, or philosophical approaches, competed. Each of these, moreover, had an intricate history of its own. As we will see in chapter 1, American idealism, concerned with a quasi-religious (indeed, quasi-Christian) ideal order, had been the country's dominant philosophical tradition until the late nineteenth century. By the beginning of the Cold War, it had faded for philosophical reasons and had largely been replaced by the more down-to-earth (or "naturalistic") approach of pragmatism. As the Cold War heated up and external pressures became stronger, pragmatism found itself doing battle with the early version of analytical philosophy that I will call "logical positivism," which had been imported from Europe after the rise of Hitler.[9] Also in the background, but unable to break into the intellectual centers of American philosophy, was existentialism, which later developed into what is today called "continental" philosophy.

We thus confront a wide variety of what Foucault would call relations of force impinging upon a plurality of what he would call forms of knowledge. Uncovering the "definite historical connections" among them that Sidney Hook, the distinguished pragmatist philosopher who later turned avid Red hunter,[10] postulates in my epigraph above means seeing whether a given

relation of force favored one form of philosophical knowledge above its competitors. Direct evidence for this, in the form of explicit avowals by practitioners of the influence of political forces on their work, are, as noted above, for
the most part lacking. Therefore, I proceed by a "differential" method that
begins by identifying a sociopolitical pressure or relation of force (such as the
religious pressure against Max Otto). Having identified this, I turn to the field
of independently identified, competing philosophical approaches, or forms
of knowledge, which it would have affected. The question is then whether
the identified pressure would have differentially favored one or more of those
forms of knowledge. These identifications will require that we adopt what
Foucault calls a "positivistic" attitude to the subject-matter: the relevant facts
of the case—the political pressures and the various discourses they may have
affected—must be identified not only separately but above all correctly, and the
inferences drawn from them must be warranted by these descriptions (Foucault 1972, 125–27; McCumber 2000a, 132–36).

It is instructive to see how the differential method leads, with respect to
pragmatism, to results differing from those of Joshua Rayman (Rayman 2010).
Rayman focuses on explicit attacks and reaches the conclusion that since pragmatism, unlike what later came to be called "continental" philosophy, was not
loudly attacked during the McCarthy Era, it did not suffer problems as serious as its continental competitor. There is, however, more than one way to
kill a paradigm: sometimes attacks on it are less effective than simply praising
it faintly or ignoring it altogether. That pragmatism did go into at least some
eclipse is documented both by historical eyewitnesses (Bernstein 1989, 11) and
by historians (Hollinger 1985). My method permits us to see that the difficulties it faced were at least in part political in nature.

Finally, as I noted above, the positive contributions of Cold War philosophy's various components, and the good reasons many had for converting to it,
perforce get short shrift here. Cold War philosophy, like its descendent, "analytical philosophy," certainly had much to offer individual investigators, and
many of its achievements (such as Quinean holism and Rawlsian social theory)
will, I think, stand as permanent; but those achievements, and the arguments
that led to them, are already well documented.[11]

STRUCTURE OF THE INVESTIGATION

Cold War philosophy is laid bare here via three interrelated probes, each
keyed to the Foucaldian distinction between relations of force and forms of
knowledge. The book therefore comprises three pairs of chapters. In each pair,

the first chapter identifies a social or political pressure on academia, and the second discusses its differential impact on the then-available forms of knowledge. Overall, the first two of these pairs are ordered by the fact that Cold War philosophy, like many modern philosophical approaches, views subject and object—mind and reality—as very different from one another, and therefore gives very different accounts of them.

The first probe, comprising chapters 1 and 2, treats the impact of the early Cold War on philosophical views of nature as the object of rational investigation. I argue that the view of nature that won out in philosophy did so, in part, because it responded successfully to "sticks" wielded by religious fundamentalists seeking to keep atheism (which they equated with naturalism) from being taught in the university. These sticks, I argue in chapter 1, required philosophers, like other academics during the Cold War, to become "stealthy"—to act in ways unclear to outsiders. The resulting form of knowledge, to be discussed in chapter 2, took shape as what I will call "stealth philosophy"—a type of naturalism that privately viewed reality in naturalistic (and even atheistic) terms but was able to avoid open confrontation with religious leaders by postponing, so to speak, open assertions of naturalism.

The postponement was achieved, first, by a displacement: by avoiding talk about nature and concentrating instead on science, viewing it as hierarchized in such a way that its most basic level, that of physics, took precedence; higher levels—chemical, biological, psychological, and social—were to be "reduced" to physics, if at all, only subsequently. The truly philosophical question, then, was not one of whether soul (for example) was a kind of body, but the safer one of whether *talk* of "souls" could be reduced to *talk* of "bodies." Answering that kind of question turned out to require the definitive empirical ascertainment of the scientific laws governing both the lower and the higher levels in play— which meant, in effect, that the whole issue was indefinitely deferred. In the early Cold War, a time deeply haunted by fear of atheism, this displaced and deferred form of naturalism contrasted favorably with its main philosophical competitor, which I call "pragmatic" or "humanistic" naturalism. Pragmatic naturalism began, not from a foundational account of physics, but from human interactions with nature—interactions that were premised from the outset on the "atheistic" view that humans are wholly natural beings. Thus, for pragmatic naturalists, atheism came first and explicitly; for the stealth naturalists, it came late and murkily.

The second probe treats Cold War philosophy's theory of the mind, or "subject," which was influenced by establishment "carrots" encouraging an approach that accorded with the ideological imperatives of America's global battle against Communism. Chapter 3, following the work of S. M. Amadae and others, argues that rational choice theory (RCT) provided the favored model. With the support of governmental and academic elites, RCT quickly took over the discipline of economics and made strong inroads into political science. But as a theory of market and voting behavior, it presupposed contested elections and free markets—the very things that needed justification as against Marxism. RCT thus had to be expanded into a theory of the human mind as such, from which it would follow that free markets and contested elections were—the world over—part and parcel of the mind's proper functioning. Chapter 4 discusses the form this expansion took in philosophy, which coincides with what Hans Reichenbach called "scientific philosophy." The resulting form of knowledge again had the advantage over pragmatism, which had inherited from its idealist forerunners an "edifying" view of philosophy according to which the prime function of the human mind was not to make rational choices but to integrate itself into a larger cosmic or social order—in the early days of the Cold War, a fatally collectivist imperative.

These two favored forms of knowledge had, to be sure, a number of problems. RCT, for example, has long been criticized for its strong idealizations of human mental functioning—it did not take the financial crisis of 2008 to show that humans are not rational in the ways that it requires and that their choices are usually heavily constrained by cultural and social factors. The hierarchy of the sciences had even worse problems. As a general structure of science, it ought to capture something about nature itself; otherwise, science was no more than the systematic imposition of its own overall structure onto nature. But the claim that nature exhibited a hierarchical stratification corresponding to the one exhibited by science—a layering of natural phenomena themselves into levels that were physical, chemical, biological, and so forth—was a metaphysical thesis and so was disallowed by the anti-metaphysical commitments of those who forwarded it. The stratification of nature, the "objective correlative" to the hierarchy of the sciences, was thus philosophically unacceptable but never quite went away. Much of the job of chapter 2 is to trace the contortions philosophers went through to *avoid* committing to it without sacrificing its politically advantageous aspects.

In addition to their separate problems (and there are others), the two forms of knowledge did not go well together. Not only were they logically independent (RCT was not, for example, intrinsically naturalistic or even antireligious: what could be more rational than a preference for eternal salvation?), but their conjunction exhibits, if not outright contradiction, underlying tensions and fault lines. Explaining how Cold War philosophy, their uneasy amalgam, came to dominance in so many American universities is the job of chapters 5 and 6. While there can be no doubt that what Kuhn calls "conversion" played a large role in this—philosophers of the time saw Cold War philosophy's commitment to mathematical logic, in particular, as promising to solve a great many philosophical problems—the rise to dominance was also enforced by a particularly draconian set of institutions, collectively known in California as the "California Plan." Emulated elsewhere to various degrees, this was a three-level vetting system for job candidates that virtually guaranteed that only those who adhered to the basic tenets of Cold War philosophy could be hired anywhere in the state. Chapter 5 discusses the general functioning of the California Plan as a strategy of force, and chapter 6 discusses the form of knowledge that it provoked—its own rationalization. Only when rationalized did the California Plan become acceptable to professors otherwise dedicated to intellectual freedom; their willing adherence thus completed their own subjectivation.

SELECTION OF LOCALES: ACADEMIC PHILOSOPHY AND UCLA

As with Foucault, the diversity of the developments I discuss, as well as of the kinds of evidence for them, requires me to restrict myself to specific cases. This means, happily, that I will spare the reader any Herculean pretensions to uncover the overall effects of the early Cold War on American intellectual life in general. It demands, however, that the cases in question be selected with care. I confine myself to events concerning the discipline of philosophy at UCLA, and to events elsewhere that cast light on them.

There are a couple of reasons why philosophy, among the academic disciplines, is a promising place to probe for political influence on intellectual work. In spite of its current reputation as one of academe's more remote backwaters, philosophy is in fact uniquely situated at the confluence of the natural sciences, social sciences, and humanities, for the basic doctrines of any discipline tend to be philosophical ones. What happened in philosophy thus stands to illuminate what happened in a broad array of other academic fields. In addition to this intellectual centrality, philosophy held point position in some of the major cultural battles of the Cold War. Domestically, as we saw in the prologue, philosophy departments were identified by right-wing forces as the only places in the university where atheism could be promulgated. Internationally, highly placed intellectuals such as Friedrich von Hayek, Karl Popper, and Joseph Schumpeter felt that the Cold War needed to be fought on a philosophical level—on which the "free world," in their view, was losing (Amadae

2003, 15–22). Academic philosophy in America and elsewhere thus came in for heavy, and so more readily visible, pressure from both inside and outside the intellectual establishment.

The emphasis on UCLA requires lengthier justification. One set of reasons for it has to do with the unusual accessibility of information about the institution: not only is UCLA relatively well archived, but because it is a public university, those archives are easily accessible.[12] One reason for this that UCLA is so young. Strictly speaking, it did not exist until 1952. Prior to that, Berkeley was senior; UCLA was merely the University of California's southern campus. After 1952, UCLA enjoyed "autonomous" status equal to Berkeley's within an overall system whose two main universities (today grown to ten) would share a president, while having their own chancellors.[13] Thus, where other universities were weathering an anti-Communist maelstrom, UCLA was actually birthing in the middle of it. This made it all the more important to guarantee that the fledging university was not attacked in its cradle by Communistic influences. As we will see in chapter 6, the fear of such attacks, and of their becoming public, was a major factor in the hiring of UCLA's first chancellor.

Other factors combined with UCLA's newness to make it one of the most politically scrutinized campuses in the nation. Both main campuses of the University of California were clearly in that league by 1950, as the much-publicized California Oath controversy shows.[14] During the early Cold War, UCLA itself was taken by many Red hunters to be a paradigm case of Communist infiltration. According to a 1950 article in *The Saturday Evening Post*, "The record of Communism at UCLA is worth studying as a case history of what has been done at many schools, and can be done anywhere, by Communists or any other cohesive group which invades a school with a definite and continuing purpose."[15]

By that time, indeed, so much McCarthyite attention had been drawn away from Berkeley and toward UCLA that the state's main Red-hunting agency felt obliged to explain the reasons. Like such committees in other states,[16] this one (of which we shall hear much in the sequel) was modeled on the federal government's House Un-American Activities Committee, commonly called HUAC. California's version bore the unwieldy name of "California State Senate Fact-Finding Subcommittee on Un-American Activities," and was variously called, after its chairmen, the [Hugh] Burns or the [Jack] Tenney Committee. Its activities under both chairmen exhibit enough continuity to call for a single name; my choice, CUAC, has the modest advantage of rhyming with that of its exemplar, HUAC.

In its annual report for 1951,[17] CUAC stated that important Communist activity in Berkeley had gone deep underground as far back as 1942, when serious work started there on the atom bomb. In order to concentrate on infiltrating the Manhattan Project, CUAC claimed, the Communist Party had closed its office in Berkeley and set up a super-secret group of operatives who did not carry party cards or attend party meetings, and who avoided associating with the party and its other members in any overt way. Their efforts were for the FBI to uncover, which left CUAC with little to do in Berkeley. UCLA, widely known as the "little Red schoolhouse in Westwood," had—according to CUAC—experienced a "surge in recruiting" for the party when its Berkeley operation was closed down and had become the "epicenter of the earthquake."[18] CUAC's subsequent efforts, then, mainly targeted UCLA. They began with a report dated June 9, 1951, which accused administrators at the University of harboring Communists. This report, which attracted nationwide attention,[19] was followed by many subsequent efforts to "clean up" the campus. Their ultimate discovery was that Communist infiltration at UCLA was basically mythical: the only Communist faculty member CUAC would ever find on the UCLA faculty was a woman who played piano for exercises in the woman's gym (Hamilton and Jackson 1969, 119–20). UCLA thus indeed furnishes a "case history"—not of Communist subversion, but of the efforts to stop it.

The extent to which we can generalize from what happened at UCLA to other colleges and universities across the country remains, however, unclear, for the pressures on UCLA were in several respects qualitatively different from those at other institutions. To be sure, even if events at UCLA had been wholly unlike those that occurred at any other university in the country during the early Cold War, they and their effects would be worth uncovering; UCLA is a great institution, and its story should be told—especially at a time when, in Philip Mirowski's words, "consideration of the local fallout [of the Red scare] on specific disciplines and schools is still in its infancy" (Mirowski 2002, 246). But UCLA's uniqueness, and that of its California setting, should not be overstated. The University of California has long served throughout the world as an example, widely imitated, of public education at its finest; and as the system expanded from one campus to its present ten, it was UCLA—the first of Berkeley's offspring—that served as the model for its siblings.

Some of the attacks on UCLA, as we will see in chapter 1, invoked its status as a public university. While generalizing from public to private universities must, like all generalizing, be conducted with care, it does not follow that what happened at UCLA had no analogues at private institutions. Kevin Starr has shown that by the time of the Cold War, the Board of Regents of the university had come to resemble the boards of trustees of many private institutions in being largely composed of conservative business leaders (Starr 2002, 313–14), and while pressures from private boards of trustees were often quieter than those from public universities, there is no evidence that they were any less intense. E. Wilson Lyon, president of the elegantly private Pomona College from 1941 to 1969, captures the situation at private institutions in moving words: "The tensions and fears of the McCarthy period led to unfair criticisms of the economic and political views of faculty, [to] attempted interference with academic appointments and [to] objections to distinguished outside speakers . . . The grave problems were handled so discreetly, by both the president [i.e. by Lyon himself] and the trustees that *the faculty and students were totally unaware of them*" (Lyon 1977, 410–11; emphasis added).

When we turn to the outside pressure groups themselves, we find that anti-Communist hysteria was fomented across the nation as in California: by politicians, businessmen, and religious leaders who were sometimes sincere and sometimes merely opportunistic. Attacks on academics amounted to a nationwide wave, and research has shown that their goals and tactics were much the same everywhere (see Hofstadter and Metzger 1955; Lewis 1988; McCumber 2000b; Schrecker 1986).

Still, we should generalize from UCLA to other institutions, and from philosophy to American intellectual life as a whole, only with caution. This book aims to avoid hasty generalization by noting special circumstances at UCLA when they become relevant and asking whether the pressures involved were unique in kind or only in visibility and degree. But a final answer to such questions—and a final judgment concerning the effects of sociopolitical pressures on American intellectual life during the early Cold War—can only come from the readers of this book, when they compare developments at UCLA to whatever institutions they are acquainted with.

THE WIDER CONTEXT: REORIENTING AMERICAN SOCIETY

Focusing on the early Cold War at UCLA can hardly mean excising consideration of wider contexts, just as focusing on its philosophy department during that time hardly allows us to ignore developments in the university as a whole. It does mean, however, minimizing such considerations. In this section, I discuss, minimally, the widest sociopolitical context for the rise of Cold War philosophy—the Cold War itself and its effects on American society in general. The next section narrows the focus to some of the early Cold War's effects on American academia.

To place something on a new basis, not because it is broken but because it must perform new tasks, is to "reorient" it. American society, I suggest, went through such a reorientation after World War II. The years between 1945 and 1989 were dominated by a global contest between the United States and the Soviet Union, for which the overall name is the Cold War; its domestic first phase, for purposes of this book, began in 1947, with the first major postwar attack on UCLA philosophy. That first phase is usually called the "McCarthy Era," but the name is problematic. It is not only offensive to the Irish and to Catholics generally, but masks important connections between domestic McCarthyism and global developments. Indeed, focusing on Senator McCarthy localizes the damage even more, to the depredations of one man and to the city in which he worked—Washington, D.C. In fact, the transformations in American society triggered during the McCarthy Era went beyond the senator, beyond Washington, and indeed beyond the federal government altogether. The transformation of UCLA philosophy was largely complete by about 1959, which thus signals the end of the "early Cold War"—at least in Westwood.

If the British legendarily acquired their empire in a fit of absent-mindedness, the Americans got theirs in a panic attack. Garry Wills has shown that even if there had been no such person as Stalin and no Communist threat, the postwar period would have been socially transformative because of the sudden appearance in world history of the atomic bomb (Wills 2010, 1–53). As of the Trinity Test on July 16, 1945, the United States was in possession of a weapon of unimagined destructive power, the sudden fruit of a feverish campaign to beat the Nazis to it.[20] But the bomb was useless without the means to deliver it around the world, and the airplanes of that time were incapable of doing that from bases inside the United States. Thus came the need for an enormous (and still largely secret) archipelago of foreign military installations from which the bomb could be launched into use. The care and keeping of these bases, in turn, required close policing, not only of the archipelago itself, but of the host countries in which its components were located. It required, in short, nothing less than a modern re-performance of the main foreign policy tasks that James J. O'Donnell assigns to the Roman Empire: "to establish economic relations, form a friendly alliance, send troops to join its allies against attacks from beyond, and finally assimilate and consolidate new holdings" (O'Donnell 2008, 80).

As Wills documents (Wills 2010), this produced far-reaching changes in the American system of governance, for only a massively enhanced presidency, operating under drastically reduced oversight, could hope to manage this burgeoning realm. Presidents, though still elected and still often thwarted by Congress on domestic measures, ceased to be genuinely democratic leaders and became commanders in chief, not merely of the military, but of the entire country.[21] Cold War mobilization also went far beyond matters of governance and politics, and changed the daily life of every American. The interstate highway system, for example, today binds the country together economically and is commonly used by Americans just to navigate around their own cities and towns. But its official name is "The Dwight D. Eisenhower National System of Interstate *and Defense* Highways" (emphasis added). It was authorized by the National Interstate and Defense Highways Act of 1956, and part of its stated purpose was to facilitate the rapid movement of troops and equipment around the country in the event of Soviet attacks.[22] Similarly, the American television networks, which quickly came to dominate the country's popular culture, were set up in part to disseminate government announcements to the American citizenry (Bernhard 1999). What they disseminated was sometimes more like propaganda. A personal example comes from my childhood afternoons in central Illinois—a commercial which began suddenly with the image of a mustachioed commissar in a heavy cloth coat, swinging his arm in denial and shouting "Nyet!" The commercial's message was that if the Communists took over, we children would not be allowed to watch Howdy Doody or the Lone Ranger. It was a fearsome thought for nine-year-olds.

That the national highway system and the broadcast television networks are creations of the federal government, rather than of free-market entrepreneurs, introduces us to what Wills calls the "dirty little secret" of American capitalism: that for achieving many goals, government sponsorship is far more efficient than free markets (Wills 2010, 9). This fact, though obvious enough, caused problems during the postwar period because governmental control was precisely what the United States was supposed to be fighting *against*. One way to get the American people to accept such federal intrusion in the economy and daily life was to scare them: a certain amount of social regulation could be justified as being necessary to fight something far more frightening—in this case, Communism. Fear of Communism was thus encouraged and manipulated in the service of the Cold War. Senator Arthur Vandenberg made this strategy explicit, telling President Truman, with regard to proposed American intervention in Greece in 1947, that "the only way you are ever going to get this is to make a speech and scare hell out of the country" (Wills 2010, 72).

Truman gave the required speech on March 12, 1947, and it had the desired effect. As diplomatic historian Robert McMahon has written, "Using hyperbolic language, Manichean imagery, and deliberate simplification to strengthen his public appeal, Truman was trying to build a public and Congressional consensus not just behind this particular commitment but behind a more activist American foreign policy. . . . The Truman Doctrine thus amounted to a declaration of ideological Cold War along with a declaration of geopolitical Cold War."[23]

Viewed from above, the early Cold War thus amounted to the mobilization of the American people, still recovering from their World War II victories, into a populace disciplined enough to support the suddenly needed establishment of global American hegemony. In this perspective, Red hunting appears as a gigantic, orchestrated effort to frighten the American people into accepting far-reaching changes in their nation and in their own lives. But appeals to fear could hardly be expected to work if fear were not already abroad in the population. When we look at the domestic front of the early Cold War from below, that is exactly what we find: a societal body contorted into a massive, chaotic spasm of alarm and suspicion. Many reports of the time convey things that seem, to contemporary ears, to be not merely skittish or harebrained, but unfathomably bizarre. Well-meaning citizens denounced Groucho Marx to the FBI because they thought he *might* have referred to the United States as the "United Snakes" on his radio show; Albert Einstein was said to have joined with ten former Nazis to witness a beam of light melt a block of metal.[24] That such reports were not taken overly seriously at FBI headquarters only testifies to the genuine frenzy among the populace and to an important fact about the early Cold War: much of the damage in the country was done, not by government agencies such as the FBI, HUAC, and CUAC, but by earnest citizens who were terrified of Communism and, in the words of the *UCLA Daily Bruin*, of "anything which . . . might faintly resemble it."[25]

In fact, much of the hysteria gripping the country in the early fifties, while rhetorically couched in terms of anti-Communism, in fact had other targets. These included Jews (Litvak 2009), homosexuals (Johnson 2004) African Americans (*TD*, 22),[26] and feminists (Storrs 2013). In some cases these other battles actually took precedence over the one against Communists. A Congressman from Michigan told his colleagues in 1950 that his constituents "tell me they are concerned before they get to the issue of Communism or loyalty with this issue of morality and decency," while in the State Department, according to officials, more than twice as many employees were fired for being homosexual as for being politically disloyal (Johnson 2004, 2).

As the Michigan Congressman's reference to "morality and decency" suggests, a major strand in the tapestry of fear concerned religion. Where the associations of Jews, African Americans, homosexuals, and feminists with Communism were largely mythical, Communism itself had long trumpeted its atheism and opposition to religion. In a country as religious as the United States, this was a key aspect of Communism's general hatefulness well before the beginning of the Cold War. It may even have been *the* key element: in the words of Mark Toulouse, "The anti-communism of earlier decades, in the popular mind at least, expressed a deep-seated belief that the Cold War represented a religious battle more than a political one" (Toulouse 1993, 268; for a general account, see Wald 1994). This cannot truly be called religious fervor, because in the first instance it was not for religion but against atheism. It persisted through the early Cold War, which saw the words "under God" added to the pledge of allegiance in 1954 and "in God We Trust" placed on paper currency in 1957 (Crouse 2002). It lasts into the present century, where recent polling indicates that atheists still constitute America's most despised minority and where the movie *God's Not Dead*, about an atheistic philosophy professor who receives his due comeuppance, has spawned a sequel. [27]

The "panic attack" that reoriented America thus went far beyond anti-Communism. While the onset of the Cold War hardly created anti-Semitism, racism, homophobia, antifeminism, and anti-atheism in America, it saw traditional streams of hatred against Jews, African-Americans, gays, feminists, and freethinkers flow together into a single paranoid torrent, sweeping many different things and people into its current. From this point of view, McCarthyism appears, not as a strictly anti-Communist mobilization, but as a desperate fight to keep the United States out of the hands of those who were not straight, white, and Christian. When German composer Hanns Eisler, who had fled from the Nazis to the United States, reported that his appearance before HUAC showed him "fascism in its most direct form" (Betz 1982, 107), he was neither joking nor exaggerating.

THE NARROWER CONTEXT:
REORIENTING ACADEMIA

Common sense tells us that it would have been strange indeed if all this had spared universities. There is plenty of evidence that it did not. One obvious transformation wrought in academia during the early Cold War, for example, was the arrival of massive government funding for certain disciplines and approaches. The governmental build-up of hard science had begun under the pressures of World War II and by 1945 had reached the point that Yale philosopher Brand Blanshard could write: "Mathematics, physics, engineering, medicine—all the sciences, theoretic and applied, that have to do with the art of war are riding high; the humanities, including philosophy, have gone into temporary eclipse" (Blanshard 1945, 8; see also Hollinger 1996b, 101).

Designing and maintaining the bomb and its required infrastructure called for a virtual army of scientists. This led, in 1950, to the creation of the National Science Foundation, which itself was not exempt from the politics of fear—it explicitly warned applicants against "social reform movements and welfare activities" (Schrecker 1998, 407). When the World War was replaced by the Cold War, Blanshard's use of "temporary" above revealed itself to be false optimism; as Wills, Philip Mirowski (Mirowski 2002) and many others have shown, the privileging of militarized hard science was in fact the new normal.

Social sciences were similarly affected, if to a smaller degree, because much of their funding was from private foundations. Here, too, however, the mentality of the times prevailed: between 1950 and 1960 not one important foundation awarded a major grant to study race relations (Schrecker 1998, 407). The civil rights movement thus took academia largely by surprise—as did, in turn, the student revolt of the late sixties, the collapse of Communism in 1989, and the near collapse of capitalism in 2008. In part because their funding depended on their thinking about other things, American social scientists no more anticipated any of these than the St. Petersburg aristocracy anticipated the Russian Revolution.

Though vast amounts of government funding were hardly an issue for the humanities, they were not wholly exempt from all this. As Schrecker writes, "The academy lost its critical edge. College teachers embraced a cautious impartiality that in reality supported the status quo. . . . Literature was put on a pedestal, where it was either treated as a storehouse of abstract ideals or else subjected to psychoanalysis" (Schrecker 1998, 404–5). In the humanities as in the social sciences, the dominance of politically narrowed mind-sets prevented the recognition of changes on the horizon. What the social scientists failed to predict were major changes in American society and the world. The changes confronted by the humanities, by contrast, were smaller and closer to home—in the nature of the humanities themselves. In the seventies and beyond, philosophy and literary studies were suddenly overwhelmed by critical imports from Europe, mainly France. Understood without regard to their origins in the European intellectual climate, which, unlike that in the United States, was heavily inflected by Marxism (see Cusset 2003), these approaches would be taught as if they had somehow dropped from heaven (or risen from hell), leading to a humanistic academy beset by all too many rigid applications of semi-understood ideas, on the one hand—and by useless efforts to dismiss those ideas on the other.[28]

In many aspects of American life, critical reflection on the distortions introduced into it by the early Cold War has begun to undo some of the damage. The subsequent histories of African Americans, gays, Jews, and feminists show that the early Cold War efforts to suppress them ended in utter failure. Such critical reflection has, however, been largely missing from academia, where attention has been directed mainly to the unwarranted suffering of individuals such as Morris Judd, who was summarily fired from the University of Colorado philosophy department in 1950 and spent the rest of his career working as the office manager in a nearby junkyard.[29]

Whether Cold War philosophy was really new or improved, and to what extent, I leave to the reader. One thing both Foucault and Kuhn got wrong, in their zeal to free reason from the strictures of global accounts of its nature, concerns the degree to which individual investigators inhere in their respective paradigms or dispositives. Pace Kuhn, such inherence is not an incorrigible matter of the "fundamental components of immediate experience." Pace Foucault, it is not a matter of how one is "subjectivated" into one's very selfhood. Even those most deeply involved in a particular approach have the capacity, if they wish to exercise it, to question its presumed authority and to disengage its real limits.

They have the capacity, in other words, to philosophize about it.

* Part 1 *

The Cudgels of Freedom: Cold War Philosophy's Theory of Objects

CHAPTER 1

Academic Stealth in the Early Cold War

Economic facts are important, but they will never check the virus of collectivism.... The only antidote is a revival of American patriotism and religious faith.

H. S. PRENTIS, President, National Association of Manufacturers, 1938

Political and religious pressures of the early Cold War required, I have suggested, a certain amount of conscious dissimulation, or academic "stealth," from both administrators and professors. In the case of philosophy at UCLA, such stealth primarily concerned the movements of philosophers into and out of the philosophy department. Hiring a professor potentially unacceptable to the right wing had to be carefully managed so as not to arouse opposition, while departures, such as Max Otto's, had to be handled so as not to give the impression that UCLA had succumbed to outside pressures.

One problem with uncovering cases of academic stealth is that in order to work, stealth must be as close to invisible as those engaged in it can make it. The argument in this chapter thus proceeds by an accumulation of cases. I present four cases of administrators and professors at UCLA acting in what appear to be stealthy ways for the benefit, as they conceived it, of its philosophy department. If no one case is definitive, the overall pattern is clear.

These four incidents represent the early Cold War phase of what in fact was (at least) two decades of conflict between conservative religious forces and the philosophy department at UCLA. The conflicts began in 1947 with the public outcry against the hiring of Max Otto and ended after the 1967–69 controversies surrounding Angela Davis. In between we find the successful hiring of continental philosopher Hans Meyerhoff in 1948; a strangely incomplete "defense" of philosopher Hugh Miller during the California Oath controversy in 1950; a 1953 effort by the UCLA dean to get the university's philosophy department to hire a non-naturalist philosopher; and a 1965 denunciation of Patrick Wilson, who was teaching philosophy of religion in a manner deemed by clergymen to be insufficiently respectful. The Davis and Wilson affairs postdated the early Cold War, and I mention them only briefly. The four earlier cases, none of which has been publicly known, require closer investigation if we are to understand the tactics imposed not only on UCLA philosophy but throughout academia by the political pressures of the early Cold War.

Academic stealth, finally, could exert political pressures of its own: it tended to favor those individuals and approaches that were most easily hidden from outside pressure groups. These were not necessarily the approaches those groups favored. The religious forces whose efforts to keep atheism out of philosophy occupy much of the next two chapters, for example, failed completely to install the jingoistic Christianity they favored; science-based "naturalistic" approaches carried the day. But that does not mean that those efforts were altogether without effect. As we will see in chapter 2, some versions of naturalism, such as Hans Reichenbach's, were more easily concealed from outsiders than others—such as Max Otto's.

1947: THE MAX OTTO AFFAIR AT UCLA

That hiring Max Otto to the Flint Professorship at UCLA would produce strong protests should not be surprising. As the epigraph to this chapter indicates, American society had long been washed by strongly conservative currents of opinion founded mainly on religious and anti-immigrant sentiments—and economic self-interest. Such currents had come to the surface in the Palmer Raids of 1919 and 1920 and in the case of Nicola Sacco and Bartolomeo Vanzetti, which ended with their execution in 1927. They had also flowed into philosophy, most notably in 1940, when (as noted in the prologue) City College in New York attempted to appoint Bertrand Russell to a position in its philosophy department. But the Russell case, like the others, was relatively clear: there is no sense of mystery about the motivations of the parties involved.[1] When we look further into the Otto affair, however, what we find is a deeply confused situation in which not everyone was honest about his goals and tactics, while a complex smokescreen was apparently devised to enable Otto to back out of the professorship without giving the impression that doing so was a capitulation to right-wing forces.

We begin with a closer examination of the nature of the protest itself, as conveyed in the letters attacking Otto. For present purposes, these exhibit five important features. First, as we saw in the introduction, several of them specifically targeted philosophy as a discipline, because only there could atheism be promulgated to students.

Second, while most of the letters were written by individual citizens, rather than on organizational letterheads, those citizens were very religious people who presumably belonged to churches, and there is reason to think that the campaign was to some degree orchestrated by religious leaders. To be sure, the letters do not exhibit the identical wording that often signals a planned campaign. They tend, however, to follow the *Examiner* in identifying Otto as an "atheist," rather than as a "humanist" or "naturalist," the terms philosophers tended to use of him (Kennedy 2005; Schulz 2002, 114), and different letters often resort to the same metaphors. Most of them, moreover, share the odd argument that the United States has made war on Germany and Japan, not because of their military aggressions or maniacal genocides, but because of their atheism—an evil which, the writers claim, both countries had now renounced. The United States, in the minds of the protestors, had not sacrificed billions of dollars and thousands of lives only to see its war on atheism lost at home.

Evidence that at least some of the letters were not wholly the work of their authors is provided by a Mr. and Mrs. Swanson: "As a Professor of Theosophy, . . . [Otto] would be a detriment to society in being in a position to easily poison the minds of young youth [*sic*] along the line of his teachings."[2] If the Swansons do not know the name of Max Otto's field, how can they know that it provides a place where the "poison" of his teachings can be introduced into young minds? The presumption is strong that someone has told them. Moreover, this "someone" is not the *Los Angeles Examiner*, which made clear that Otto was a philosopher and not a theosophist. "Philosophy" and "theosophy" do not look alike—but they may sound alike, when heard, for example, from a pulpit.

Third, the letters slightly predate full-blown McCarthyism. Truman's fearmongering speech on Greece, mentioned in the introduction, was still three weeks away when the *Examiner* article appeared revealing the Otto appointment. Government operations against Communists would begin ten days after that, with Truman's March 22 Executive Order # 9835 (Schrecker 1986, 4–5). Joseph McCarthy's famous Wheeling Speech, which began his national demagoguery, was not given until 1950 (Caute 1978, 48).

In early 1947, many still thought of the Soviet Union as a wartime ally. Only seven of the letters even mention Communism; the standard foreign connection attributed to Otto is with Germany and Japan, not with the Soviet Union. Though one writer opines that Otto is a "relative of Marx,"[3] Otto's main sin even in that letter is identified as atheism, not Communism. The letters of protest thus illustrate how the anti-Communist fervor that was about to erupt was preceded, not merely by earlier versions of anti-Communism, as evidenced in the Palmer Raids, but by wider suspicions about challenges to religious doctrine. What counted as "religious," moreover, was given a broad interpretation. As one writer put it, in words whose echoes have still not died away, "our Constitution is a sacred document."[4]

Fourth, the problem is not Otto's beliefs but that he is being given an opportunity to "teach" them. Several of the letters go out of their way to reiterate that Otto himself, as an American, is free to hold whatever beliefs he wishes. However, "We do not want our American youth to be taught any atheistic doctrines because without firm faith in God our nation and the world will sink beneath the waves of barbarism."[5] As we will see shortly, the *Examiner* article itself made clear that Otto's aim was not to persuade students of his philosophy, but to engage them in independent thinking. This failed entirely to register with the protestors.

Fifth and finally, the letters generally come, not only from outside academia, but from far outside. Stanley Thatcher's letter, quoted in the prologue, is one of the most ominous because its author is well enough informed to know how to forward his letter to the regents, or at least to say he is doing so. The complaint of Mr. and Mrs. Swanson, who do not know the difference between philosophy and theosophy, exhibits a more usual level of unfamiliarity with academia. Other writers typically have little connection to UCLA, or apparently to any university; while a few identify themselves as alumni, the most that is usually claimed is that the writer is the parent of small children who will (or may) one day attend UCLA. A number of the letters are written on ruled paper, presumably appropriated from schoolchildren in the family. However uninformed the latter writers may be, however, they are very sincere in their concern, and some of the letters are quite moving. The philosophy department chair, Donald Piatt, attempted to answer them; but in those days of carbon paper and mimeographs, he seems to have given up after about half a dozen. His responses give no ground. They stoutly defend Otto both as a philosopher and as an American, and assert, in no uncertain terms, the department's right to hire him.

Piatt's efforts, however, were for nothing. After teaching for UCLA's summer session, Otto resigned the Flint Professorship on August 15, 1947, before taking up any of its functions.[6] The stated reason was his inability to find a place to live in Los Angeles. Piatt opposed the move, partly on the grounds that for Otto to resign the professorship would give rise to gossip that he had been forced to, meaning that UCLA had capitulated to political pressures.[7] Otto thought about it some more, but on August 25, in a letter to Piatt's home adress, he made his resignation definitive.

Piatt's worries about how the resignation would be perceived soon proved justified: rumors that Otto had been forced to resign because of religious opposition spread quickly across the nation. On September 11, 1947, Otto's friend, the psychologist Harry A. Overstreet, wrote him from Bennington, Vermont:

Dear Otto:

This is the most sickening thing I have heard of! What could the vigilantes and cultists of Los Angeles have against *you*? It makes me more deeply ashamed than ever of my native state. Too bad that your half-year of good work had to be ditched because of a parcel of intolerant half-wits. . . .

Some day send me the inside story of this California stench. I have friends out there and I should like to get to the bottom of the mess.

In any event we hope that you will have a happy and productive half-year in a less fanatical region.[8]

The rumors had spread all the way to Vermont in just over two weeks. They were still abroad in December, when Otto's friend, the New York adult education pioneer Eduard C. Lindeman, wrote bluntly: "What happened in California? I hear contradictory reports."[9]

It is easy to see why the stated reason for the resignation, Otto's inability to find a home, should have aroused skepticism. UCLA was a major university in a major city, and some of the 296 regular professors listed in its *General Catalogue* for 1947–48 must have been going on leave. There are no records of other Flint Professors encountering housing problems, and as President Sproul said in his offer letter to Otto, the Flint Professorship carried the very highest level of prestige—surely a motivation for the university to find something for the Ottos.[10] Moreover, Piatt had charged the wife of UCLA Provost Clarence Dykstra with finding a home for the Ottos back in January.[11] Problems doing so would have been evident by the time Otto arrived for the summer session, but he had come anyway. More than skepticism was expressed by another friend of Otto's, philosopher Dickinson S. Miller, who had retired to Boston and who wrote him on October 2, 1947: "I am *astounded* by the conditions you tell me of at Los Angeles which forced you to resign the Flint Professorhip. It seems *incredible* that the University could not have arranged something."[12]

The implausibility of the resignation's stated reason is not the only puzzling matter about it. Otto's effort, in his letter of August 25, to reassure Piatt that his sudden resignation will not give rise to damaging rumors also rings strange: "And I shall be extremely sorry if, as you feel sure will be the case, unfounded rumors will be spread as to the reasons for my resignation, reasons reflecting unfavorably on freedom of teaching at U. C. L. A. However, such rumors, I believe, will soon be dissipated, since they can only thrive if those responsible for the freedom of educational ideals betray their trust, which I see no reason to anticipate." It was Otto's resignation and so, presumably, his job to explain it. But his letter does not reassure Piatt by promising that Otto himself will make clear to the world that the failure to find housing, rather than political pressures, was responsible for the resignation. Instead, Otto immediately displaces the task onto "those responsible for the freedom of educational ideals"—that is, the university's leaders. The rest of the sentence is an admonition to those leaders not to "betray their trust."

The behavior of one of those leaders, UCLA provost Dykstra, deepens the puzzlement. Dykstra had been chancellor of the University of Wisconsin from 1937 to 1945, and was apparently a friend of Otto's from those days; in the correspondence surrounding the original offer of the Flint Profesorship, they are "Dyke" and "Max." But a letter from Otto's longtime dean at Wisconsin, George Sellery,[13] written just two days after Otto's letter of resignation to Piatt, suggests that Dykstra had ongoing qualms about Otto's appointment. Sellery writes, "I agree in thinking Dyke relieved at your decision not to take the semester appointment [i.e., the Flint chair]. But I very much doubt that the alleged taxpayer would bring suit, since he ought to know—he or the R. C. Hierarchy—that he would have to be licked in defense of *Lehrerfreiheit*. You, of course, have given the thing up because 1). No home; 2). No business teaching all summer and next semester."[14] According to Sellery, a lawsuit was being threatened by someone associated with the Roman Catholic hierarchy, and both Otto and Sellery believed that Dykstra was worried about this.[15] Given the outcome of the Bertrand Russell case seven years earlier, Dykstra had good reason to be "relieved" when Otto turned down the Flint Professorship— and good reason to hide his relief from Otto, who as an old friend and fellow academic needed and deserved Dykstra's wholehearted support. Dykstra, in other words, was being less than honest—stealthy—with Otto (and perhaps with Sellery) about his real feelings in the matter.

Not finding a home for Otto was an embarrassment for UCLA. But it brought real hardship to Otto, who had rented out his house in Wisconsin and had no place to go back to.[16] Dykstra solved the problem with an act of extreme personal generosty: he offered his weekend home at Laguna Beach to Otto and his wife, who spent the fall there.[17] Laguna Beach is about sixty miles from Westwood and so, in those pre-freeway days, out of range for regular commuting.

The possibility then arises that Dykstra, worried about further opposition to Otto and a possible lawsuit, but unwilling openly to ask Otto to resign, undermined the appointment by stalling help for Otto's housing search from both his own wife and from UCLA. This would explain the odd wording in Otto's August 25 letter to Piatt: he is calling on Dykstra to honor a commitment, open or implicit, to find Otto a place to live for the fall. It would explain as well UCLA's puzzling inability to find housing for the couple, and Dykstra's spectacular offering of his own weekend home to them for a period of several months.

What this all signals is stealth upon stealth. Otto himself may have behaved stealthily in putting forth the housing problem as the reason for his resignation, when it was really a matter of fear that actually taking up the Flint Professorship would reawaken right-wing opposition. Dykstra clearly engaged in conscious dissimulation in not expressing his doubts about the appointment openly to Otto, who surmised them anyway. Dykstra may even, moreover, have engineered the whole housing fiasco in order to keep Otto out of the Flint Professorship without seeming to capitulate to right-wing forces—a piece of chicanery that he then recompensed by giving his weekend home to the Otto's for a period of several months. We cannot know for sure, of course, that such was the case. It is possible, though unlikely, that none of the hundreds of professors at UCLA was going on leave in the fall of 1947; or that Mrs. Dykstra had been dilatory in her efforts; or that UCLA was too disorganized to find out about available properties.

A somewhat clearer indication of academic stealth in connection with the Otto Affair can be found in some complex iconography in the UCLA *General Catalogue*. Between the academic years 1939–1940 and 1970–71, fifteen issues of the *General Catalogue* list a Flint Professor of Philosophy. His name (they were all men) is given in alphabetical order among the names of the regular full professors until 1963–64. After that, it is given after the list of regular faculty, along with those of other temporary faculty. In the remaining issues, there is no mention whatever of a Flint Professor, and we may conclude that in those years the position went unfilled.[18] Finally, when a Flint Professor's name is given in the catalogue's faculty listing, it is also placed next to the courses he is scheduled to teach. Thus, a general policy emerges: when there is no Flint Professor, there is no mention of the position at all; when there is, his name is printed both somewhere in the faculty listings and with the courses he is to teach.

The *UCLA General Catalogue* for 1947–48, published on July 1, 1947—before Otto's resignation—is different. It does not identify a Flint Professor for that year. Neither, however, does it entirely omit mention of the position. Nor does it indicate the professorship with a dash at the end of the faculty listings. That year, and that year only, we find a dash and the words "Flint Professor of Philosophy," not at the end of the listing but between the names of the full professors Miller and Piatt—i.e. in the place where "Otto" would come alphabetically. No courses are identified as being taught by Max Otto; indeed, his name does not appear at all, even though he was still, at the time of publication, scheduled to be the Flint professor. General university catalogues, of course, are widely distributed and available to the general public.

That academic stealth was really at work in the Max Otto Affair becomes more plausible when we consider the further examples of it to be adduced in the rest of this chapter. Before doing so, however, we must understand the Max Otto Affair a bit better, by seeing Otto's problems at UCLA in the context of his entire philosophy. The *Examiner* article that started the whole thing quoted some of Otto's views in boldface:

> "Practical faith in the non-existence of God," he wrote, "has worked better than faith in His existence did—the consequences of giving up belief in God have not been disastrous; they have been beneficial. . . .
>
> "Yes, I disagreed with Chapple's God. I didn't believe in Him and I don't believe in your God either, or anyone's God. Everyone has his own philosophy and it's his job to broaden and deepen that philosophy regardless of my personal opinions."[19]

This quotation should have made four things abundantly clear to the article's readers. First, Otto was unafraid to be bluntly and publicly provocative. Second, he believed that religious faith should be evaluated, at least in part, in terms of its consequences. Third, such evaluation in his view showed religious belief to be counterproductive. And fourth: he had no intention of imposing his views on his students. Rather, he was explicitly concerned to help students develop their own philosophies, "regardless of my personal opinions." In the event, as we have seen, only three of these points got through; the last of them escaped a number of religious conservatives, who did not distinguish between "teaching" and the advocacy of one's personal views.

Finally, Otto's atheism was not merely a view he held independently of his views on other topics, but a basic premise of his entire philosophy. This is conveyed by an affectionate portrayal of him, four years earlier, in *Time* magazine (hardly a socialist rag):

Years ago Wisconsin's stubby, pragmatic bon vivant, Philosopher Max Otto, stood on the bank of the upper Mississippi one Sunday sunset to ask himself again what force it was that prevented the technology of the modern world from being used to the greater happiness of the plain man. Afternoon darkened into evening; the shining silver of the river blurred in the darkness; lights began to appear in the village.

Modern man's strength is greater than his knowledge or his will, thought this aging Midwestern professor. "The vast economic material body of the world lacks a mind to match it, and is not animated by a commensurate moral spirit. This backwardness is the tragic inadequacy of our time. It is the basic problem which the agencies of aspiration and intelligence have to solve."[20]

The crucial problem posed by science is not one of what science is, or of how it works, but of how science can better the life of the "plain man." This problem arises, not from a purely philosophical perplexity, but from history itself: The "strength" of the human race, its capacity to change nature, is not currently matched by intellectual or moral capacities. The result is that human interactions with nature, especially economic ones, have been unguided: "the . . . material body of the world lacks a mind to match it."

For a religiously oriented thinker, philosophy's problems would look very different. The world would not lack a mind, for one thing, because God's mind would be there to guide it. Moreover, if the true destiny of the human being were to achieve salvation in the afterlife, our treatment of nature would hardly be our "basic problem;" getting to heaven would. From the very first, in the way it sets its "basic problem," Otto's philosophy is bound up with his denial of God. On that issue, the protestors were entirely right.

1948: THE HIRING OF HANS MEYERHOFF

Outside scrutiny of the UCLA philosophy department for possible atheism was not a mere nuisance. In 1953, Donald Piatt would write to Lewis E. Hahn that the members of the department were themselves, "almost to a man, hard-boiled naturalists."[21] But the UCLA *General Catalogue* for that year indicates that the makeup of the department had not changed greatly since 1947 (see appendix). The same hard-boiled crew was therefore already in place during the Otto Affair. What could its members have made of the citizenry's easy reduction of naturalism to atheism and its consequent outrage? What were they to think in later years, when (as we will now see) the regents, the local campus administration, and finally their own dean successively joined the ranks of the attackers? To say that the department in general was not to some degree disquieted by the Max Otto Affair and its various sequels would be to attribute to them a foolhardy *insouciance*—or arrogance.

That the department was free of such vices is shown by the care with which it hired Hans Meyerhoff, who taught what is now called "continental philosophy" at UCLA from 1948 until his death in 1963. This approach, which by now includes philosophers like Giorgio Agamben, Hannah Arendt, Alain Badiou, Simone de Beauvoir, Judith Butler, Gilles Deleuze, Jacques Derrida, Michel Foucault, Georg Hegel, Martin Heidegger, Friedrich Nietzsche, Jean-Paul Sartre, and Slavoj Žižek, was already, as World War II ended, the most famous and important philosophical tradition in the world. But the anti-atheist pressures of the early Cold War strongly disfavored that kind of philosophy. Its most influential representative, then and now, was Karl Marx; no other philosopher has ever had more than a billion people living by his teachings, or even claiming to do so.[22] As we see from the letters opposing Otto, Marx's Communism would not have been, in 1947, a major problem; his atheism, however, was. And many of the other famous names in the tradition at that time—Nietzsche, Beauvoir, and Sartre, to mention a few—were not only atheists, but atheists whose atheism, like Otto's, was central to the rest of their philosophy. Even worse, these world-famous figures were public about their atheism; the world at large was well aware of what they advocated.[23] It is not surprising, then, that Walter Kaufmann would in 1956 identify existentialism's association with atheism as hindering its arrival in the American university system.[24]

The problem, then, was this: on the one hand, hiring someone to teach continental philosophy risked provoking further outrage among religious conservatives. On the other hand, that kind of philosophy, then under the label of "existentialism," was already recognizable as an extremely significant philosophical approach. The need to educate students about it was patent.

There was, however, a way out of this dilemma; for if the philosophy department was under outside eyes, the observers, certainly in 1947, were not well informed about the arcane customs of academia. The people who protested the hiring of Max Otto, as I have noted, in general had little contact with universities. They did not know how to go looking for atheists in the academy; in order to cause trouble, one's atheistic views had to be placed squarely before them—as Otto had done, first with his provocatively titled *Is There A God?* and, later, when news of his UCLA appointment made it into the *Los Angeles Examiner*. More private venues were relatively unproblematic. Thus, philosophy department chair Piatt could write in a personal letter in 1952, "I am a thoroughgoing naturalist, and have no use other than a purely symbolic one for the term God, [so] there is for me no problem of evil, I speak of good and bad, but do not need, in place of the latter term, evil."[25] We can imagine the problems Piatt would have encountered had these sentiments been published in the *Los Angeles Examiner*. Religiously controversial philosophical ideas, such as atheism and naturalism, might thus have a chance at UCLA, but they would have to be "stealthy"—that is, handled in such a way as to keep outsiders to the academy from knowing about them.

It was in this context that, a year after the Max Otto Affair, UCLA hired Meyerhoff. Given what has been established above, his hiring should have been controversial, but it seems to have been handled with unusual delicacy. Consider, to begin with, Meyerhoff's publications. One's first major publication, especially in the humanities, normally comes out of one's thesis. Meyerhoff's thesis, however, was never published. It resided, as it does today, in the remote section of the UCLA library devoted to dissertations, under the innocent title "Types of Ethical Premises." Only when we examine it physically do we see that it contains a detailed discussion of Nietzsche—a discussion that ends with a judgment on Nietzsche that is severely critical, but not only of Nietzsche: "Nietzsche was not justified in rejecting all traditional values *in toto* simply because they failed to provide for adequate organic satisfaction. . . . Nietzsche's own 'naturalism in morals' may turn out to be as unbalanced as the Christian 'supernaturalism in morals' against which he crusaded."[26] Calling Christian supernaturalism "unbalanced" and equating it with Nietzsche's atheism would not have pleased the anti-Otto letter writers; but they were scarcely the kind of people to haunt the card catalogue in the UCLA Library or to be provoked by an investigation of "ethical premises."

Meyerhoff did publish one book during the early Cold War, *Time in Literature* (1955). It is an elegant and insightful meditation on literary treatments of time, to which I return in chapter 5. Relevant here is that "literary" time for Meyerhoff is wholly "subjective," and so sharply distinguished from the "objective" time of physics (*TL*, viii). The kind of philosophy with which such literature is allied, which includes "all varieties of phenomenology and existentialism," is likewise concerned only with "subjective" aspects of human existence (*TL*, 138). As an attempt to illuminate the human condition, such philosophy is asserted to have close ties not only with art but with religion— even when the writer in question is an atheist (*TL*, 143–44). Meyerhoff's appeal to the "illumination" of the human condition thus opens a place for religion (without actually endorsing theism). This delicate treatment of religion is in direct contrast, not only to Otto's blunt dismissals of belief in God, but to much of the existential-phenomenological tradition with which Meyerhoff allies himself: Heidegger, for example, illuminates human existence for hundreds of pages in *Being and Time* without any reference to religion. Sartre goes further: "There is no human nature, because there is no God to have a conception of it" (Sartre 2001, 28): human subjectivity *cannot* be illuminated from a theistic standpoint.

In addition to the circumspection of his writings, Meyerhoff's appointment can be considered as "stealthy" in that he had been on campus for several years before his hire, having received both his BA and his PhD from UCLA (in 1936 and 1942 respectively). Hiring one's own graduates was an astute move in the early Cold War, because someone already on campus had a network of friends and supporters on campus who could raise an outcry in case of attacks from outside. This brought some protection, as we will see in chapter 5, from even CUAC, the most rabid of California's Red hunters. It seems to have become something of a policy for the UCLA philosophy department as regards junior hires, which (as we will also see in chapter 5) were the most vulnerable kind. Thus, Abraham Kaplan (hired 1952) was, like Meyerhoff, a UCLA PhD. Donald Kalish (hired 1950) and Richard Montague (hired 1955) had both studied at Berkeley. This hiring from home, while more common then than it is today, was something of an innovation at UCLA. The older two generations in the department had mainly done their graduate work in the East—John Elof Boodin, Charles Rieber, and J. Wesley Robson at Harvard, and Ernest Moore and Donald Piatt at Chicago. Hans Reichenbach had received his PhD from Erlangen, in Germany.[27]

The discretion concerning Meyerhoff continued after his appointment. Unless a professor was unfortunate enough to attract journalistic attention, as Otto had, the main way to find out about what she was teaching was, in those pre-Internet days, via the course listings in her institution's annual catalogue. During Meyerhoff's first four years at UCLA, its *General Catalogue* lists him as teaching, not courses explicitly in phenomenology and existentialism, but "Introduction to Philosophy" and "Philosophy of Religion." In 1952–53, he began teaching a course called "Nineteenth-Century Idealism and Romanticism," which included Nietzsche—strangely enough, since Nietzsche, an uncompromising materialist, is neither an idealist nor a classical romantic (see del Caro 1989). In 1955–56, the year after Meyerhoff got tenure,[28] he added a course in existentialism, but again it was a strange course, giving Buber and Marcel—a Jew and a Catholic—equal time with the more famous and far more philosophically influential non-theists Heidegger and Sartre.

Marxism itself was not taught in the philosophy department until 1958–59, when Jósef Bochenski, the Flint Professor for that year, taught a course called "Dialectical and Historical Materialism in Russia." Bochenski was himself Polish; he was also a logician and a Dominican priest, and so could hardly be accused of advocating things like dialectics and materialism in the classroom.[29]

1950: THE OATH AND SOME PHILOSOPHERS

Another apparent case of stealth concerns the California Oath controversy. The core puzzlement here is the strangely incomplete defense offered by philosophy professor Hugh Miller when he was attacked for not signing the California Loyalty Oath. The California Oath controversy was a major incident in the history of American higher education, and its basic facts require only brief summary.[30] The Board of Regents of the university had long had a policy that no Communist could be employed at the University of California, and a loyalty oath had long been required of state employees.[31] On March 25, 1949, the regents decided to enforce the policy by revamping the oath. The new oath was for university employees only, and it contained an explicit statement that the signer was not a member of the Communist Party.

Just why the regents took this course at this time is, like so much else about the early Cold War, unclear. The immediate trigger was an invitation to fired University of Washington philosophy professor Herbert Phillips to speak at UCLA (*TD*, 28). But some suspected that starting a battle of this kind was part of an attempt to weaken President Robert G. Sproul to the point where UCLA could be separated off from Berkeley and made into an autonomous university (which indeed happened in 1952).[32] John Caughey, a history professor who refused to sign the oath, pointed out another possible ulterior goal, and one with better empirical support. In an article in *Harper's Magazine* for November, 1950, Caughey recounted a telling exchange at a Board of Regents meeting, between California Governor Earl Warren, an *ex officio* member of the board, and one of the regents: "Do I understand," Governor Warren asked, "that we are firing these people merely because they are recalcitrant?" "It is not a question of Communism," said Regent Arthur J. McFadden, "but one of discipline" (Caughey 1950).

The regents may, of course, have had multiple goals. If one of them was to assert their authority over professors by forcing them to do something they did not want to do, it was achieved, for the oath was extremely unpopular even with professors who eventually signed it. According to a report to the Berkeley

Academic Senate, "The faculty of one of our greatest universities—now no longer so—has been cowed and beaten so that hundreds of the most brilliant people in this university have been forced to accept conditions they resent and intellectually reject. . . . Very few volunteered to take this oath. It was rammed down their throats."[33] It is easy to understand the faculty's vehement reaction. The oath, required of university employees only, questioned their patriotism *en masse* and without evidence; it amounted to a gratuitous insult. Moreover, as a weapon against Communism the oath was simply silly. If Communists were the lying subversives the regents claimed they were, the idea that they would reveal themselves by refusing to sign an oath of any kind was absurd. If they were not, the loyalty oath was unnecessary.

So some faculty members refused to sign.

The regents, enraged by their disobedience, declared on February 24, 1950, that anyone who had not signed as of the following April 30 would be automatically off the payroll as of the next day. As Caughey pointed out in his article, this meant that non-signers were treated far more harshly than Communists, who were at least entitled to due process in the form of a hearing. The immediate peril in which non-signing faculty now found themselves was made clear by Rudolph Carnap in a letter to Hans Reichenbach in October, 1950, after declining the Flint Professorship because of the controversy. Carnap explains that he does not hold Reichenbach's signing of the oath against him, going on to say that if he were presently employed at the university, he would probably sign it too, because of concerns for his family.[34]

In the face of this dire threat to their colleagues, the University of California Committee on Privilege and Tenure secured from the regents permission to hold hearings, with the aim of determining whether any given non-signer should be retained by the university or not. The Southern (UCLA) committee promptly interviewed twenty-seven non-signers, and cleared twenty-six of them (Schrecker 1986, 121). After much prevarication, the regents changed their minds, rejected the committee's findings, and went ahead with some of the firings. In October 1952, however, the California Supreme Court decided that it was unconstitutional to force faculty to sign an oath not required of other state employees, and ordered the non-signers reinstated. The original oath was also reinstated (I took it upon arriving at UCLA in 2001), and the controversy subsided, though the non-signers did not fully settle with the university regarding back pay until March 1956.

Five of those twenty-seven non-signers were members of the philosophy department—an extraordinary record of courage for such a small department in such a large university. One of them was Christopher Jackson, a Briton who was at UCLA only for a single year and had left by the time the committee completed its work. The others were Donald Kalish (the only non-signer not to have tenure), Abraham Kaplan, Hugh Miller, and Donald Piatt.[35]

In its zeal to acquit the non-signers, the Privilege and Tenure Committee frequently used their professional opinions and activities as evidence that the professors in question were not Communists or fellow travelers. Thus, in its letter to the regents concerning Kenneth Roose, an economist, the committee stated, "His professional research has been in the fields of employment, income, and business cycles. He stated that he opposes redistribution of wealth; he believes that 'the profit motive is the guide for where resources should go— there should be rewards for initiative and innovation.'"[36] This is not a simple report of Roose's field and opinions; the information is included in the letter for the express purpose of clearing Roose of Communistic associations.

Hugh Miller had also expressed—indeed, published—anti-Communist views. Chapter 10 of his 1939 *History and Science* contains a harsh refutation of Marxist dialectics—as Miller understood them. Marxism, he writes, represents a "materialistic regression into a dogmatic and fatal rationalism" and resorts "to a mess of fantastic dogma to support this inadequate social analysis" (Miller 1939, 168, 166). These criticisms come from Miller's basic claim that everything is temporal, so that "every natural occurrence, however small, has a temporal as well as a spatial dimension; and in this way even observed occurrences are short histories" (Miller 1939, 7).

This is, paradoxically, actually rather close to Marx's definition in *Capital* of "dialectics" as thought, which "includes, in its comprehension and affirmative recognition of the existing state of things . . . also the recognition of the negation of that state, of its inevitable breaking up; because [such thought] regards every historically developed social form as in fluid movement, and hence takes into account its transient nature not less than its momentary existence; because it lets nothing impose upon it, and is in its essence critical and revolutionary" (Marx 1906, 26). Everything historical is impermanent, including capitalism, which is destined to disappear. Marx's philosophy then builds on this foundation to ask what it is about capitalism that will make it disappear.

Miller, then, shared Marx's view of dialectics, and shared as well his corresponding view of the impermanence of social arrangements: "Our age," he wrote, "is admittedly one of transition" (Miller 1939, 1). When Miller criticizes Marx, it is because he reads him along Stalinist lines, so that dialectics is no longer merely the presumption that everything is in time but becomes itself atemporal—the infamous "iron law" of economically determined historical development via thesis, antithesis, and synthesis. Miller can thus be read as proposing a *more* comprehensive version of social change than the one he attributes to Marx. Indeed, he writes, Marx's account of the "observable facts" of social realities was, though incomplete, not entirely false:

> Thus [for Marx] industrial society, ruled by a capitalistic class, produces an exploited and disprivileged proletariat, which enters into conflict with its exploiters, the struggle being resolved by the establishment of a new economic order. . . . That there is some truth in this portrayal of the contemporary scene is evident. . . . The error of the Marxian dialectic does not lie in the observable facts it appeals to. It lies in the supposition that those facts . . . are the whole truth and in its resort to a mess of fantastic dogma to support this inadequate social analysis (Miller 1939: 166).

Moreover, Miller was not (in 1939) without sympathy for the Soviet Union: "Let it be said here that the new sociological emphasis on economic factors, and the political movement of revolutionary Russia, are not meant to be included in this indictment of the pseudo philosophy which is their ostensible basis" (Miller 1939, 163). While finally harsh, Miller's philosophical critique of Marxism is both nuanced and contextualized: as a concrete diagnosis of the current state of history, Marxism has "some truth," and the Soviet Union's efforts to put it into practice, when not founded on this "pseudo philosophy," are not targets of his criticism.

What is interesting for present purposes is the use the Committee on Promotion and Tenure made of Miller's writings: none at all. In contrast to their procedure with Roose, they made no mention of Miller's disagreement with Marx and Marxism. Either they decided to pass over it in silence, or they did not know about it; and if they did not know about it, it was because Miller and his allies did not tell them—and so themselves decided to pass over it in silence. Given that the aim of the committee was to acquit Miller of Communist views and that the committee elsewhere used professional opinions for that purpose, this seems strange indeed—until we remember that one staple of the McCarthy Era was the use of quotations from the distant past, taken completely out of context, to convict people of Communist sympathies. The last two quotations above would likely have been enough to convict Miller of such sympathies, no matter how they were balanced in the rest of his discussion. Miller's problem, then, was not that his philosophical opinion of Marxism was positive, for overall it was not; it was that it was nuanced.

Nuance was not a problem for Donald Kalish, who, as I have noted, was the only untenured non-signer and whose extraordinary courage on matters of principle would shine forth again, sixteen years later, when he was department chair during the Angela Davis affair. Kalish's argument against signing, an ingenious one, was that he had come to the conclusion that the philosophical foundations of Marx's Communism were "balderdash."[37] If his students knew that he was required by oath to say this, the status of his view as a philosophical truth reached by impartial inquiry would be impeached in their eyes.

If this one-word dismissal of Marx sounds like Reichenbach's denigrations of "unscientific philosophy" (to be discussed in chapter 4), it is a long way from logical positivism's original self-assignment in Europe, which, as George Reisch puts it, was to "clean Marxism's stables of the metaphysical elements lurking within dialectical materialism."[38] Unlike Miller's nuanced condemnation, which is closer to what the original positivists had in mind, Kalish's blanket dismissal was happily reported by the committee in its letter for him. Being able to make blanket dismissals of people like Marx, and to present those dismissals as professional (i.e., objective and impartial) opinions, was clearly a good survival tactic.

Here we have the reverse of the usual situation: instead of giving public lip service to capitalism while criticizing it among friends, as many did, Kalish expresses his anti-Marxism privately to the committee, while he publicly aligns himself with leftists (if not Communists) by refusing to sign the oath. Given what we know of Kalish, his private statement cannot have been insincere; but that he made it at all suggests that in his view, and certainly in that of the Privilege and Tenure Committee, nuance had no place in the American academy during the early Cold War.

1953: THE NON-NATURALIST HIRE

In late 1952, Abraham Kaplan took over from Donald Piatt as chair of the UCLA philosophy department. In January 1953, almost six years after the Otto affair, the new chair found himself confronting a challenge that came, not from outside the university, but from the Westwood campus itself—indeed, from the college's own dean, Paul A. Dodd. In a letter Kaplan wrote that month to his colleague Hugh Miller, who was on leave in Austria,[39] he explained that when meeting with the dean earlier that month on another matter, he had been surprised to hear him offer the department a permanent new line, on condition that they make it in metaphysics or philosophy of religion.

Within weeks of the dean's offer, several members of the department began writing letters to colleagues around the country soliciting recommendations for the new position. Piatt, in one of these, wrote to Lewis E. Hahn that "we are looking for a young man who specializes in metaphysics and, even more, philosophy of religion. . . . As you may know, we are, almost to a man, hard-boiled naturalists, and we have rightly been criticized by the local clergy and others for giving religion a bad break."[40] The mention of criticism "by the local clergy" may have been a reference to the Otto affair itself, but that is unlikely; it was now six years in the past, and almost all of those letters had come from laypeople. More likely is that various "local clergy and others" were continuing to speak out against "atheism" in the philosophy department. Until Dodd's offer to the department, however, their speech appears to have had little effect. Kaplan's surprise at the dean's offer suggests that he had either discounted the ongoing criticism or had actually been unaware of it.

Though some of the letters, especially those from Piatt, seem to go to some length to suggest that the dean's demand was at least partially justified (as in his letter to Hahn quoted above), all of them make clear that in the final analysis the hire is being forced on the department. Thus, Robert Yost wrote to Walter Kaufmann at Princeton, "The general motive behind the creation of the post is the desire for balance in the Department's course offerings. But, of course, the Department must be satisfied that the person it nominates is a good philosopher."[41] Yost does not specify to Kaufmann whose desire it was that the department should have more "balance." Abraham Kaplan, writing to his UCLA colleague Hugh Miller, was clearer in locating the desire for balance outside the department: "I think I am fairly reporting the attitude of the Department if I say that . . . there are others whom we might prefer to appoint if we had completely free choice for the particular fields for which the position was intended."[42] The other letters soliciting recommendations, including several more from Kaplan to various people, make sure to mention, in a somewhat embarrassed way, that the impetus is coming from the dean—behind whom, according to Piatt, stood the "clergy and others."

The department had thus agreed on two things: that it did not want to make this hire, and that it would do so anyway. There is evidence, to be sure, that the department was not of one mind as to how to respond. No letters from Hans Reichenbach appear in this context, and he may have boycotted the search altogether. Piatt seems to have been at odds with himself. Letters in which he solicits recommendations from professors at other universities refer to the department as "guilty" of a naturalistic "bias," and he even says that the clergy

has "rightly" criticized this; but it is a bias that in other cases he admits to shar-
ing, and with some pride.[43] Kaplan also wrote to solicit recommendations, and
his letters—his alone—say that the prospective hire must actually *be* a non-
naturalist, presumably in the sense of actually believing in a supernatural order
rather than merely studying and teaching the works of others who do. The
letters from the others either avoid that issue altogether or merely say that the
successful candidate must take non-naturalism seriously.

This incident raises two questions that need consideration here. One is that
of just why Dodd made the offer of a non-naturalist position when he did. This
seems to have been something of a mystery even to Kaplan, who, as we saw, was
surprised by the offer. Dodd may have had his reasons, however. Earlier that
month, the *UCLA Daily Bruin* had warned a number of times that Senators
Patrick McCarran and Joseph McCarthy were planning hearings on Communist infiltration in universities and that the University of California was "likely to
be hit;"[44] it may be that Dodd was trying to preempt these by tossing a piece of
good news to religiously inspired Red hunters. It is also the case that in March
1952, less than a year before Dodd made his offer, the university had put into
place the California Plan, which (as chapter 5 shows) was designed to insure
that no subversives would be hired to the faculty. Dodd may have decided that
the time was right to go beyond this "negative" achievement and start the hiring
of the "right" people. Or it may be that he was told to do this by higher officials.

This helps contextualize, if not explain, the department's somewhat puzzling acquiescence in the dean's initiative. The department's clear view, as reported in the letters soliciting recommendations, was that non-naturalism had
no important place in the future of philosophy. Whether this view was right or
wrong (I personally think it was right), it was the department's prerogative—
indeed, its scholarly duty—to act on it. Dodd's offer thus constituted blatant
interference in the department's affairs—all the worse because it was openly
provoked by forces outside the university. But not only did the department
cooperate with the search; Kaplan's letter to Miller reports no resistance at all,
not even in the form of a private argument with the dean. This sudden lack of
spine is strange indeed coming from a department whose members had behaved so heroically with regard to the California Oath controversy.

But things had changed at UCLA. In contrast to the Otto Affair six years
before, in which the administration was publicly silent, anti-atheist forces now
had the explicit support of the dean. This illustrates an underlying dynamic of
the McCarthy Era. Though, as Ellen Schrecker shows, the federal government
was involved in Red hunting before McCarthy himself even entered the scene

(Schrecker 1986, 4–5), on the state level the pattern was somewhat different. M. J. Heale puts it as follows: "Conservative and maverick elements tended at first to operate on the political fringes, but around 1950 governments were being recruited to a more vigorous embrace of the anticommunist cause. . . . Such pre-emption of the issue, however, sometimes by authorities of a moderate disposition who hoped to control it, could result in the unlocking of a Pandora's Box" (Heale 1998, 7).

As seen from the UCLA philosophy department, this gradual "recruitment" exhibited four stages. After the Max Otto affair came the extremely complex California Oath controversy. Crucial here is that the controversy was precipitated, not by outsiders but by the university's own regents, who undertook to preempt outside pressures by loudly instituting their own version of academic repression—the loyalty oath. Two years after that, in March 1952, the California Plan, to be discussed chapter 5, was introduced; with it, the active cooperation of UCLA's higher administration with Red hunters was institutionalized. And ten months after that came Dodd's offer to the philosophy department. As the years went by, then, outside forces were joined in turn by the regents, the UCLA higher administration, and finally the dean of the college. Attacks were clearly coming from closer and closer to home, as administrators adjusted to the increasingly powerful anti-Communist elements in American government and society. As wall after wall crumbled, resistance must have looked more and more futile.

A sense of futility is suggested by the willingness of the department's faculty members, in their letters soliciting recommendations, to state openly that they were giving in to this sort of administrative pressure. During the Max Otto Affair we found, particularly on the part of Donald Piatt, an extreme concern that UCLA not be perceived as giving in to right-wing forces; yet now he is writing to colleagues and openly admitting such capitulation as if it were a matter of course. This suggests that the situation was not unusual around the country, and the resulting picture is depressing indeed: one of a department facing repeated attacks for its "atheism," now without protectors within the university, and confronting the fact that this situation is so prevalent nationwide that open capitulation will be viewed as reasonable. The department itself thus seems, by 1953, to have opened the "Pandora's box" of cooperation with right-wing forces. Such cooperation was only prudent. Departmental resistance to the dean would clearly, if word of it got out, bring yet more criticism from the "local clergy." Other sticks, in the form of threats to punish the department if it did not accept the new position, may have been brandished or implied.

But happier factors may also have played a part. The offer of a free position on a permanent line, even when the job itself is unpalatable, is a carrot not easy to refuse. Still cheerier (but not incompatible) is the possibility that the writing of so many letters, and the subsequent hiring of a one-year interim professor in the field, were consciously dilatory—a stealthy effort to at least delay the hire.

It was Hans Reichenbach who eventually stopped it—not stealthily, but in the most costly possible way: he died suddenly of a heart attack on April 9, 1953. By that time the department had made a one-year stop-gap appointment, and it speedily decided, as Yost wrote to Kaufmann on July 1, that its first priority now had to be replacing Reichenbach.[45] This was accomplished the next year—and spectacularly—with the hiring of Rudolf Carnap. Carnap had, to be sure, signed some improvident petitions since coming to America, but his arrival at UCLA, unlike Otto's, did not make the newspapers, and the matter was left in the relatively professional hands of the FBI. The investigation lasted until 1955 but turned up nothing significant (see Reisch 2005, 271–79).

Criticism from the clergy would not quickly abate. Sniping from the pulpits would be renewed in 1960–64, when Patrick Wilson was teaching philosophy of religion at UCLA from a "naturalistic" point of view, and was denounced by both a prominent Los Angeles rabbi and the Catholic archbishop.[46] The hiring of Communist Party member Angela Davis in 1967 would provoke a national firestorm. As Foucault might say, there was no shortage of citizens peering into the academic Panopticon to see if the philosophers, at least, were doing their job. Atheism and "disrespect" for religion were truly an open sore that attracted right-wing attention to the UCLA philosophy department for decades.

CONCLUSION

The cases discussed in this chapter show the UCLA philosophy faculty and administrators moving adroitly to salvage respectable (naturalistic) philosophy at the university without provoking outside forces among the regents, the clergy, and society at large. If Clarence Dykstra did sabotage the Otto's house hunting, he made up for it by giving them his own house for several months. As for Otto himself, present evidence does not permit us to know whether he himself fully believed the housing problem was real; he announced it as his reason for resigning the Flint professorship but never said it was his only reason. The department's careful treatment of Hans Meyerhoff's dissertation and its careful wording of his course listings in the *General Catalogue* were eventually successful, as Meyerhoff went on to a distinguished teaching career (he is commemorated today in Meyerhoff Park, the free speech area on the Westwood campus). Its equally careful defense of Hugh Miller avoided drawing attention to the favorable things he had said about the Soviet Union, and while this precluded using some exculpatory statements he made in his book, what remained was enough for his vindication by the Committee on Privilege and Tenure. And finally, the department's slow acquiescence in the non-naturalist hire, if intentional, was simply brilliant. This is a story of heroism and subtlety. I am proud to have told it.

But in the anguished tumult of the early Cold War, were heroism and subtlety enough?

CHAPTER 2

Reductionism as the Favored
Form of Naturalism

Nature loves to hide.

HERACLEITUS

Chapter 1 showed religious conservatives, spurred on by their view that philosophy departments were the only places in universities where "atheism" could be promulgated, deploying various strategies of force against the philosophy department at UCLA. These included newspaper articles, letter-writing campaigns, and threats of lawsuits. By 1953, the department's own dean was aiding the religious forces to the extent of imposing on the department a hire it did not want to make. The department seems, in response, to have assumed a "stealthy" stance characterized by hiring in-house, publishing controversial (i.e., "atheistic") views in places where they would not be found easily or at all, and editing the university catalogue in very careful ways.

The pressures, we saw, worked against the importation from Europe of the largely atheistic "continental" philosophical tradition (as it is called today). They also, I argue in this chapter, affected the philosophical approaches already being practiced in America, favoring some and disfavoring others. Approaches that could be presented as neutral between atheism and religion, such as rational choice theory (to be discussed in chapter 4), or whose commitment to naturalism could be disguised, such as the "stratified" naturalism to be explored here, had political winds at their backs, favoring them at the expense of their alternatives.

These were several. As the United States reoriented itself to fight the Cold War, no fewer than four different philosophical dispositives played roles in its secular intellectual life. They included various versions of idealism and materialism, as well as two versions of naturalism. One of these was a humanistic naturalism associated with many pragmatists, which I call "pragmatic naturalism." The other was the eventual winner, a more oblique version of naturalism presented in Hans Reichenbach's *The Rise of Scientific Philosophy* (*Rise*), which I call "stratified naturalism."

Unlike the situation today, when analytic and continental approaches are largely closed off from one another, the different approaches during the early Cold War engaged in mutual dialogue. Indeed, the boundaries among them were so fuzzy that it can be hard to tell exactly what distinguished pragmatists, in particular, from idealists and materialists. The real contest, however, was between the two "naturalistic" approaches. Adherents of both defined them polemically—that is, by contrasting themselves with adherents of the other approaches. Thus, for all of Hans Reichenbach's assertions in his 1951 *The Rise of Scientific Philosophy* that philosophy must become "scientific," his account of the actual nature of "science" is at best only casual (see chapter 4). His book in fact presents, not an "internal" balance sheet of scientific philosophy's doctrines and prospects but the polemical story of its contrast with, and triumph over, other approaches. Pragmatic naturalism, for its part, was also clearer about what it was against than what it was for—or, at least, so says William Dennes, in his contribution to the important pragmatist anthology *Naturalism and the Human Spirit*.[1] A complete understanding of these four dispositives lies far beyond the scope of this work, and my discussion aims merely to give a sense of the relevant contrasts among them.

IDEALISM

By the time of the Cold War, American idealism was consummating a very long death. It features here, not in its own right, but as an antiquated foil for both types of naturalism, as well as for materialism. In contrast to these, idealism included all philosophy that posited a spiritual order of some kind. As ideal, this spiritual order was both ethically supreme and metaphysically unalterable, with the result that the basic task of human individuals was to integrate with it. This approach had a long history in America and claimed to go back to the Greeks. Some discussion of that history is necessary to understand its academic position in the early Cold War.

As Bruce Kuklick puts it in his masterful *A History of Philosophy in America* (Kuklick 2001), in the eighteenth century and for most of the nineteenth, the mission of American philosophers "was to support theoretically the concerns of the divinity-school theologians and the most serious ministers on the hustings. The philosophers were invariably ministers and committed Protestants themselves. Often the presidents of their institutions, they had captive students and easy access to publication" (Kuklick 2001, 1–2) . American philosophical idealism was thus firmly rooted in American religiosity. After the Civil War, however, a change occurred, as idealism outside Catholic universities began to take on a Germanic cast. Advanced training in theology had long been common for American idealists; now, many of them got it in Germany (Kuklick 2001, 111). It was not the Bible but Kant, these Americans held, who had definitively established the existence of an immaterial, spiritual order. But the strict Kantian dualisms regarding nature and mind left them uneasy and led them further into German terrain (Kuklick 2001, 113), which meant a break with traditional views of a personal God. By the time the Americans reached Hegel's Absolute, the loving and righteous God of the Bible had evanesced into what was (and is) generally read as a set of metaphysically creative, supra-temporal logical structures. Thus, as one of idealism's California exponents, George Holmes Howison, put it in 1895, "Our common philosophy is Idealism—that explanation of the world which maintains that the only thing absolutely real is mind; that all material and all temporal existences take their being from mind" (quoted at Kuklick 2001, 113). A traditional Christian would likely have written "God" in place of "mind," but the underlying commitment—to an atemporal rational order as the foundation of reality (and so of value, for values are real)—is similar.

Hegelian mind (*Geist*) expressed its divinized conceptuality in the spirit (*Geist* again) of a people (*Volk*), which to the Americans meant submerging the individual in a divinized collective. As opposed to this, American idealism found its mission in the valorization of the individual human spirit (Kuklick 2001, 113–15). Just how this replacement was carried out need not concern us, for the individualistic emphasis of the Americans meant, in practice, that they spared themselves much of the work. The job of the philosopher, for them, was not metaphysical theorizing but of a more practical order: indeed, for Howison, ethics itself is "first philosophy" (McLachlan 2006, 239). Philosophers were not to argue for idealism's basic premises—these were, as Kuklick notes, presupposed (Kuklick 2001, 112–13)—but to articulate them so that others could come to identify their worth as persons with their integration into a larger, spiritual order: "Those idealists . . . interested in morality promoted 'self-realization ethics'—the moral being developed a communal sense of harmony with the greater self, and in time the best human selves would mimic the growth of the world-defining soul" (Kuklick 2001, 113).

Thus, Howison, whom James McLachlan calls "by all accounts . . . one of the great philosophical teachers of his age," failed to develop any positive doctrine (Kuklick 2001, 114; McLachlan 2006, 224). The idealists seem generally, in fact, to have been better teachers than researchers, engaged in a pedagogical project of inculcating a sense of the individual's inherence in a larger whole. I call this project "edification," not in Richard Rorty's sense of bringing about a healthy skepticism or (in Jaegwon Kim's telling gloss) of fostering an individual's "capacity for self-expression,"[2] but in that of bringing the student to an educated appreciation of her place in, and so her duties to, a larger order.

By the time of the Otto Affair, idealism was represented in the UCLA philosophy department only by two emeriti, John Elof Boodin and Charles Rieber. The UCLA memorial notes for each convey the spirit of their thought. According to Boodin's statement, published in 1950, his work constituted a "sustained and masterful effort to preserve the long tradition of philosophical idealism from Plato to Royce, within the framework and the materials of our contemporary science. . . . He brought historical perspective and breadth of knowledge into our present human situation, and refused to regard that situation as one of subjective and arbitrary values as over against objective and stubborn facts. The wholeness of things would not permit such a dualism."[3] Boodin's refusal of the fact/value distinction in this form meant that he regarded values *as* facts, as objective characteristics of an ideal order. This order, being both good and unchangeable, was something the student had to harmonize with, like it or not—a thoroughly "Platonic" view. Rieber's lineage was also traced back to Plato: "In his philosophy he was an adherent of the school of modern idealism, looking back through Royce and Howison to the epistemology of Kant and the idealistic metaphysics of Fichte, but his idealism was closer in spirit and intention to that of Plato, who used logic and metaphysics to gain direct access to that height where intellectual comprehension is the support of artistic genius and religious vision."[4] At such a height, logic and metaphysics were merely tools in the service of "artistic genius" and "religious vision." They, and with them philosophy itself, had no status to criticize belief in spiritual realities, and philosophy could only—as for Boodin—preach to its students the necessity to integrate themselves with the ideal order.

That idealism by 1947 was represented at UCLA only by emeriti testifies to its almost complete rejection by American philosophers. So does the philosophy department's 1957 reaction to a bequest from Boodin's estate to provide for the publication of some of his writings: "Because much of Prof. Boodin's work in philosophy is seriously outdated and subject to almost no interest today, normal publication of his works would be wasteful and uneconomical."[5] The language is brutal, but accurate. Apart from its religious roots, idealism had in fact had little recommend it, either theoretically or practically. Theoretically, the very existence of its quasi-divine ideal order, which it had baldly taken from Kant, was undermined in various ways by its move to Hegel; for Kant's identification of that order began from his doctrine of synthetic *a priori* propositions, a doctrine Hegel rejected (see McCumber 2014). And its practical project of individual edification carried whiffs of a tea-time elitism in which the person edified is assumed to be not only intelligent, but white, male, and Christian.[6] It became untenable after World War II, as students became more varied in skin color, gender, and religion. As a result of these philosophical and social changes, many idealists gradually slid into pragmatism. The prime example is John Dewey, who by 1947 had transformed his early commitment to neo-Hegelianism into a view of the larger order as "human nature itself, in the connections, actual and potential, that humans sustain to one another in the natural environment."[7]

The quasi-divine Hegelian Absolute has thus been replaced by a web of human interconnections. Correspondingly, the UCLA philosophy department's idealist visionaries had by 1947 been replaced as active faculty by a more down-to-earth set. Philosophy at UCLA, as in the rest of the country, thus seems to have undergone something akin to a Kuhnian paradigm shift. In this case, it was a change in intellectual orientation so profound that the writings of someone on the far side of it, such as John Elof Boodin, were viewed as containing almost nothing of value.

PRAGMATIC NATURALISM VERSUS IDEALISM

We have now uncovered three relevant characteristics of idealism's position in the philosophical constellation of the early Cold War. First, it was, philosophically speaking, all but dead: its loss of credibility with the younger generation of philosophers had been virtually complete. Second, its illustrious history meant that it still had to be engaged with: philosophers still had to explain why they were no longer idealists. And third, though the rhetoric could be harsh (as with Boodin), a clear doctrinal line between idealism and pragmatism is surprisingly hard to draw. The cosmic mind of the idealists, though decked out in theological language, was already of unclear ontological status, and between it and the social network of the pragmatists were many ontological gradations, just as there had been between the personal God of the Christians and the cosmic mind of the Hegelians.

We can understand what the participants of the time viewed as the radical break between idealism and naturalism by looking at Dewey's response to a 1939 essay by UCLA's Donald Piatt on Dewey's logical theory. In it, Piatt argued that logical laws are postulates of inquiry and that "when inquiry turns in upon itself it finds that, to produce warranted conclusions it must proceed according to certain rules or stipulations; . . . if one thinks, one is obliged to follow the *a priori* forms of thought shown by inquiry to be implicit in all previous rational inquiry and necessary for further inquiry" (Piatt [1939] 1951, 110; punctuation updated). This is somewhat muddy, because Piatt has not explained what sort of inquiry shows that the "*a priori* forms of thought" are implicit in all previous rational inquiry or how it can establish that they will be necessary in the future: what does it mean for inquiry to "turn in upon itself?" The argument was definitely unconvincing to Dewey, who responded that "the kind of '*a priori*' which Mr. Piatt mentions (and which is involved in my theory) is so radically different from the fixed *a priori* located in and furnished by the inherent nature of Mind, *Intellectus Purus*, Reason as *Nous*, figuring in the history of thought, that it seems to me that the words rationalism and *a priori* should be either avoided or else used only with explanatory qualifications" (Dewey 1951, 538, n. 22). What Dewey is objecting to here is the view that the *a priori* is "fixed"—that is, unchanging and so above time. Such an *a priori*, Dewey claims, can be "furnished" by nothing less than an *intellectus purus* or *nous*—that is, it is necessarily rooted in a supernatural form of reason. For Dewey himself, by contrast, the logical order, like everything else, is natural—and so capable of change as our knowledge grows.

The bone of contention between the naturalists and the idealists thus lay in their differing conceptions of the cosmic order. For the idealists, that order was beyond the vicissitudes and transformations of nature. Only from that position could it be viewed, in Howison's words, as "giving being" to nature. For the naturalists, the cosmic order was part and parcel of nature. Yet it was, nonetheless, a "cosmic" order: a set of properties of the whole, now social, to which the individual must conform her thought and submit her actions even as she tried to improve it. Thus, pragmatic naturalism retained the idealistic view that philosophy should be edifying. An example of this is furnished by the third emeritus in the UCLA Department as of 1947, Ernest C. Moore, a philosopher of education (and the first provost of UCLA). Moore, who had retired in 1941, was no idealist.[8] He had been a student of Dewey's at Chicago. Yet he had, like Boodin and Rieber, an elevated view of philosophy as an edifying pursuit. The final paragraph of his last published book includes the following exhortation: "Shall men tell the truth? Or resolve to live by lying? . . . We need a Socrates to teach us what words mean, but more to teach us what conceptions mean. That is what philosophy does, when it is not deadlocked over the barren problem of realism versus idealism. It is a kind of perspective of life, a sailing chart which helps us to find out how human undertakings are related to each other, where dangers lie, and how to sound the depths and keep to navigable waters."[9] The "wholeness of things" to which Boodin appealed has thus, as with Dewey, survived its naturalization to become the mutual interrelations of human undertakings. Within this context, however, philosophy is still a sort of rational edification in which science, logic, and metaphysics are not philosophical ends in themselves, but tools for leading the mind to a higher moral vision of a supra-individual order.

This view of philosophy as an incitement to think beyond oneself was represented in the next generation of UCLA philosophers by Piatt's contemporary, Hugh Miller. The last paragraph of his *History and Science* sounds edifying notes similar to Moore:

> In the strength of these names and as a story of human progress, let us write history! But let us make history, too! No men, in any epoch, have been more signally called upon than we are to resolute action, determining irrevocably what the past shall have meant and the future shall be . . . Righteousness is a crusade. Action is our last honesty. Let us act—we have surmised enough—and show what our hearts are bent upon Let us allow the appeal to history, and in the name of history fight! (Miller 1939, 200–201)

Miller here sounds virtually Heideggerean in his call to resolute historical action. Philosophical edification for him is no mere appreciation of the preexisting wholeness of things, but a rallying cry in the face of history. It is not merely an individual but a social process.

PRAGMATIC NATURALISM VERSUS MATERIALISM

As against idealism, then, pragmatic naturalism denied the existence of a supernatural order, whether in theistic form or in that of a quasi-Hegelian cosmic mind somehow inherent in individual minds. Its rejection of a supernatural order placed it in the same camp as idealism's traditional enemy, materialism. Materialism was not the kind of force on the American philosophical scene that idealism was (see Kuklick 2001, xii–xiii), and I will not go into its long history here. But some discussion of how Americans understood it at the time is in order because understanding pragmatic naturalism requires seeing how it defined itself against materialism. Once again, sharp doctrinal contrasts are hard to draw. Indeed, in a scathing critique of naturalism published in the *Journal of Philosophy* in 1947, Yale philosopher W. H. Sheldon denied that materialism and pragmatic naturalism could be coherently distinguished. Referring to the authors in *Naturalism and the Human Spirit*, Sheldon argued that "their naturalism is just materialism under a softer name" (Sheldon 1945, 254).

It is understandable why philosophers in 1945 would wish to avoid "accusations" of materialism (Sheldon's word: Sheldon 1945, 251), and Sheldon considers two ways in which they attempted to distinguish themselves from the materialists. The first of these, most powerfully stated by Dewey, takes matter and mind to be a conceptual pair whose members originated together and are defined in terms of each other, so that to reject either consistently means to reject both: "Since 'matter' and 'materialism' acquired their significance in contrast with something called 'spirit' and 'spiritualism,' the fact that naturalism has no place for the latter also deprives the former of all significance in philosophy" (Dewey 1944, 3). Naturalism is not for Dewey a "softer" version of materialism, but another animal entirely; indeed, he claims, it is materialism, not naturalism, that is a halfway escape from idealism, for while materialism rejects idealism's nonmaterial, spiritual order, it retains its traditional denigration of matter. This view of matter as in "stark opposition to all that is higher" (Dewey 1944, 3) means that matter is incapable of grounding value. Naturalism, by contrast, allows values to be drawn from nature: "[It] finds the values in question, the worth and dignity of men and women, residing in human nature itself, in the connections, actual and potential, that humans sustain to one another in the natural environment. Not only that, but naturalism is ready at any time to maintain the thesis that that foundation in man and nature is a much sounder basis than is or can be any foundation alleged to exist outside the constitution of man and nature" (Dewey 1944, 9).

The second way of distinguishing between naturalism and materialism is most forcefully advanced by Sidney Hook: "Despite the variety of doctrines which naturalists have professed from Democritus to Dewey, what unites them all is the wholehearted acceptance of scientific method as the only reliable way of reaching truths about the world of nature, society, and man" (Hook 1944, 45). For Hook, materialism is a metaphysical doctrine and, like all such, is to be eschewed (Hook 1944, 45). On his view, naturalism is just adherence to the scientific method—an allegiance professed by a number of the writers in the Columbia Manifesto. As Sheldon puts it, "It is not so much the conclusions of science that they stress, as the method" (Sheldon 1945, 258). But, as he goes on to point out, the Manifesto writers are notably vague in defining the "scientific method" (Sheldon 1945, 257–61). Dewey, for example, characterizes it as the "systematic, extensive, and carefully controlled use of alert and unprejudiced observation and experimentation in collecting, arranging, and testing evidence" (Dewey 1944, 12). This, we may note, is broad enough to vindicate even what Dewey calls the "out and out supernaturalism of the Roman Catholic Church" (Dewey 1944, 1)—as long as we follow the Scholastics in accepting the opinions of the Bible and eminent theologians as our "evidence."[10]

Sheldon goes on to argue that the main constraint the naturalists introduce on scientific method is that what is scientifically observed must be public, which again reduces naturalism to materialism: "Scientific method thus means, to the naturalist, that observation of the non-public has no sense or meaning. Publicity is the test; the private and hidden is ruled out of court. And the only publicly observable things are the physical things" (Sheldon 1945, 262). The one meaningful constraint on what constitutes "scientific method" thus reduces, in Sheldon's view, to an outlook keyed to physical things, if not to explicitly stated materialist doctrine.[11]

The pragmatists' refusal to define scientific method was, it should be noted, a principled one. Piatt expresses this well. The most basic epistemological phenomenon, he argues, is neither science in general nor knowledge as such, but the individual "inquiry." Inquiries are, roughly, attempts to determine what exists independently of us. They are always provoked by and in concrete situations; inquiry is one of our ways of coping with the fact that "the world is in its own right precarious, hazardous, challenging." It follows that inquiry can have no single methodology. "All thought must follow the lead of its subject matter" (Piatt [1939] 1951, 108, 109). This view was not unique to pragmatism; its lineage includes the Vienna Circle's own Otto Neurath and stretches back, before him, to Nietzsche and to Karl Marx,[12] for whom the fundamental fact of science is human interaction with nature, in the form of labor (Marx 1906, 197–98).

We may thus characterize pragmatic naturalism in mid-twentieth-century America as an attempt to found values exclusively on the lives we lead with others as natural beings. Such naturalism distinguishes itself from materialism in that it retains idealism's advocacy of a larger moral order and distinguishes itself from idealism in maintaining that the larger order in question is social rather than divine. When either distinction is rejected, pragmatic naturalism loses its very identity and merges with one of the other approaches. Maintaining both together, however, required it to formulate its project of edification as a break with traditional religion; and that break, moreover, could not be merely individual. For as long as the social order was publicly viewed as predicated on immutable divine truth, it was neither intellectually acceptable nor something an individual student could hope to improve. The break with religion thus had to attack the very status of religion in American society; hence Max Otto's fateful decision to engage theologians in the public pages of the *Christian Century*. Pragmatic naturalism was thus as publicly and intrinsically atheistic as existentialism, and no more politically digestible in the early Cold War. The difference was that by that time, it was already established in American philosophy departments, having arrived on its philosophical merits at a time when political pressures on philosophy were fewer. It is far more comfortable to excoriate European thinkers, such as Hegel and Sartre, than one's own colleagues.

If we measure idealism, materialism, and pragmatic naturalism against the political pressures involved in the Max Otto Affair and its sequels, we see that none of the three was wholly congenial to religious forces, for none upheld belief in a personal God. But all were not equal, either. Idealism, positing a supernatural spiritual order if not a living God, would have been the most tolerable (were it not moribund); materialism, clearly, the least. Pragmatic naturalism, denying a spiritual order but not all values as such, placed itself somewhere in the middle. But the center could not hold, as the Otto Affair showed. Otto clearly had strong moral values, as the writers at *Time* magazine had found; no Russellian hints of scandal in his personal or professional life were charged against him. To those who opposed him, however, an atheist was an atheist, and an atheist should not be in a philosophy department.

STEALTH AS AN AUTHORIAL PRINCIPLE: THE ABSENCE OF RELIGION IN *THE RISE OF SCIENTIFIC PHILOSOPHY*

There was, however, another kind of naturalism at hand in the UCLA philosophy department and elsewhere in the country. This version of naturalism traded on a view of nature as "stratified" into distinct layers (starting from the bottom: physical, chemical, psychological, etc.). Advanced as a component of logical positivism,[13] it was articulated (though the word, we will see, misleads) in many mid-twentieth-century publications, of which the first to be considered here is Hans Reichenbach's 1951 *The Rise of Scientific Philosophy* (*RSP*). Reichenbach's thought on the relevant issues remains sketchy, so I turn for clarification, though briefly, to Carl Hempel, concluding with a short discussion of Paul Oppenheim and Hilary Putnam's 1958 "The Unity of Science as a Working Hypothesis" ("*US*").

Reichenbach's book was no stealth publication. It was not only brilliant but clearly written for a general public, and, according to Michael Friedman, it had by 1960 been translated into German, French, Spanish, Swedish, Italian, Japanese, Polish, Yugoslavian [*sic*], and Korean (Friedman 2000, 75). In the United States it played an enormous role in establishing the various permutations

of what would later be called analytical philosophy as the dominant dispositive in most American philosophy departments. As *The Directory of Modern
American Philosophers* puts it, "*The Rise of Scientific Philosophy* was one of
the best-selling introductions to philosophy of science of [its] day. It helped to
establish the reputation of philosophy of science as a vibrant field dealing both
with traditional philosophical problems and with new questions in response
to exciting developments in the sciences" (Schook 2005, 232). Many young
Americans who would become philosophers read it early on and were, as Kuhn
might say, "converted" by it; as late as 1981, according to Richard Rorty, most
American philosophers still believed that it was Reichenbach who gave their
philosophy the "scientific" character it retains to the present day (Rorty 1982b,
211–12). Though it was, in Kuhn's terms, not a textbook but a popularization
(see *SSR*, 136), *RSP* in fact functioned as the kind of textbook that inculcates
paradigms. As Rorty put it in 1982, "Most of today's teachers of philosophy in
American colleges and universities assimilated some version of Reichenbach's
picture of the history of philosophy in graduate school" (Rorty 1982b, 215).

Though it is written with an unsurpassed vivacity, *RSP* remains, on some
levels, a riddlesome work. In places its discourse becomes strangely oblique.
One of these, as we will see, concerns the "doctrine" of stratified nature itself.
Another concerns its treatment—or rather nontreatment—of religion. One
would think that a book detailing the rise and merits of "scientific" philosophy would make some critical comments about religion, and certainly earlier
public writings of the logical positivists had done so. A. J. Ayer's *Language,
Truth, and Logic* (Ayer 1936), for example, was blunter than Max Otto when
talking about religion, and in this attack, Ayer reported later, he was following
the lead of the original Vienna Circle, whose members had waged a veritable
"war of ideas" against the Austrian Catholic Church (Ayer 1977, 129).

Ayer's book was written in Britain just before World War II; Reichenbach,
writing in America in 1950, is notably more circumspect. Indeed, religion
escapes criticism entirely; even the few critical remarks on mysticism in Reichenbach's 1938 *Experience and Prediction* (Reichenbach 1938, 58–59) have
no counterparts in the later book. *RSP*'s polemics are in fact overwhelmingly
restricted to competing, "unscientific" paradigms in philosophy itself. Here
the main enemy is Hegel, who was already unpopular not only because of the
painful difficulty of his texts but also because of his association with Marx and
the "totalitarian" tradition generally.[14]

Reichenbach discusses Hegel, not in terms of totalitarianism, but as one in
a long line of philosophical idealists, tracing back to Plato. Reichenbach thus,
like the pragmatists, defines his approach partly by contrasting it with idealism

(though not with the American variety: people such as Howison and Royce are not mentioned in *RSP*). Three of those contrasts are important here. First, post-Kantian idealism, unlike earlier versions, was the rejection of a better path of scientific philosophy that was then available: "Those older systems [of Kant and Plato] were expressions of the science of their time and gave pseudo answers when no better answers were available. The philosophical systems of the nineteenth century [including Hegel's] were constructed at a time when a better philosophy was in the making; they are the work of men who did not see the philosophic discoveries immanent in the science of their time and who developed, under the name of philosophy, naïve systems of generalizations and analogies" (*RSP*, 122). While the sins of philosophers up to Kant can be excused because the science of their times could not provide the answers they sought, later philosophers had modern science available to them and rejected it. Hegel, the most extreme idealist, is not even a philosopher; he is a "fanatic" (*RSP*, 72).

Second, while idealism, for Reichenbach, cannot be justified philosophically, it can be explained psychologically. Thinking of Plato, Reichenbach writes, "The symbol of the idealist is the man who resorts to daydreaming because he in unable to enjoy reality in all its moral and aesthetic imperfections. Idealism is the philosophical brand of escapism; it has always flourished in times of social catastrophes, which have shaken the foundations of human society" (*RSP*, 254). Idealism thus arises from a psychological inability to accept the imperfections of reality.

Third, the situation is worse for Hegel because, instead of escaping reality, he wants to control it: "[Hegel] wishes to construe knowledge in such a way that it supplies a basis for moral directives; he wishes to construct for knowledge a certainty which sense perception can never attain, with the intention to construct a parallel to such certainty in an absolute ethical knowledge" (*RSP*, 67–72). This attribution to Hegel of a desire to provide moral directives is in some tension with Reichenbach's claim that idealism in general is a form of escapism. It also directly contradicts what Hegel himself says in one of the most famous passages he ever wrote, in the preface to his *Philosophy of Right*—the book in which, if he ever formulated "ethical directives" he would have done so: "A further word on the subject of issuing instructions on how the world ought to be: philosophy, at any rate, always comes too late to perform this function. As the thought of the world, it appears only at a time when actuality has gone through its formative process and attained its completed state . . . The owl of Minerva begins its flight only with the onset of dusk" (Hegel 1991, 23). But Reichenbach's attack on Hegel poses a bigger question than that: Why cannot everything that Reichenbach has said about Hegel not be said of religion?

As Ayer and the Vienna Circle recognized, religion is a much more redoubtable enemy of scientific philosophy than an incomprehensible Berlin professor from the early nineteenth century; however prestigious Hegel may have been as a philosopher, he could not have begun to match the influence of the major religions when it came to fighting science. As Nietzsche famously pointed out in detail,[15] religion often embodies a flight from reality that paradoxically seeks to control everyone's lives. Indeed, it would presumably have helped Reichenbach's argument to point out that, for the Germans as for the Americans, much of idealism's prestige was derived not from its philosophical strengths but from its alliance with religion—an alliance that Hegel himself cultivated at every opportunity (see Fackenheim 1967).

It would seem, then, that a forthright account of the rise of scientific philosophy would want to take account of its triumph over religious opposition. But Reichenbach keeps silent about such matters, turns only to Hegel, and excoriates him all the more savagely. When we see that Reichenbach's dismissal of idealism as the resort to a "daydream" by those who cannot bear "reality in all its . . . imperfections" carries religion along with it, we see that the main contrast between his endorsement of naturalism and that of the pragmatists is between his obliqueness and their bluntness. In light of what had happened to Max Otto in Reichenbach's own department four years before the appearance of *RSP*, who can blame him?

STRATIFIED NATURALISM AS STEALTH PHILOSOPHY

Doctrines of the stratification of nature, for their part, go back to Aristotle, who had a robust metaphysical warrant for it in terms of the operations of form on matter (cf. Randall 1960, 32–38). *RSP*'s presentation, in line with Reichenbach's positivistic anti-metaphysical stance, is oblique. On the one hand, Reichenbach strenuously *avoids* claiming that nature is stratified; his strict empiricism can hardly tolerate such blanket claims about nature as a whole. Yet, for reasons that remain to be explored, he and his fellow logical positivists cannot escape the stratification of nature altogether. They seek instead to displace it onto the sciences themselves, which they think of as standing uncontroversially in a hierarchical order corresponding to the problematic levels of nature. Thus, instead of physical *reality* being asserted as fundamental to the higher natural levels of chemical reality, biological reality, and the rest, physics is asserted to be the basic *science*, with chemistry, biology, and the rest layered above it. But the stratification of nature does not go away, as we see when we ask why the sciences are themselves ordered hierarchically. For scientific realists such as the logical positivists, it is reasonable to hold that science captures something about nature, not merely in its individual statements and theories, but on the larger level of the organization of science itself. The question then arises of what that "something" is, and the most natural answer is that if the branches of science exhibit hierarchical order, it is because nature does as well—that it exhibits some type of stratification (see Dupré 1996, 103).

This, too, is unappetizing. But the alternative—to claim that nothing we can know about nature shows us why the sciences are hierarchically ordered—is unpleasant as well. We can see this by looking first at Reichenbach's views on the beginning point of epistemology, as presented in his *Experience and Prediction*, published in 1938, the year he arrived at UCLA. An empiricistic philosophy cannot begin, as Kant does, with an *a priori* "theory of the subject" in the classical sense—with an account of how the human mind functions independently of its experiences of objects. Rather, it must begin in humbler fashion, with the only kind of knowledge it recognizes: empirical knowledge. Its first job is then to give an empirical account of empirical knowledge—that is, of our cognitive capacities as displayed in actual experience:

> Every theory of knowledge must start from knowledge as a given sociological fact. The system of knowledge as it has been built by generations of thinkers, the methods of acquiring knowledge used in former times or used in our day, the aims of knowledge as they are expressed by the procedures of scientific inquiry, the language in which knowledge is expressed all are given to us in the same way as any other sociological fact, such as social customs or religious habits or political institutions. . . . Knowledge, therefore, is a very concrete thing; and the examination into its properties means studying the features of a sociological phenomenon (Reichenbach 1938, 3).

The nature of knowledge, like everything else, must be understood empirically. Hence, Reichenbach begins, not with an overall account of the human mind, but with what he claims is an empirically adequate conception of science. So if the motivation for idealism's *a priori* starting point was the view that the mind constitutes knowable objects, we are entitled to suspect that Reichenbach rejects that as well. Which, of course, he eventually does.[16] He is not only an empiricist, but a thoroughgoing realist.

Or almost; for Reichenbach's prose above slides into a cranny where idealism seems still to linger. It does so in the second sentence, when it moves from "the aims of knowledge" to "the procedures of scientific inquiry," and we can unpack it as follows: Suppose Reichenbach is right, and knowledge is what is gained by scientific procedures. Then anything that we may experience but that cannot be known by those procedures cannot be an object of knowledge; it can be experienced, let us say, but not known. But what, then, is the difference between the "empiricist" view that science informs us whether some experience, or aspect of an experience, can give rise to knowledge, on the one hand, and the idealist (Kantian) view that science "constitutes" an experienced object as to some degree "knowable," on the other hand? The methods and procedures of science itself, it appears, have taken over from Kant's categories of the understanding.[17] Just as the Kantian categories pick out those of our intuitions that can be interconnected into objects, so science picks out from the overall field of our sensory data those of its components that can give rise to knowledge. If this were his view, Reichenbach would have abandoned the idealistic view that the mind constitutes its objects only to give science itself the power to determine which objects are scientifically knowable. His empirical science would function as did Kant's transcendental mind: idealistically.

Reichenbach avoids such residual idealism by saying that the procedures of science do not constitute experiences as knowable because there is nothing in experience that is *not* scientifically knowable; scientific procedure applies, from the start, to everything we experience. Thus, he strenuously denies that the basic presuppositions of science, such as those of logic and mathematics, place any significant constraints upon what can be known. For Reichenbach, they are entirely empty (*RSP*, 125); as such, they make no demands on reality and can constrain nothing—which means that nothing escapes them, and gives them absolute validity.[18]

Reichenbach now has achieved the needed contrast with the other relevant approaches. As against both Kantian idealism and its American offspring, he has first turned to science, instead of to the nature of the human mind, as the foundation of knowledge, and then has denied that its basic components, logic and mathematics, play any role at all in constituting things as knowable. His naturalism, at this point, remains in the general spirit of Sidney Hook's definition cited previously: though he never quite says so in *RSP*, Reichenbach clearly believes that knowledge of nature can be given only by the scientific method.[19] But then he brings in something foreign to Hook (and, as we will see, to the pragmatists generally): the fact that science is divided into a number of special sciences, or "branches," such as physics, chemistry, biology, and the like, which are hierarchically arranged. This in turn slides into the view that nature itself exhibits a similar hierarchy:

Physics is not a parallel of biology, but a more elementary science. Its laws do not stop short of living bodies, but include both organic and inorganic bodies, whereas biology is restricted to the study of those specific laws which, in addition to physical laws, govern living organisms. There is no exception to physical laws known in biology. Living bodies fall down like stones if not supported; they cannot produce energy from nothing, they verify all the laws of chemistry in their digestive processes—there is no physical law which has to be qualified by the clause "unless the process occurs in a living organism." If living organisms display properties which require the formulation of specific laws, *to be added to those of physics*, there is nothing strange in such addition. But it appears inadmissible to assume that living matter possesses properties which contradict those of inorganic matter (*RSP*, 193; emphasis added).

Physics, then, is the basic empirical science. Above it, in Reichenbach's view, are, successively, chemistry and biology, to which we can add psychology (for which, see *RSP*, 270–71). Each level contains all the laws of the lower levels and adds some of its own. Other philosophers, at that time and subsequently, would have similar versions of this hierarchy, often bringing in at the top the social sciences of economics, political science, and sociology; *RSP* (stealthily?) stops short of this.[20]

But there is now another slide in Reichenbach's prose, this time not from knowledge to science but from science ("physics is not a parallel of biology") to nature itself ("its laws . . . include both organic and inorganic bodies")—and back ("there is no exception to physical laws known in biology") and back again ("living bodies fall down like stones . . .").[21] The hierarchy of the sciences is thus not firmly distinguished from the stratification of nature, and Reichenbach is in a position akin to the one that Kant assigns to Locke (*CPR*, B, 127–28): the objective and subjective sides of the situation have not been fully disentangled. As long as that is not done, the hierarchy of sciences remains what it is here: an obscure amalgam of "subjective" and "objective" factors whose origins, dispersed among those two domains, cannot but be unclear—which, in turn, allows the unquestioned status of the hierarchy to migrate to the stratification.

FROM REDUCTIONISM TO FICTIONALITY: HEMPEL, OPPENHEIM, AND PUTNAM

Disentangling the two, however, only exposes an underlying dilemma. If, in particular, we do not wish to appeal to the stratification of nature to explain the hierarchy of the sciences, perhaps we can reverse the direction of explanation and say, "idealistically," that the strata of nature result from the way science is hierarchized. But then, as noted above, we have to say that science does not describe nature as it really is, but interprets it in light of its own framework. How, then, can we say that science informs us about how nature is organized? The answer has to be that science's hierarchical structure is not intrinsic to it, but merely provisional. Science will eventually learn to do without the hierarchical framework, an idea which takes mid-twentieth-century philosophy of science into a new and extremely complex area, that of reductionism. The naturalistic thesis that there is no supernatural order is now converted into the view that all sciences will eventually be "reduced" to physics, so that naturalism will become what Quine calls it: "physicalism" (cf. Kuklick: 354, 356).

Explorations of this have given rise to an enormous and growing body of literature, one early strand of which I am following here.[22] A salient feature of that strand is what can only be called the hope that as, science progresses, the lines between physics and the other sciences will eventually, as Carl Hempel will put it later (1966), become "blurred."[23] But expressing a hope brings the question of whether it is possible to realize it, and if so how. The stratification of nature thus comes yet back again in a classic article by Reichenbach's associate, Paul Oppenheim, and his PhD student Hilary Putnam,[24] "The Unity of Science as a Working Hypothesis." Published seven years after *RSP* (1958), this article is explicitly motivated by the fact that earlier discussions "have been expressed in a more or less vague manner and without any very deep-going justification" ("*US*," 27–28), which certainly applies to Reichenbach (who is unnamed here). Establishing reductionism, even as a mere working hypothesis, requires careful thinking about the hierarchy of the sciences and about what in nature may justify it.

To do that, we must first understand what unifies a given science. Any science must exhibit some sort of unity, Oppenheim and Putnam claim, for unless that is the case we must allow, trivially, that "a simple conjunction of several branches of science" ("*US*," 4) may constitute unified science itself. But in what does that unity consist? This, again, is not an issue for Reichenbach; in terms of *RSP* (193, quoted above), chemistry adds a set of laws—call it {C}—to the set of all laws of physics {P}. The unity of each science would then require that, ideally at least, no member of {C} could be added to {P} unless all of them were. Reichenbach does not articulate this clearly; nor does he ask why it is the case. Oppenheim and Putnam attack the problem by beginning (at "*US*," 5) on the still more local level of scientific theories, whose unified structure is relatively well understood. A "branch" of science, such as physics or chemistry, is then a set of theories ("*US*," 5, 28). The question, then, is what unifies this set, and their answer is that it is the type of object with which each branch deals: "We must suppose that corresponding to each branch we have a specific universe of discourse" ("*US*," 6).

The stratification of nature now makes its third entrance into our story: the objects in different universes of discourse are related by a part/whole relation such that for any two adjacent universes, the objects in the lower one are proper parts of the objects in the higher one ("*US*," 6, 9). Nature is stratified by part/whole relations.

This requires, to be sure, the "metaphysical" claim that all objects of scientific discourse, except those of the lowest level, have proper parts. But Oppenheim and Putnam, like Reichenbach, want to avoid metaphysics. They argue, familiarly by now, that this view of the natural basis for unified science is not a claim about nature at all, but merely a directive for the reductionist project: ascertaining the parts of objects in any stratum of nature is a matter, not of how the levels are given, but of how they are "chosen" ("*US*," 9). Thus, their account of the strata of nature speaks, not of how things are, but of how they "must" or "should" be if reduction is to be viable as a scientific program or "working hypothesis" (ibid.). The levels (as they call them) must, to be sure, be "natural" (ibid.), but that does not mean corresponding to levels actually existing in nature; the discussion to which Oppenheim and Putnam refer (Oppenheim and Hempel 1936, 107, 110) takes "natural" and "artificial" to be points on a continuum rather than a dichotomy. Finally, this construal of the natural basis for the hierarchy of sciences does not result in the sciences as we know them today. Physics, for example, deals with several such levels, and so does biology. The special sciences as we have them are thus "largely, fictitious" (OP 28). The fiction, to be sure, is a valuable one because it furnishes, if something less than a realistic account of either nature or science, something more than a hope: a viable "working hypothesis" of the unity of science.[25]

Oppenheim and Putnam thus present the following conundrum: If we attempt to justify the stratification of nature by invoking the hierarchy of the sciences, we must explain the unity of each science. If it is to be more than arbitrary, that unity must be grounded in something in nature—viz., in the part/whole relations among natural objects. But what these relations lead to is not the current (1958) hierarchy of sciences, but another one that cannot be understood until the part/whole relations have been worked out.

WHY STRATIFIED NATURE?

The stratification of nature thus haunts logical positivist philosophy of science: it cannot be accommodated, but it will not go away. Stated forthrightly, it is unacceptably metaphysical; but attempts, like Reichenbach's, to ground it in the undoubted hierarchy of the sciences inevitably leave it in place as what, somehow, grounds that hierarchy. Depriving it of that role leaves the hierarchy without a realist justification and lands us in a different kind of metaphysics—a version of idealism. The escape route from this is to suggest that the hierarchy of sciences itself is merely temporary, eventually to be overcome by the reduction of all sciences to physics. Careful examination of how this should come about finally reveals that reductionism is no more than a "working hypothesis" that, unlike most such hypotheses, is known to be based on a "fiction."

In fact, the hierarchy of sciences has subsequently run into trouble. Kuhn's approach to science in terms of mutually incommensurable paradigms has no place for it, and by 1975 Paul Feyerabend was arguing that science did not even exhibit methodological unity (Feyerabend 1975; see also Hacking 1996, 51). Further developments have supported this, in that the sciences have proliferated in complex ways uncapturable by the metaphor of a hierarchy. Some (like neuroscience) have colonized others (like psychology); others (like ecology) have split off (from biology) and brought other investigations together under their umbrellas. Trans-, inter- and multidisciplinary investigations are the buzzwords and increasingly the norm. It turns out that the special sciences are not located in a stable hierarchy but are formed and re-formed by interactive processes of separating from and rejoining one another. Reductionism remains, of course an important component of many scientific research agendas; what else are we to call it when neuroscientists seek to correlate behavior with brain states? But there is a difference between reductionism pursued in the context of individual research programs, and reductionism as an overall project.

Sandra Harding characterizes the current situation of science in the following terms:

> Science is not singular, either in practice or in principle. . . . Scientific elements are not even actually or ideally always "harmonious. . . ." This multiplicity and discordance are both problematic and fortuitous. It can be useful to link together different kinds of observations and discordant theories as, for example, Darwin did. Discordances between knowledge systems characterize the conceptual shifts ("paradigm changes") through which scientists reorganize most of a field of existing data into illuminating new patterns. Moreover, such discordances mark the valuable distinctive positional, interest, discursive and organizational resources that different fields, disciplines and cultures bring to their attempts to understand their allotted or chosen environments. (Harding 2006, 153)

But here lies another riddle: Harding's account sounds much more like the pragmatists' inquiry-driven view, expressed, as I have noted, by Piatt and shared with people like Marx, Neurath, and Nietzsche, that the fundamental things to understand about science are not the "foundational" laws uncovered by physics, but the variegated domains of human interactions with nature—the interests and resources we deploy to try and understand our environments. This brings us to a question that has been haunting this entire discussion: If the stratification of nature and the hierarchy of the sciences were so problematic and alternative views to them were known, why were they so tempting in the first place?

One answer has to do with establishing the proper contrasts between logical positivism and pragmatic naturalism. Unless science has some organizing principle for which humans are not responsible, its various undertakings must be understood as just that: human undertakings. There is then no organization to them other than what humans give them. The organization of the sciences is itself a human artifact, and as such is part of the way humans interact with nature. The fundamental data on which philosophy of science must reflect are thus not immutable laws of physics but diverse human interactions with nature, which originally constituted science as hierarchical and subsequently gave rise to the dynamic multiplicity of what Harding calls "knowledge programs." In short, unless the hierarchy of the sciences has some nonhuman grounding (i.e., some grounding in nature itself), we fall back into pragmatic naturalism. To avoid this, we must see science as organized via some sort of principle independent of concrete human projects and intentions. For Reichenbach and the logical positivists generally, that principle was the assumed hierarchy of the sciences, together with its objective shadow, stratified nature. These were thus part and parcel of the polemical jockeying for position that defined "scientific philosophy" in the early Cold War; abandoning them meant some sort of amalgamation with pragmatism.

This can explain why the hierarchy of the sciences continued to be asserted (and stratified nature toyed with) by the logical positivists in spite of its problems: it established a needed contrast with the pragmatists. But that does not answer the question of why, with the contrast established in such a problematic way, logical positivism went on to gain the day. Here, the political pressures identified in chapter 1 (plus another quick look at Oppenheim and Putnam) can shed some light.

The thesis that there is no supernatural order has, for the logical positivists, been converted, as we have seen, into the thesis that all other sciences can eventually be reduced to physics. But such reduction is a long road. First, the laws and basic terms of a science must be understood before they can be shown to be equivalent to those in any other science. The assertion of any overall naturalistic thesis must thus be deferred until the laws governing the relevant branches of science are completely known. Moreover, Oppenheim and Putnam argue, reduction must first be achieved on adjacent levels: "It would be utopian to suppose that one might reduce all of the major theories or a whole branch . . . to a theory concerned with a lower level, *skipping* entirely the *intermediately* lower level" ("*US*," 10). We cannot credibly undertake, for example, to reduce biology directly to physics; we must go by way of chemistry (or whatever the equivalent sciences would be in a nonfictitious undertaking based on objects and their parts).

Not only must all the laws of any two branches be fully understood before reduction can take place; the laws of any and all intermediate branches must be ascertained as well. The kind of knowledge we would need to carry out a reductionistic program is thus, except in the case of chemistry and physics, a long way off. Hempel points this out in *The Philosophy of Natural Science*: "The physical and chemical theories and the connecting laws available at present certainty do not suffice to reduce the terms and laws of biology to those of physics and chemistry. But research in the field is rapidly advancing and is steadily expanding the reach of a physico-chemical interpretation of biological phenomena" (Hempel 1966, 105–6). The situation is similar for the reduction of mind to the behavior of human bodies (Hempel 1966, 108–9), and for the reduction of social phenomena to those of individual psychology (Hempel 1966, 109–10). Whether naturalism is anything more than a working hypothesis cannot be decided until the laws of nature have been definitively established.

We see that when the view that there is no ideal or spiritual order above nature is converted into the issue of reductionism, *it is indefinitely postponed*. In the meantime, naturalism can arise only tentatively and hypothetically. It is hard to imagine even the Otto protesters having a quarrel with naturalism if it is merely a "working hypothesis" guiding scientific research. And for the logical positivists, it will be a long time before it is anything more.

The pragmatists were not so well placed. Their attempt, *contra* materialism, to vindicate human values in art, politics, and even religion (Lamprecht 1944) without appeal to supernatural entities meant that they had to talk, from the start, about how natural processes and events impact us and we them; and those impacts can come from any level of nature or from many at once. A car crash, for example, presents a concatenation of physical, chemical, biological, and psychological phenomena that are not neatly layered but impact each other in ways almost impossible to separate out (see Dupré 1996, 103–4). So do pollution from a factory, mind-altering drugs, and any number of issues that arose in the late 1960s.

Pragmatic naturalism not only had to confront issues of naturalism first off and directly, but—even worse—it had, as we have seen, to do so publicly. For the view that it had to contest—the view that a supernatural order exists and is the source, even the only possible source, of moral value—was not a technical view confined to Hegel and his lotus-eating followers. Fighting atheism had long been integral to the fight against Communism, and with the arrival of the Cold War, fighting Communism became one of the *raisons d'être* of the United States. In view of this, the fight for naturalism had to be carried into the public sphere, as John Dewey, Max Otto—and A. J. Ayer—had done. As the Cold War went on, and theism became ever more central to American identity, the political pressures on philosophy entered the academy itself, as we have seen, and so became even harder to resist. Stratified naturalism countered these pressures by making it possible to be a naturalist without having to say in public that there is no such thing as God or an immortal soul.

The *Los Angeles Examiner*'s story on Otto's appointment as Flint Professor has thus led us to uncover American philosophy in the early Cold War as a broad discursive field in which a variety of dispositives jockeyed for position. It is not, I fear, wholly accidental that the winning discourse was the one whose explorations of the nature of science, begun decades before in Europe, had best equipped it cope with the challenging American political climate.

* Part 2 *

The Carrots of Reason: Cold War Philosophy's Theory of Subjects

CHAPTER 3

The Politics of Rational Choice

> But it is as in a house, where the freemen are least at liberty to act at will, but all or most things have been prescribed for them, while the slaves and the animals do little for the common good.
>
> ARISTOTLE, *Metaphysics*

If stratified nature was Cold War philosophy's account of "the object," what I call "rational choice philosophy" is its account of the properly operating human mind—its "theory of the subject."[1] Like Cold War philosophy in general, this theory is hard to see. One reason for the obscurity is that rational choice *philosophy* is easily confused with rational choice *theory* (RCT), which is a well-established and widely applicable theory of market and voting behavior. RCT today receives its clearest statements and most vigorous defenses in departments of economics and political science, where it has provoked a vast amount of discussion but where its philosophical implications are largely passed over.[2] American philosophy, for its part, tends to view itself as originating in Central European reflections on mathematics and physics, which obscures its later affinities with free-market economics and political theories of electoral democracy.

As S. M. Amadae has shown in her acclaimed study of the Cold War background to RCT, exigencies of the Cold War favored the rise of rational choice *theory* (Amadae 2003). Those exigencies, I argue, also required that certain doctrines of RCT be elevated from an empirical theory applying to a relatively determinate object domain (chiefly market and voting behavior) into a philosophy that applies to the human mind as such, everywhere and always. The results of this generalization were given their most rigorous and systematic expression in Hans Reichenbach's "scientific philosophy," which is discussed in the next chapter.

As we saw in chapters 1 and 2, the fear of atheism—indeed, of its mere appearance—worked "negatively" at UCLA: it disfavored pragmatism and continental philosophy, but it did not support the winning dispositive, logical positivism. Logical positivism, indeed, was just as naturalistic as the other two; but it was better able to hide its naturalism from those outside the academy by resorting to the multiply stealthy strategy of stratification. Rational choice theory was similarly stealthy. It was not overtly atheistic, and indeed its assumption of the universal and therefore timeless truth of mathematics counts in some quarters as a kind of deification.[3] Indeed, as RCT rose to prominence in the fifties, religious life itself was often reduced to a single choice: Billy Graham pleaded with millions to make a "decision for Christ" (Aikman 2007, 256).

As opposed to the heartfelt but sometimes uninformed concerns of the Otto protestors, the external pressures that influenced Cold War philosophy's account of the subject were conveyed by a vast and prestigious network comprising the federal government (including its increasingly important military arm), think tanks, foundations, and eventually universities. Rational choice philosophy was not something grudgingly accepted, like the loyalty oath, but something new, promising, and glamorous—a dispositive that academics *wanted* to join. This, perhaps, helps explain some of its relative staying power. Where doctrines of stratified nature are fading away as the sciences become less stably hierarchical, RCT has endured long after the end of the Cold War; some of its later avatars are discussed in the epilogue.

THE RISE OF RCT

Like the previous story, this one begins humbly. In the summer of 1948, Kenneth Arrow, an intern at the RAND Corporation in Santa Monica, CA, received an assignment from philosopher Olaf Helmer, a former student of their fellow RAND employee Hans Reichenbach. The assignment was to develop a "preference profile" for the Soviet Union.[4] Such a profile was a single ranking of the preferences of a group of individuals, so that one could say what that group as a whole preferred. Producing a preference profile thus amounts, as Arrow put it in his subsequent *Social Choice and Individual Values* (*SCIV*), to "passing from a set of known *individual* tastes to a pattern of *social* decision making" (*SCIV*, 2; emphasis added). The aim was to do this by purely formal (i.e., mathematical and, in particular, logical procedures (*SCIV*, 11).[5]

This assignment, like most academic assignments, had a couple of presuppositions. One of these was that intercultural understanding is possible in the first place. Otherwise, what business does a young American have trying to figure out what citizens of the Soviet Union prefer? A second presupposition was that such understanding can be achieved using only the formal tools of mathematics and logic. Could a mathematical function take us from the many different preference rankings of individuals to a single preference ranking for their whole society?

Given that the population of the Soviet Union at the time was approximately 182 million people[6] and that their preferences were not only distorted by massive government indoctrination but, under Stalin, counted for very little anyway, the assignment seems not only presupposition-laden but absurd. It may merely have been an excuse to allow an obviously brilliant student to work on his doctoral dissertation. In any case, what he produced was not the assigned preference profile, but a mathematical demonstration that any such profile was impossible unless various more or less implausible or uncongenial conditions were met. And this achievement proved to be unusually fecund.

As Amadae points out, we cannot really see the intellectual climate of the early Cold War with contemporary intellectual eyes. Though it is taken for granted by many across today's intellectual universe that, as William Greider puts it, "Marxism is utterly vanquished if not yet entirely extinct, as an alternative economic system" (Greider 1997, 28), far less triumphalist views were common long before the end of World War II: "During the 1930s and 1940s there was a pervasive sense of dismay and defeat among the intellectuals of the West over what they took to be the inevitability of the triumph . . . of fascist or communist alternatives to democratic capitalism."[7] In the aftermath of World War II, with fascism firmly on history's rubbish heap, what Alex Abella, in his popular *Soldiers of Reason*, calls Marxism's "philosophical prestige" (Abella 2008, 49) was winning it adherents across the world: "Soviet style communism, with its faith in a Hegelian movement of history that culminated in a Marxist workers' paradise, was seen as the inevitable wave of the future. Even though history or the spirit of the times manifested itself through individuals, adhesion to the collective will was to be the ruling principle of all society" (Abella 2008, 29). The "pervasive sense of dismay and defeat" to which Amadae refers thus included, after the war, the feeling that the West needed, but did not have, a compelling philosophical alternative to Marxism. In order to understand how RCT gave birth to such an alternative, we need first to understand a bit about what made Marxism, in the early Cold War, so attractive. What were the sources of its "philosophical prestige?"

Marxism, to be sure, is many things. I am asking about the Stalinist version promulgated by the Soviet side in the early Cold War (and after). Much of the philosophical attraction of such Marxism was in fact imported from other domains. These included still-vivid memories of capitalism's failures during the Depression; sympathy for the impoverished majority of human beings;

the bandwagon effect of the string of Communist victories in Eastern Europe after World War II; and the sight of guided missiles being paraded through the streets of Moscow on major holidays. Two further attractions of Stalinistic Marxism, however, were more intellectual.

First, it had a strong pseudoscientific façade, in the form of the so-called laws of history: the supposedly necessary development from thesis to antithesis to synthesis, which rendered the triumph of Communism necessary and so predictable. The fact that these "laws" are largely absent from Marx (who did not need them to write, for example, his *Communist Manifesto* [Marx 1988]) suggests that they were window-dressing; but they were, as such, quite seductive.

Second, the Marxist narrative of history had a power that its capitalist counterpart simply could not match. As Friedrich von Hayek points out, the capitalist story of gradually increasing wealth is too slow for many; the Stalinist story of capitalist contradictions building to revolutionary cataclysm promised a much faster transition to a society of general abundance (Hayek 1994, 21–23). In addition, I have argued elsewhere that philosophical narratives in general can be judged on their comprehensiveness—that is, on the number and variety of the different stages they bring together, and on the transparency of the connections they establish among those stages (McCumber 2004, 78–83). The Marxist narrative met these criteria far better than its capitalistic counterpart. It began with primitive hunter-gatherers and extended through ancient, medieval, and early modern stages of society, to arrive finally at the contemporary situation; it thus encompassed the whole of human history.[8] The capitalist narrative, by contrast, began only around the sixteenth century, with the rise of the free market. Moreover, the unifying Marxist notion—that of class struggle—is not only very easy to understand, but much more exciting than the organizing concept of capitalism, that of increasing profits. Where the capitalist story leaves us with the sober figure of the shop owner settling accounts at the end of the day, the Marxist one provides the far more glamorous image of the revolutionary heroically risking his life on the barricades. Since capitalism could not compete with this, it needed a counter-discourse that did not need to.

Rational choice theory offered promise on all counts. Where Marxist dogma was formally dressed up in dialectical wizardry, RCT was presented by way of mathematical formulas, which were impressive enough that grand historical narratives could credibly be dismissed as unneeded. In addition, it met the Marxist challenge on its self-proclaimed home ground—that of economic theory. As to its actual content, RCT contained, as it happened, a series of point-for-point contrasts with Marxism. Where Marxism claimed that history and society were shaped by large-scale social forces, RCT directed attention to market and voting behavior, where the only thing that ever happened was that individuals made free choices in order to maximize their utility. Where Marxism demanded subordination of individual aspirations to the common good (often as defined by the party), RCT held that there is no such thing as a "common good" (except as a preference of individuals).

Besting Marxism on a philosophical level cannot have been part of Arrow's original intention as he set out on his assignment for RAND; indeed, if his expectations had been fulfilled, the result would have been far more favorable to collectivism, if not specifically to Stalinism. Moreover, Arrow's version of RCT, formulated almost by accident as an academic exercise, needed major changes before it could serve the national purpose in the Cold War. In particular, the very fact that RCT worked well as a theory of market and voting behavior meant that it presupposed the very thing at issue in the intellectual struggle between Marxism and capitalism: the existence of free markets and elections in the first place. Thus, Arrow simply assumes, as "apparently reasonable," that dictatorship is bad and that citizen sovereignty is desirable (*SCIV*, 28–30)—the exact points that Stalinist propagandists would want to contest.

In order to furnish philosophical arguments against Marxism, RCT needed to be reoriented from an empirical theory of voting and market behavior, dealing in uniformities that, Arrow claims, were "discovered" by RCT to hold in a "certain part of reality" (see *SCIV*, 21, n. 18), into a theory of the proper operation of the human mind as such—into a theory of rationality. Only then could the claim be made that democratic elections and, especially, free markets were needed in all societies, regardless of their historical background and culture. And only then could the United States credibly assume the global mission of defending free markets and voters' democracy wherever they existed, and of bringing them to places where they did not.

In order to function in this way, rational choice philosophy also needed to be disseminated not only to economics departments but through the academy in general; then through American society itself; and finally across the world. This job was undertaken at first, as Abella and Amadae have argued, by the RAND Corporation (Abella 2008; Amadae 2003, 31–47). RAND hardly acted alone—the Ford Foundation, which had helped bankroll it, was an early ally (Amadeae 2003, 35–39)—but its contribution was notable. Growing out of operations research at the McDonnell Douglas Company in Santa Monica, California, RAND had important allies in the worlds of both business and government. It could give internships to brilliant young scholars (such as Kenneth Arrow), invite others to prestigious seminars, and employ a remarkable raft of people. These RAND protégés "went from their humble origins as contractors for the U.S. Air Force to controlling enormous budgets, influential departments of government and universities, and key federal initiatives affecting all Americans."[9] Lyndon Johnson's Great Society programs spread RCT through the federal government (Amadae 2003, 27–31), and from there it reached into academia. By 1978, "the influence and institutionalization of these tools spread even further as the professional schools of leading universities, such as Harvard's Kennedy School of Government, reorganized their structures and curricula around RAND-style policy analysis" (Amadae 2003, 28). As Amadae sums it up, "Rational decision technologies gained legitimacy not on paper or in intellectual debate, but *because* they became institutionalized in practice and played the role of transferring authority, rationalizing ponderous decisions, and shaping the reality of peoples' lives" (Amadae 2003, 72).

The transformation of RCT into rational choice philosophy was not only speedy, but widespread and enduring. We can glimpse its subsequent scope and influence by looking at two military examples of it. Esther Mirjam Sent has traced the way the strategy of "controlled escalation," shaped by economist Thomas Schelling, became American policy in the Vietnam War. It presupposed that the Viet Cong were rational choosers: when the war became too painful for them, they would stop fighting it.[10] A similar view was still motivating the American military in 2010. Bob Herbert, writing in the *New York Times*, quoted one "Capt. Dan Kearney of Battle Company," speaking to a group of Afghan elders: "You know, 5 or 10 years from now, the Korengal Valley will have a road going through it that's paved and we can make more money, make you guys richer, make you guys more powerful. What I need, though, is I need you to join with the government, you know, provide us with that security—or help us provide you guys with that security—and I'll flood this whole place with money and with projects and with health care and with everything" (Herbert 2010). Like the Viet Cong, the Afghans are assumed to think about war in the same way that Arrow's Western capitalist voters think about candidates. They are assumed to believe that they confront a choice, that of whether or not to join (or help) the Americans, and it is assumed that they will make that choice on the basis of their expectations of utility. The uniformities that Arrow claims to have "discovered" in a "certain part of reality" have been replaced by uniformities assumed to hold across very different cultures and in very different situations.

Philosophers played a role in this. Over the years, RAND employed a startling array of logically oriented philosophers, who often went on to have brilliant careers. George Reisch lists Rudolf Carnap, Donald Davidson, Olaf Helmer, Carl Hempel, John Kemeny, J. C. C. McKinsey, Paul Oppenheim, W. V. O. Quine, Hans Reichenbach, Nicholas Rescher, Patrick Suppes, and Alfred Tarski.[11] Most of these philosophers would publish in and on rational choice theory and its interaction-oriented cousin, game theory, helping bring them to the attention of philosophers across the country.[12] Though Rescher himself qualifies Reisch's view that RAND affected the nature of American philosophy as "bizarre" (Rescher 2005b, 192), Philip Mirowski has put it differently: "The professionalization of American philosophy of science in the immediate postwar era grew directly out of the soil of Operations Research [at RAND]."[13]

The RAND alumni, highly educated and usually brilliant, could hardly have been more different from the earnest but uninformed Otto protestors we have already seen. Their success was not always a matter of their prestigious résumés, however. A letter written by the University of California Privilege and Tenure Committee on behalf of Abraham Kaplan, a UCLA philosopher who was in trouble for refusing to sign the California Loyalty Oath, refers to his work for RAND as grounds for exculpating him.[14] During the tumult of the early Cold War, employment at RAND could provide a valuable defense against academic Red hunters.

BARE BONES OF RCT

Rational choice philosophy, in its broad outlines, can be derived from RCT by generalizing some of its core doctrines. Though the generalizations involved are not particularly complex, they need to be excavated with care, and I do so in three stages. In the rest of this section, I give a "bare bones" account of RCT's philosophically salient doctrines as these are articulated in Kenneth Arrow's 1951 *Social Choice and Individual Values* (*SCIV*). In the rest of this chapter I spell out a few of the further implications of these doctrines for the traditional philosophical disciplines of epistemology, ontology, and ethics. Finally, in the next chapter I examine the congruities—and some important discrepancies—between those implications and some core features of Hans Reichenbach's account of "scientific philosophy" as presented in *The Rise of Scientific Philosophy* (*RSP*), which also appeared in 1951. Many of Reichenbach's views on science, to be sure, have not been sustained by subsequent work in the philosophy of science—and several of the most troublesome of these turn out to accord, not with the ways scientists actually work, but with a Cold War view of science as a global exercise in rational choice.

Arrow proceeds from a voters' paradox originally set forth by the French philosopher Nicolas de Condorcet in 1785 (*SCIV*, 93–94). It postulates three voters (call them 1, 2, and 3) trying to decide among three alternative policies (call them A, B, and C). Voter 1 prefers A to B and C; 2 prefers B to A and C; and 3 prefers C to A and B. No policy can win a majority of the votes, because each policy is disfavored by two of the voters. The core job of Arrow's mathematics (*SCIV*, 46–59) is to generalize this to situations where the number of voters and of policies is greater than three.

In this paradox, and in RCT generally, an individual is presented as having a number of values or desires, which are expressed in binary terms as preferences, such that for any two alternatives x and y, xRy, where R means "is preferred to or is indifferent to." The binary preference-or-indifference relation R is stipulated to be *transitive*, so that for any three alternatives x, y, and z, xRy and yRz imply xRz. It is further stipulated that the preference pattern is *complete*—that is, all relevant preferences are ranked. The completeness of the pairwise rankings means that for any two alternatives x and y, xRy. The result is a weak ordering of the entire system of preferences, or a "preference pattern."[15] In such a pattern, all alternatives are ranked against each other, and this may in practice require complex considerations of such things as the probability of a given alternative actually leading to a desired outcome and of how choosing one alternative would require the forgoing of others. The comparative benefit brought to the chooser by a given alternative is its "utility," and the rational chooser chooses in such a way as to maximize her overall utility.[16]

Since an individual equipped with such an ordered preference pattern is "rational," human rationality is here represented as "an ordered system of preferences" (*SCIV*, 19; Amadae 2005, 736). The proper activity of reason is thus to produce, from a pair of sentences xRy and yRz, the sentence xRz. This gives us a thesis that is philosophically salient enough to be stated separately: (1) "RATIONALITY" IN RCT IS THE CAPACITY TO RANK PREFERENCES WITH REGARD TO COMPLETENESS AND TRANSITIVITY.

This definition, though narrow, is not wholly unrelated to philosophical tradition. Consider Aristotle's definition of the syllogism as "a discourse [*logos*] in which, certain things beings stated, something other than what is stated necessarily follows" (*Prior Analytics* 24b18–20). In RCT, what is stated are the two preferences xRy and yRz, and what follows from them, by transitivity, is xRz. The difference is that for Aristotle, the syllogism is not the whole of reason but a tool for one of its functions. Thus, reason for Aristotle also has the function of grasping the "simple objects of thought"—that is, universals (*de*

Anima 2.6.430a26). Since syllogisms require universals for their formulation, the latter function of reason is for Aristotle more basic than the former one.

One way to understand the kind of generalization that turns RCT into rational choice philosophy is to see it as the dropping of the qualifying phrase "in RCT." This means, as we will see in the next chapter, that rational choice philosophy generalizes this view of reason from a theory about how people behave rationally under the circumstances envisioned by RCT—those of making choices—to a theory of how people behave rationally all the time—that is, to a theory of rational performance, or indeed of rationality itself. For the moment, what we see is that rationality in RCT is defined as a matter of ranking preferences, and so ultimately of choice. The account of "collective rationality" at *SCIV*, 28 presents it that way, and *SCIV*, 19 extends this to individuals, yielding a second relatively salient thesis: (2) A "RATIONAL" INDIVIDUAL OR COMMUNITY FOR RCT IS ONE THAT MAKES RATIONAL CHOICES.

Choosing follows from ranking in the following way: "The [chooser] orders the . . . alternatives according to its . . . preferences once for all, and then chooses in any given case that alternative from among those actually available which stand highest on this list" (*SCIV*, 2). The highest alternative (or set of alternatives, should several be ranked equally high [*SCIV*, 12]) is the one that maximizes the chooser's overall utility. The choice thus follows immediately from the preference ranking.

The only characteristic of preferences with which RCT is concerned is that they are rankable; issues of how they are formed in the first place and of how strong they are do not, as we will see, enter in. Since what is ranked must remain stable, preferences are taken as fixed. The "once for all" requirement above expresses this basic axiom of RCT: "individual values are taken as data and are not capable of being altered by the nature of the decision process itself" (*SCIV*, 7). Thus, we have a third philosophically salient thesis of RCT: (3) PREFERENCES IN RCT ARE FIXED. The fixity of preferences is highly counterintuitive, and many later discussions of rational choice attempt to incorporate changing preferences. It is in fact empirically obvious that preferences vary; for RCT, when they do, the choice itself also changes.[17] Preferences are thus *held* fixed for the duration of a given choice.

Since reason is now a matter of ranking, and ranking does not create what it ranks, preferences are basic data; how they are formed is not a matter of concern. Just why Janice prefers staying home and studying to going out for ice cream is a complex matter involving local givens such as her physiology and moral values, the layout of the neighborhood, the weather, the costs of not studying, and so on. Rationality comes in for RCT only once the preferences have been fixed. What we might call the "context of preference formation" is thus excluded from RCT.[18] This gives us a fourth philosophically salient thesis: (4) PREFERENCES IN RCT ARE GIVEN.

Also excluded from RCT are questions of how strong preferences are on any "absolute" scale (*SCIV*, 9–11) a rank-ordering of preferences among themselves is all that is needed. This exclusion of "cardinality" is made on good positivist grounds: "The viewpoint will be taken here that interpersonal comparison of utilities has no meaning and, in fact, that there is no meaning relevant to the welfare comparisons in the measurability of individual utility. . . . The only meaning the concepts of utility can be said to have is their indications of actual behavior" (*SCIV*, 9).[19] A human individual thus consists of a ranking procedure operating under the norms of transitivity and completeness, plus a number of preferences whose origin and "absolute" strength are irrelevant.

Notably missing from this early version of rational choice theory are emotions, history, and culture. Emotions are excluded along with cardinality. My desire for *x* may be raging, while my desire for *y* is merely a mild whim; what matters for RCT is only that *x*R*y*. The exclusions of history and culture can be seen by considering two real-world phenomena that Arrow discusses: "imposition" and "dictatorship." In imposition, some preferences cannot be expressed because of customs and codes prevalent in society; they are "taboo" (*SCIV*, 28–30). In dictatorship, the preferences of one individual, and only those, are given weight in a particular ranking. These two are allied for Arrow in that imposition tends to lead to dictatorship because sacred codes require interpreters, who gradually assume dictatorial power (*SCIV*, 1 n.1). Arrow's exclusion of imposition thus tends to bring the exclusion of dictatorship with it, though dictatorship is also excluded because it is not really a procedure for "social" choice at all; in a dictatorship, all relevant choices are made by one individual (*SCIV*, 30–31).

Such an "individual" may consist of several or many actual human individuals; the point is that they function as a unit. This points to a deeper counterintuitive assumption in RCT: since the mathematical ranking procedures are the same for everybody, what distinguishes one person from another can only be their differing preferences. If two people have the same alternatives and preferences, as, for example, members of the Soviet Politburo were supposed to, they count as the same "individual" (see Davis 2012, 464–69).

The general principle for excluding imposition is given the name "citizen's sovereignty," which captures the fact that it is derived from the concept of "consumer sovereignty" (*SCIV*, 30). Consumer sovereignty is taken over by

Arrow, but not argued for (Amadae 2003, 107–8); the concept of it was originally developed (though Arrow does not say so) by the Austrian economist Ludwig von Mises (Mises 2009). According to such "sovereignty," (5) IN RCT, EACH INDIVIDUAL IS SOLELY RESPONSIBLE FOR HIS OR HER PREFERENCES. Consumer sovereignty, originally introduced in *SCIV* as a desirable norm, thus becomes a presupposed fact: only where it holds does RCT apply.

In addition to violations from imposition and dictatorship, citizen's sovereignty may also be "violated" by the rational choice theorist, who may decide that some preference patterns held by individuals are "inadmissible" into her account. Arrow's discussion of admissibility (at *SCIV*, 24) is notably opaque, but in a later article endorsed by Arrow (*SCIV*, 92), William Vickery puts it as follows: "By an admissible ranking is meant one with which the social welfare function is required to be capable of dealing, in combination with other admissible rankings selected on a particular occasion by other individuals. Certain rankings may be excluded, for example because they appear inherently inconsistent by some test, or they are deemed contrary to the patent interests of the individual concerned" (Vickery 1960, 509). The rational choice theorist thus has some leeway as regards the givenness of preferences: preference rankings that are inconsistent with each other or with the "patent interests" of the ranker can be eliminated from consideration. Not every empirical preference that someone holds needs, then, to be taken up in RCT; and this, along with the overall doctrine of consumer sovereignty, allows for the elimination of historical forces and circumstances from considerations of rational choice: "The social choice at any moment is determined by the range of social states available (given the preferences of individuals); there is no special role given to an alternative because it happens to be identical to or derived from a historically given one" (*SCIV*, 119).

Individuals may, of course, prefer an alternative social state that is closer to the current one and so can be reached with less disruption than one that is more distant; but that kind of consideration is outside the purview of RCT, being adequately captured by those individuals' (given) preferences. Social choices are thus entirely determined from individual preferences and take effect only insofar as they affect those preferences. Arrow asserts that this captures the individualism of the "classical liberal creed" as stated by F. H. Knight: "*Liberalism takes the individual as given*, and views the social problem as one of right relations between given individuals."[20]

RCT thus contains a bare-bones theory of a kind of rational subjectivity that treats the individual human mind as independent of culture, emotion, and history, and as consisting of a number of given and fixed preferences plus a mathematically oriented procedure for ranking them. I call this view "mathematical individualism." It is individualistic in that individuals are entirely responsible for their preference rankings; it is mathematical in that those rankings are established as rational via the mathematical characteristics of completeness and transitivity.

RCT EPISTEMOLOGY

That RCT does philosophical work has long been known (see Amadae 2003). What has gone largely unnoticed by philosophers, if not by Amadae, is that its philosophical work is systematic. RCT does not merely supply piecemeal insights into various philosophical problems, but propounds or implies a series of positions, of varying complexity, in the three basic philosophical disciplines of epistemology, ontology, and ethics. All of these positions depend on its narrow view of reason and, with that as background, can be readily extrapolated.

Arrow does not spell out the epistemological implications of RCT in detail. He operates, as we have seen, in terms of a positivistic epistemology that allows only for factors that make observable differences in behavior. The epistemology of the rational chooser herself is somewhat more complex, and we can approach it by asking what sorts of knowledge a person must have in order to be able to make rational choices.

As Rudolf Carnap put it in 1966, "Free choice is a decision made by someone capable of foreseeing the consequences of alternative courses of action, and of choosing that which he prefers" (Carnap 1995, 221). This places constraints both on epistemology and ontology. Knowledge, for its part, must be individualized, in the sense that it is considered as present in the mind of a single person, the one making a decision; if I am ignorant of some fact relevant to my choice, it does not help if someone else has knowledge of that fact unless that person communicates that knowledge to me. Knowledge must also be predictive, which means that reality itself must contain predictable sequences of events, with each such sequence having both a unitary beginning in the form of a decision and a unitary ending or "outcome"—the state of affairs which choosing it will (likely) bring about. In RCT these sequences are called "alternatives"; when generalized in the context of rational choice philosophy, they become what are often called "causal sequences."

There are, I suggest, two types of knowledge involved in prediction, of which the simpler is knowledge of the prediction's initial conditions (i.e. of conditions currently obtaining). This helps the chooser discriminate relevant from irrelevant alternatives: because I know I am currently in Los Angeles, I do not have to consider whether to take the elevator to the second level of the Eiffel Tower or go all the way to the top. Such knowledge is observational. But in RCT, where one alternative is to be chosen from a number of them, the current conditions as observed are insufficient to individuate alternatives: that is, from any observed set of current conditions, more than one outcome is possible, for otherwise there is no choice. Also required for a rational choice, then, is predictive knowledge: the chooser has to know that if she chooses to bring about state of affairs A ("getting in the car"), then B ("driving to the grocery store") and C ("buying dinner") will probably follow. Thus, the knowledge relevant to a particular rational choice includes knowledge not merely of the current state of affairs but of various possible sequences of events, all of which can begin from the current actual state.

This knowledge must, like the chooser's preferences, be fixed. Any new information obtained in the course of a rational decision would be relevant to the choice only if it changed the chooser's preferences. Since that has already been excluded, new knowledge is as well. Finally, in order to be fully rational, the chooser must know that she has evaluated all relevant alternatives, since ignorance of relevant alternatives impeaches the rationality of a choice. While such "complete" information is often assumed in discussions of rational choice (see Hargreaves Heap and Varoufakis 2004, 31–32), I do not require it here for a "rational" decision—only for a "fully rational" one.

Rational choice knowledge thus includes the following: (a) an individual's observational knowledge of current circumstances; (b) her predictive knowledge of what sequences of events will probably follow on a given set of initial conditions;[21] (c) her knowledge of her own preferences; and (d) her knowledge of the relevant mathematical ranking procedures. Item (a) is openly empiricist, and empiricist accounts also apply for (b) and (c): my knowledge of probabilities is garnered from my past observations, while my knowledge of my own preferences comes from either "internal" observation of my own feelings or from "external" observations of my own behavior. The ranking procedures, since they apply to any preferences whatever, must be entirely empty or formal; as we saw, they are no more than the requirement of transitivity plus the further stipulation of completeness. This gives us three more philosophically salient theses: (6) KNOWLEDGE IN RCT IS PREDICTIVE IN PURPOSE; (7) THE INGREDIENTS OF KNOWLEDGE IN RCT ARE OBSERVATIONAL (CURRENT CONDITIONS, PROBABLE SEQUENCES) AND MATHEMATICAL RANKING PROCEDURES; and (8) THESE RANKING PROCEDURES ARE EMPTY IN THAT THEY DO NOT CONSTRAIN THE PREFERENCES THAT CAN BE RANKED.

RCT ONTOLOGY

As matters stand, we have only an account of what Kant would call theoretical mind; in order to understand the practical dimensions of mathematical individualism, we must turn from preferences, which are subjective, to objects that are preferred or chosen: alternatives. In Arrow's essay, where examples come mainly from voting (as with Condorcet), the set of alternatives among which a choice is made is a set of candidates; when we generalize beyond this, as Arrow sometimes does,[22] alternatives become rather mysterious. There are, however, some constraints on them.

- Alternatives are not parts of the rational chooser, but are "presented" or "available" to her (*SCIV*, 2, 11, 12). They are thus "objective" in the sense that they are located in the external world rather than in the thinking and choosing subject.
- Since alternatives are what is preferred or chosen, the fixity and givenness of preferences migrates to them: if an alternative changes importantly, it changes the chooser's preferences, and the choice becomes a different one.
- Alternatives must, as we saw, be attainable, or "feasible" (*SCIV*, 109–10): an alternative therefore includes actions that a particular individual is capable of performing.[23]
- The alternative outcomes presented to a chooser for a particular rational choice must be mutually exclusive (*SCIV*, 12), since otherwise there is no choice among them. Earlier members of the sequence may not be mutually exclusive: my decision to get out of bed this morning led both to my eating breakfast and to my reading the newspaper, but neither of these led to the other. Thus, we must distinguish between the current state of the chooser and the "initial" state of affairs of an alternative, which is how I will designate the first state of affairs incompatible with other alternatives.

An alternative is thus a sequence of events that (a) can be reached from the current state of the chooser and (b) properly begins with a set of initial conditions incompatible with the other relevant alternatives. It leads to a probable outcome that is also incompatible with other future states, so that right now a choice among them is possible and perhaps necessary. That alternatives are *presented to* the chooser contrasts them with preferences, which are formed by the person who makes a rational choice (and, we saw, by her alone), but which, in the context of the choice itself, are assumed as given—both by the chooser and by the rational choice theorist.[24] It is easy to see that when we generalize from feasible alternatives to all sequences of events, including those that do not contain human actions, we reach the notion of a series of events that begins with a single event (in RCT, a decision) and that proceeds to another single state of affairs (in RCT, an outcome) via a series of intermediate events that are connected with each other, the initial event, and the outcome in some generally known, or lawlike, way. This leads to another philosophically salient thesis: (9) THE MOST IMPORTANT COMPONENT OF OBJECTIVE REALITY, FOR RCT, IS THE CAUSAL SEQUENCE.

RCT ETHICS

The fixity of preferences means that ethical theory, in the sense of a theory that would discriminate right from wrong, cannot be done on RCT principles.[25] To see this requires only a moment's thought about what would actually happen in the kind of situation Condorcet envisions. Voter 1 would promptly begin trying to get voters 2 and 3 to prefer A, either by arguing the relative merits of A as it stands or by adding various sweeteners to it; the other two voters would do the same. Eventually someone would give in—that is, change her preferences to match those of one of the other voters—and one of the policies would get two votes. This way of arriving at a common view of the situation and of what is to be done, which I have elsewhere called the "polishing of desire" (McCumber 2004, 162–63), is basic to human decision making in a wide variety of fields. In particular, it applies to ethics and politics and, indeed, can plausibly be held to permeate them, as by Shaftesbury: "All politeness is owing to Liberty. . . . We polish one another, and rub off our Corners and rough Sides by a sort of amicable Collision. To restrain this, is inevitably to bring a Rust upon Men's Understanding. 'Tis a destroying of Civility, Good breeding, and even Charity itself."[26] In the course of such social polishing, the individual comes to take account of the preferences of others and to match her preferences with theirs. Social polishing is thus a violation of consumer sovereignty and can be called an automatic, unconscious version of the pragmatist project of edification that I discussed in chapter 2: it brings the individual to an appreciation of her place in a wider social order.

It is not that Arrow denies the possibility of this. Rather, because of his assumption that each person is the sole ground of her preferences (citizen sovereignty), he relegates it, and indeed interpersonal relations in general, to the context of preference-formation.[27] Interpersonal relations are therefore excluded, not from RCT's conception of the mind in general, but from its conception of rationality. Along with them go politics, ethics, and social interaction in general. It now appears, in Arrow's words, that "choice is only individual; the very concept of social welfare is inadmissible; . . . only individuals can be rational" (*SCIV*, 107). But this is a view that Arrow wishes to attack. His attack begins from his statement of his general result: "If consumers' values can be represented by a wide range of individual orderings, the doctrine of voter's sovereignty is incompatible with collective rationality" (*SCIV*, 60; see *SCIV*, 69, 74, 80).

Arrow then attempts to rescue collective rationality by narrowing the range of individual preference orderings, which means invoking preferences that everyone in fact shares; if there are such preferences, orderings will be similar across society (and even humanity), and social choices among alternatives for achieving those preferences can be rational. Candidates for such preferences, he suggests, are those for freedom, national power, equality, and length of life (*SCIV*, 74–75). None of these, however, is given absolute priority by anyone. Moreover, they are largely unconscious, which means that for them to be operative across a society, they must first be made known to its members: "Any individual may be presumed to have some ultimate values, partly biological, partly specific to the culture pattern; these are, however, largely unconscious. His overt preferences are for values instrumental in achieving these ultimate values. . . . In that case, different opinions on social issues arise from lack of knowledge and can be removed by discovering the truth and letting it be widely known" (*SCIV*, 86–88).

This dissemination of truth would be a conscious counterpart to the social polishing mentioned above and would coincide with pragmatist edification. Arrow is pessimistic about it: "In our present pessimistic age, even this seems like a very difficult problem, not to be dismissed as lightly as it was by our more exuberant predecessors of the last century" (*SCIV*, 88). The "predecessors" are the "idealist" philosophers of the Enlightenment, among whom Arrow places Kant and Rousseau (*SCIV*, 81–86). The idealists, according to Arrow, held that there is a single preference ordering which, regardless of the individual's actual preferences, ought to govern her actions, and which is the same for everybody (*SCIV*, 82–83). In order for this to have empirical plausibility, there would have to be an actual consensus on the preference ordering, a possibility that can be rejected (*SCIV*, 84). If we attempt a nonempirical version of such a "true" preference order, we fall, idealistically, into some kind of moral absolutism, which is "unsatisfying to a mind brought up in the liberal heritage"

(*SCIV*, 84).[28] Arrow's pessimism here concerns the formation of preferences, and so is grounded, not theoretically, but on his view of the present state of history. Historical considerations not being part of rational choice, Arrow's pessimism cannot, on his own terms, be a "rational" ground for rejecting the project of edification.

What *is* the same for everybody is not any specific preference order, but the way preference-orderings are formed: the ranking procedure that constitutes rationality itself. Arrow's final suggestion is therefore procedural: individuals across a society may share a preference, not for specific alternatives, but for the decision procedure itself. The question is then one of what kinds of social decision procedures can be set up to capture this kind of ranking, and here, too, Arrow ends in pessimism:

> Some such valuation . . . seems to be implicit in every stable political structure. However, there is a certain empirical element in practice; individuals prefer certain political structures to others, not only because of their liking for the structure as such, but also because they have some idea of the preference patterns of other individuals in the society and feel that on the whole they can expect the particular structure in question, taken in conjunction with the expected behavior of other individuals, under that structure, to yield decisions on current matters which will usually be acceptable to themselves. Thus, we may expect that social welfare judgments can usually be made when there is both a widespread agreement on the decision process and a widespread agreement on the desirability of everyday decisions. Indeed, the sufficiency of the former alone . . . would require that individuals ascribe an incommensurably greater value to the process than to the decisions reached under it, a proposition which hardly seems like a credible representation of the psychology of most individuals in a social situation. (*SCIV*, 90–91)

Individuals thus value certain social structures, and the procedures by which those structures produce social choices, not because of the procedures themselves but because of the results they produce, which takes us back to the previous discussion and its pessimism about agreements on specific preference-orderings.

Arrow's pessimism is presented throughout as a personal assessment rather than rigorously argued for. RCT itself leaves us without ethical directives. This gives us a final philosophically salient thesis: (10) PREFERENCES, AS THE FUNDAMENTAL DATA OF RCT, ARE NOT SUSCEPTIBLE TO MORAL EVALUATION.

CONCLUSION: FROM RATIONAL CHOICE THEORY
TO RATIONAL CHOICE PHILOSOPHY

Kenneth Arrow, in *SCIV*, generally avoids philosophical considerations (which is why I have had to extrapolate them), and usually presents RCT as an economic/political theory—as, we saw, an empirical attempt "to discover uniformities in a certain part of reality" (*SCIV*, 21, n. 18). I have argued here that RCT nonetheless contains philosophically salient theses that can be extrapolated into components of a wider, more philosophical approach. On that approach, rationality is just the ranking of given preferences according to the formal norms of transitivity and completeness. These preferences are taken as given (how they are formed is irrelevant) and as fixed for the duration of the decision process. As a formal procedure, rationality is unaffected by emotions culture, and history.

Knowledge, on this approach, includes, in addition to knowledge of the formal ranking procedures, both observational knowledge of current conditions and predictive knowledge of what sorts of events are likely to follow on the making of a particular rational choice; this knowledge, being predictive, is probabilistic. Ontologically, it follows that reality must contain such predictable sequences. Ethically, the givenness of preferences means that they are not susceptible to rational criticism, so ethical theory in the usual sense—of discriminating, on the most general level, right from wrong—is impossible.

Several principles of RCT, to be sure, are controversial even within its home fields of economics and political science (for a summary, see Green and Shapiro 1994). In the real world, as the economic meltdown of 2008 made patent, people act emotionally and with imperfect information, and their preferences are inconsistent and unstable (see Ariely 2009). They often choose, moreover, against their own "patent interests" (see Frank 2005). Even so, RCT, like any good scientific theory, produces reliable predictions under certain conditions; its insights, certainly those listed above, can be reasonably held to apply to actors in a market economy or a contested election.

But it was speedily generalized far beyond this, including by Arrow himself: in 1974, for example, he assigned to the economist the role of "guardian of rationality" (Arrow 1974, 16), and in 1996 he wrote that "rationality is all about choice. . . . The rationality of actions means roughly that the alternative choices can be ordered in preference; . . . rationality of knowledge means using the laws of conditional probability, where the conditioning is on all available information."[29] Thus generalized, RCT becomes something quite different, for the generalization requires the various insights that I have extrapolated here to be brought together, articulated, and defended on a level that, being no longer empirical, counts as philosophical. This project includes three very different kinds of extension.

First, Arrow's findings on social choice must be extended from the locus of his empirical warrants—mainly, Western capitalist democracies (*SCIV*, 1)—to societies the world over. This *global* extension is invited by Arrow's use of mathematics, but Arrow himself, whose mathematics is in the service of his empiricism, warns against viewing his work in overly mathematical terms as "the drawing of logical consequences from a certain set of assumption regardless of their relevance to actuality" (*SCIV*, 21, n. 18). Arrow himself prepares the extension, to be sure, when he says that his own categories of imposition and dictatorship correspond to the more widespread categories of custom and authority, which are found well outside capitalist democracies. He makes this point in a footnote, however, (*SCIV*, 1, n. 1), and does not argue for it. I conclude, therefore, that the global extension of RCT expressed in Arrow's later writings is invited by his 1951 account of it, but not actually made in it.

A second extension is not even considered by Arrow in *SCIV*: that of mathematical individualism from voter's choice to all human (rational) activities, so that (in Arrow's later words) "rationality is all about choice." Societies without free markets and contested elections are thus impeding the human mind itself; they are, in the most profound and philosophical sense, against human nature. To be sure, neither free markets nor contested elections can lead to collective rational choice; but that is not a defect, because there is no such thing as *collective* rational choice. Reason is merely the ability to rank one's own preferences, and freedom is merely the ability to choose what one most prefers. If rationality is "all about" choice, so is freedom: "freedom of choice" becomes pleonastic.

The third extension, required by these two, is into a whole menu of philosophical topics, for the global and universal expansions of RCT require settling a number of thorny issues not encountered by RCT itself. The epistemological implications of RCT, noted above, must be spelled out and validated. RCT procedures must be extended to cover not merely choices among feasible or practical alternatives, but other types as well—in particular, choices among scientific theories. Finally, RCT's basic ethical posture—the acceptance of preferences as given—must be shown to be warranted, not merely by the premises of RCT, but by the nature of the human mind itself, and to be compatible with what humans might regard as a good way of life. These are matters, not of empirical theory, but of philosophy. They comprise the core challenges for rational choice philosophy.

To understand rational choice philosophy better, I examine in the next chapter its most rigorous and systematic philosophical formulation—the "scientific philosophy" of Hans Reichenbach. His *The Rise of Scientific Philosophy* incorporates versions of all ten of the philosophically salient theses advanced by RCT, as well as several of the systematic extrapolations and exclusions I have derived from it here.

CHAPTER 4

Rational Choice Philosophy as "Scientific Philosophy"

The search for truth promises success only in a milieu of freedom and honesty.

HANS REICHENBACH, *The Rise of Scientific Philosophy*

Chapter 3 showed how rational choice theory (RCT) functioned during the Cold War as, in Foucault's sense, a strategy of force. Its promise as an ideological counterweight to Marxism helped it become the favored dispositive in American economics and, to an extent, in political science. But as a theory of marketing and voting behavior, RCT was not up to the ideological job. While it could explain how people should (and often how they do) behave in the contexts of markets and elections, it presupposed those contexts rather than arguing for them. Its various doctrines and insights needed to be freed from their specific contexts and elevated into a unified theory of the human mind everywhere and always—a task obviously congenial to philosophers. As we will see here, however, UCLA's pragmatists (and its single existentialist) were not up to it. They were what I call "methodological pluralists," in that they believed that the mind has a variety of methods for its proper operation, and that these can change. Rationality for them was many things, and no single account of it, in terms of rational choice or of any other approach, was possible.

What Hans Reichenbach called "scientific philosophy" did not have that problem. It was committed to a unitary view of scientific method, and so of reason; this made it what I will call "methodologically monistic." This chapter begins by contrasting the different forms that methodological pluralism took in the UCLA philosophy department with Reichenbach's methodological monism. I then argue that Reichenbach's views on reason and philosophical method exhibit important features that are empirically foreign to science but can be found in RCT.

Scientific philosophy's methodological monism also served it well in the domestic struggle against "academic subversives." In chapters 5 and 6, we will see that once the proper functioning of the human mind was laid out, any dispositive that did not adhere to its norms could be condemned as irrational and so as unworthy of representation in academia. A monistic view of rational method, and only such a view, could thus justify the immediate and permanent exclusion of Communists (and others) from academic employment.

PIATT, MILLER, AND MEYERHOFF: THREE METHODOLOGICAL PLURALISTS

The relevant philosophical field here consists of the logical empiricism of Hans Reichenbach, the pragmatism of Hugh Miller and Donald Piatt, and the existential approach of Hans Meyerhoff. The idealists are excluded because they did not share one of the debate's major presuppositions: the cognitive authority of science in its own field. All of the other approaches accepted this. The analytical and pragmatic philosophers tried to appropriate scientific status for their own approaches, while Meyerhoff sought to complement science with his own kind of investigation.

Donald Piatt, whose complex trajectory I consider first, takes some steps in the direction of methodological monism in the 1939 essay I discussed in chapter 2. He begins, we saw, with the view that the most basic epistemological phenomenon is the individual "inquiry." Inquiry is one of our ways of coping with the fact that "the world is in its own right precarious, hazardous, challenging" (Piatt [1939] 1951, 108). What enables us to cope with the world's uncertainties can no more be specified in advance than can the uncertainties themselves, so it would seem that inquiry can have no single methodology. Piatt, at first, endorses this: "All thought must follow the lead of its subject matter" (Piatt [1939] 1951, 109).

He then claims, however, that when reason "turns in on itself," it discovers "*a priori* forms of thought" that are "necessary for further inquiry." This appeal to *a priori* features of inquiry that do not "follow" concrete subject matters may be an attempt to steer a middle course between Piatt's mentor, Dewey, and his new colleague, Reichenbach, who had arrived at UCLA the year before. In any case, as we saw, it drew criticism from Dewey. Twelve years later, Piatt expressed—privately—a judgment of Reichenbach's approach that was more in line with Dewey's, and indeed with pragmatism itself as usually understood. In a January 1951 letter to the provost of the as-yet-unopened campus of the University of California at Riverside, who had asked him for advice in setting up a philosophy department, Piatt wrote, "As you know, logic today is mathematical, and mathematical logicians tend to be good for almost nothing else. Some of them, like Reichenbach, are distinguished in the philosophy of science as well as logic, but in all frankness what they regard as the philosophy of science is the philosophy or rather the logic, of the physical sciences, with little or no regard for the biological and social sciences."[1] Piatt now claims that Reichenbach has taken the rules of one sort of inquiry, physics, and illegitimately extended them to all science. For Piatt, the biological and social sciences have different "logics" than physics, and need to be understood on their own terms. The criticism reads bitterly: what Piatt is saying is that Reichenbach, a man of great but apparently limited ability, has shrunk science down into something he can handle. For Piatt, as for Reichenbach, all rational method is "scientific"—but, since science is a diverse set of inquiries, just what makes an inquiry rational varies widely and cannot be specified in advance.[2]

Hugh Miller was also a methodological pluralist, but of a different type. In his *History and Science* (Miller 1939), he distinguishes "theoretical" from "historical" knowledge. As the book's title suggests, science basically sides with theory: "The theoretical hypothesis is based upon a comparison of particular occurrences, disclosing certain similarities, and leading to [structural] generalizations defining types. . . . Historical analysis moves differently. It notes not similarities among discontinuous particulars, but contiguities of particulars in space and time. It desires to see the observed occurrence as part of a larger, unobservable, but still unitary occurrence" (Miller 1939, 6).

Neither history nor science can be dispensed with; Darwin, whose theory of evolution was not a specialized theory, but a wholesale "reorientation of all theoretical knowledge towards historical fact," taught us that "all structural pattern is ultimately rooted in historical fact" (Miller 1939, 30). History is therefore basic: the patterns uncovered by theory are subject to historical change. And history, unlike theory, has no single definable method. Miller's characterization of it is in fact an expression of radical pluralism: "In our pursuit of these large historical units and their definitive characters we make use of whatever hypotheses we please. If music or poetry could be made effective, as humanly constructive patterns applicable to diverse natural manifestations, we should be wholly justified in employing them. . . . Pythagoras may yet be justified in his faith in a world built out of music" (Miller 1939, 99–100).[3] To be sure, we cannot rationally assert today that the world is "built out of music," other than as a metaphor. But if a literal understanding of it might be acceptable in the future, then the nature of reason right now is open to change, and reason itself is supremely heterogeneous.

The final example of methodological pluralism in the UCLA philosophy department was Hans Meyerhoff. In his 1955 *Time in Literature* (*TL*), Meyerhoff explores what he calls "literary" time, which is time as experienced by beings who are products of history and bound for death. Meyerhoff argues that literature, as an exploration of this kind of time, is a "legitimate source of knowledge" (*TL*, 120). Such knowledge is extracted by a kind of philosophy that seeks, not to obtain objective truth but to "illuminate" the human condition (*TL*, 143–44). Such illuminative philosophy is explicitly unscientific: it is, rather, a sort of meta-language for the "object language" of literature. Grounded in an experience of time that is either wholly or indissolubly subjective, and so sharply distinguished from the "objective" time of physics (*TL*, viii), this version of philosophy takes as its task not to follow on or complete science, but to supplement it by "making the presuppositions, modalities, and pervasive categories of subjective existence explicit and intelligible" (*TL*, 136–37). As such, it includes all varieties of existentialism and phenomenology (*TL*, 138) and has close ties not only with art but with religion—even, Meyerhoff is careful to say, when the writer in question is an atheist (*TL*, 143–44). If making explicit the hidden modalities of subjective experience is rational, then the properly functioning human mind cannot be reduced to rational choice; we can operate in rational ways that are independent of free markets and contested elections. Though such a view sounds obvious, it posed problems during the early Cold War; they are discussed in chapter 6.

Meyerhoff, Miller, and Piatt all agree, then, that reason cannot be given a single overall definition. Beyond that, however, their views differ. Piatt fragments science into a variety of heterogeneous inquiries. Meyerhoff and Miller do not question its unity, but think it needs to be supplemented in a fuller account of reason. For Miller, this supplementation takes the form of historical investigation, while for Meyerhoff, it is a matter of subjective illumination. Since both history and subjectivity are, obviously, realms where new and surprising things happen with some frequency, neither of these supplementary discourses can be definitively spelled out as to method, any more than science itself can be for Piatt. But they are also not in the epistemic state of nature where, for Arrow, preferences are formed and alternatives are presented. They have standards and criteria, but they are variable and local ones.

The three philosophers' methodological pluralism leads to a number of other contrasts with RCT. First, since rational methods are not for them universal in the sense of RCT, they are not empty and formal, either; mathematics is dethroned from the place it has in RCT and becomes merely one tool among others. Methodological pluralism is also unable to make the exclusions we saw in RCT's view of reason. Emotions for Piatt are part of the disquietude that calls forth research; for Miller and Piatt, methods of research are historically and culturally conditioned.

It is not that these thinkers were critical of RCT as a theory of voting and market behavior. What their methodological pluralism contests, however, was just what America needed in the context of the early Cold War: an approach that would maintain that individual freedom, as embodied in contested elections and free markets, was universally necessary to proper human functioning. This presupposed that rational method was unitary and specifiable. Reichenbach alone agreed with this; and uncovering how he formulates and advocates methodological monism in *RSP* suffices in itself to establish the favored place of scientific philosophy in the sociopolitical climate of the early Cold War. After locating Reichenbach's methodological monism in the context of his general view of reason, my account of his thought follows the same course as the previous chapter's philosophical extrapolations from RCT, treating in succession the views on epistemology, ontology, and ethics that are stated or implicit in *RSP* and Reichenbach's other writings of the time. These views constitute the most systematic expression we have of the main tenets of Cold War philosophy's theory of the subject.

REICHENBACH AND ECONOMICS: HISTORICAL BACKGROUND

In chapter 2, I adduced Richard Rorty's testimony that *The Rise of Scientific Philosophy* played the kind of inculcative role that Kuhn assigns to textbooks. The book does not, however, present itself as allied with free-market economic theory; in fact it does not explicitly discuss economics at all.[4] Reichenbach's own stated intention was to ground his account of scientific philosophy in a reflection not on economics but on physics and mathematics (*RSP*, viii). Moreover, the development of logical empiricism predated that of rational choice theory by several decades; the logical empiricists, like their Viennese kinsmen the logical positivists, had originally developed their doctrines in the sociopolitical context of Central Europe.

But in the intellectual hothouses of early twentieth-century Berlin and Vienna, broad intellectual contacts were common. Some of these were between philosophers and economic theorists of various kinds, and some were even familial. Wittgenstein's economist cousin Friedrich von Hayek, whom he met only on a couple of occasions, was acquainted enough with the Vienna Circle to be repelled by its dogmatism concerning truth. He gravitated instead to Karl

Popper's view that while some sentences can be falsified, none can be conclusively verified.[5] The great Austrian economist Ludwig von Mises was the brother of Richard von Mises, a Vienna Circle mathematician. Another of the Circle's mathematicians, Karl Menger, was the son of the founder of Austrian economics, Carl Menger.[6] Other relations were intellectual rather than familial: Austrian economist Oscar Morgenstern, who with John von Neumann was one of the founders of game theory, wrote in his diary in 1929, "In the evenings I read Carnap [*The Logical Structure of the World*], which is very difficult, but from which I gain a lot. I am slowly learning to think, and by doing that I come more and more into a mathematical way of thinking" (quoted in Leonard 1995, 743).

Reichenbach himself was, to be sure, associated with the Berlin logical empiricists rather than the Vienna logical positivists; but he, too, was not unacquainted with economics. According to Philip Mirowski, he made a youthful effort to mathematize neoclassical economics (Mirowski 2005, 160, 172, n. 20), and that his interest should be in neoclassical economics is not adventitious. The logical positivists of the Vienna Circle, before emigrating to the United States, had shown strong socialist commitments (Reisch 2005; Uebel 2007); Reichenbach shared this, at least in his youth, but according to Andreas Kamlah, also had a libertarian streak (Kamlah 2013; also see Mirowski 2005ß). The principles of free-market economics articulated in RCT and by its Austrian predecessors were thus hardly unknown to Reichenbach when he wrote *RSP*—or, for that matter, during his presence at RAND, when Kenneth Arrow received his fateful assignment, as we saw, from Reichenbach's former student Olaf Helmer. Sorting out these long-ago contacts and influences would be a diversionary task here, however, and having flagged them, I argue for a minimalist hypothesis: that RCT and *RSP* present separate but allied channelings of what eventually became, in America, the Cold War *Zeitgeist*.[7]

Reichenbach's views quickly gained importance at UCLA. While we cannot be sure that Piatt's turn to the *a priori*, noted above, was a response to Reichenbach, it may well have been; and his letter to the Riverside provost, discussed above, shows a deep concern with Reichenbach. It is also noteworthy that while Meyerhoff and Miller refer explicitly, in the prefaces to their books, to Reichenbach, neither of them mentions the other UCLA philosophers at all.[8]

Within a year of his arrival at UCLA, Reichenbach had thus established himself as the privileged rival to Miller and Piatt, against whom they tried to define and defend themselves; the existentialist Meyerhoff was still trying to do so in 1955. Their defenses would fail. After Meyerhoff's death in 1963, continental philosophy disappeared from UCLA and, with the brief exception of Angela Davis, would not return until my 2002 arrival in the Germanic languages department. After Piatt retired in 1965, there were no full-fledged pragmatists in the UCLA philosophy department.

REICHENBACH'S METHODOLOGICAL MONISM

Reichenbach's adherence to methodological monism is both surprisingly fervent and frustratingly vague. Though he is famously associated with "scientism" (Sorell 1991, 4)—the view that only science can give us knowledge—*RSP* never gives a detailed account of exactly what the scientific method involves.[9] He does, however, say that all knowledge is furnished either by "concrete objects" or by "scientific thought" (*RSP*, 177–78), and so constitutes "a system of inductive posits based in immediate report sentences" (*RSP*, 276, 269), and these views can be filled in a bit. Scientific method clearly, but informally, includes observation, experiment, and logical and mathematical theory construction (see *RSP*, 118). It is universal within science, as witness Reichenbach's mighty efforts—*contra* Miller—to bring the theory of evolution under it (for which see *RSP*, 197–201).

Perhaps because *RSP* is so carefully limited to developments within philosophy (see chapter 2), it does not offer a developed critique of nonscientific claims to knowledge, as A. J. Ayer's *Language, Truth, and Logic* had done in England (Ayer 1936). Though Reichenbach does say, briefly and late in the book, that Shakespeare and the Bible are properly enjoyed only by people who understand that any benefit from reading them is strictly emotional, rather than "muddled with cognition" (*RSP*, 311–12), he does not discuss the cognitive status of art and religion beyond this casual rehearsal of emotivism. Within philosophy, the fervor of his methodological monism is patent; and since philosophy's job is to analyze "all forms of human thought" (*RSP*, 308), it is clear that the standards of such analysis apply beyond philosophy to everything rational.

Reichenbach's application of those standards to nonscientific philosophy is damning. When he looks outside scientific philosophy, he finds only the "intuitive guesses and unanalyzed conjectures" (*RSP*, 311) of what he calls speculative or "traditional" philosophy. In what appears to be an oblique reference to Husserlian phenomenology, which at the time of his writing was the *dernier cri* in Europe, he writes, "And yet, there are philosophers who . . . claim that there exists an independent philosophy, which has no concern with scientific research and has direct access to truth. Such claims, I think, reveal a lack of critical judgment. Those who do not see the errors of traditional philosophy do not want to renounce its methods or results and prefer to go on along a path which scientific philosophy has abandoned" (*RSP*, 305).

This speedy reduction of phenomenology to the "errors of traditional philosophy" overlooks Husserl's many and detailed arguments as to why his approach does not fall victim to those errors.[10] The oversight, however, is a principled one: once Reichenbach has identified scientific method as the only way to get knowledge, there are only two paths for the human mind. One is that of science; the other is a mass of guesses and fallacies: "As a remnant of speculation, a haze of vagueness screens off philosophic knowledge from the eyes of those who were not trained in the method of logical analysis" (*RSP*, ix). Nonscientific philosophy, for Reichenbach, is thus a mishmash of "intuitive guesses and unanalyzed conjectures," "lack of critical judgment," and "errors," lost in a "haze of vagueness." His judgment on it is a death sentence: "It is time to put an end to this brand of philosophy" (*RSP*, 302).

Real philosophy for Reichenbach, by contrast, is a "by-product" of science, whose value lies exclusively in its contributions to it (*RSP*, 121, 123). Where, for the idealists and pragmatists (as we saw in chapter 1), science was valued as part of the overarching philosophical project of edification, for Reichenbach "edification" is purely emotional (*RSP*, 311–12). But his own fervent embrace of science has, we see, strong emotional overtones of its own.

REICHENBACH'S VIEW OF REASON

Reichenbach is thus at once casual about the specifics of scientific method and vehement about its unique validity. His views on how reason functions within it are somewhat clearer. Scientific practice for him, as we saw above, combines two elements—reason itself and the observations to which it is applied: "Scientific knowledge is obtained by the use of rational methods, because it requires the use of reason in application to observational material" (*RSP*, 31–32, 255).

This view has an impressive philosophical pedigree, for if we substitute "the understanding" for "reason" in the quotation above, we have Kant's view that knowledge is the application of the understanding to intuition—that is, to the "observational material" furnished by the faculty of sensibility. But Reichenbach is hardly an orthodox Kantian. The understanding, for Kant, contains synthetic *a priori* principles that have empirical content, but since they are to apply to all experience, they cannot be established by any number of observations. This is not the case for Reichenbach. For him, indeed, the "*disintegration of the* [Kantian] *synthetic a priori* (*RSP*, 125; emphasis in original) was the major development that freed the path for "empiricism"—not the classical empiricism of Locke and Hume, which preceded Kant, but Reichenbach's own "logical empiricism" (*RSP*, 142). In that version, there is only an analytic *a priori* coextensive with mathematics. Reason, for Reichenbach, is thus, as with RCT, mathematical in nature (*RSP*, 29, 48, 219), and he can be said to accept a generalized version of salient theses (7) and (8) from chapter 3: All knowledge requires both observational material and logical procedures that, as analytic, are empty. The latter, however, now include logic and mathematics generally, and not merely ranking procedures.

RCT's clear but narrow definition of reason as the activity of ranking all preferences in virtue of transitivity left it with only one procedure, the norms for which constituted a single monistic method. Anything that was not an operation of reason in this mathematical sense was relegated to what I called, in chapter 2, the "context of formation," which importantly included preferences. History, culture, and emotions signified only through their role in preference formation, and so reason itself operated independently of them.

The mathematical reason of *RSP*, though richer than RCT's version, is true to these crucial exclusions. Thus, the scientific philosopher is said to keep emotions separate from her work, and does not "muddle" the two (*RSP*, 36, 312). The short first chapter of the book (*RSP*, 3–4) vividly contrasts two emotional ways of approaching Hegel—the disgust of the unschooled reader at his tortured prose, and the acquiescence in it on the part of the "conditioned" philosopher—with the calm dismemberment of Hegel on the part of the trained scientist. This unemotional dissection expresses the freedom of the scientific philosopher, not only from her emotions and from Hegel, but from the history of philosophy *in toto*, which for Reichenbach is a source of error more than of truth (*RSP*, 325).

The relevance of historical circumstances was not, for its part, denied altogether in RCT but was reduced to merely another preference, to be accepted where given and forgotten where not; for Reichenbach, historical and cultural circumstances in general are allocated to the "context of discovery," a domain of hunch, guesswork, and creativity which, like preferences in RCT, "escapes logical analysis" (*RSP*, 231; cf. *RSP*, 172–73). Liberation from history and culture—that is, the establishment of a "context of justification" in which sentences do not escape but undergo logical analysis, is therefore required if logic—the philosophically relevant part of mathematics—is to have any domain at all.

Such liberation, in RCT, extended beyond the universally valid operations of reason to include the objects on which it operated—the preferences it ranked. This was expressed in RCT's principle of "citizen's sovereignty": the view that however an individual's preferences came to be formed, it was the individual alone who was responsible for constituting them *as* preferences. Both reason and its objects were thereby rendered independent of history and culture.

When we apply the notion of consumer sovereignty to Reichenbach's framework, in which mathematical reason is applied to observational material, we find it reformulated in an unusual way. Within that framework, a principle analogous to consumer sovereignty—call it "observational sovereignty"— would hold that the objects of scientific reason, the observations to which it is applied, are matters for the individual investigator alone; science hardly allows for what Arrow called "imposition" and "dictatorship." This would seem to render scientific observation strictly an individual matter, making each scientist responsible for her own observations and allowing no role either for the current scientific community or for its historical antecedents. At first blush, however, Reichenbach seems not to agree with this: "The amount of technical work involved in the solution of a problem goes beyond the capacities of an individual scientist. That is true not only for the cumbersome work of observational and experimental research, but also for the logical and mathematical construction of a theory. The social character of scientific work is the source of its strength" (*RSP*, 118).

But Reichenbach has a limited view of what this kind of scientific cooperation amounts to. The passage just quoted continues: "The limited power of the individual is supplemented by the resource of the group, the slips of the individual are corrected by his fellow workers, and the result of the contributions of many intelligent individuals is a sort of superpersonal group intelligence, which is able to discover answers that a single individual could never find" (ibid.).

Scientific collaboration is thus a sort of quantitative amplification, in which many different individuals can pool their intellectual strength because they are all, in principle, doing exactly the same thing; the proper analogy is not to a football team, in which people of very different body types and skills cooperate to bring off a play, but to a tug-of-war, in which a number of different people merely pool their strength. The scientific community, applying reason to observations, is thus not a set of clashing perspectives (for which, see the epilogue) but a sort of "superperson." Reichenbach's view of this superperson is encapsulated in a startling claim he makes about philosophy: "There can be no differences of opinion between mathematical philosophers if only opinions are clearly stated" (*RSP*, 135). This is because such philosophers all use the same mathematical (logical) procedures. Only the input of observations can vary, and since matters of fact are relatively unimportant in philosophy, such variance does not bring significant disagreement. Reichenbach thus openly expresses a principle that, we saw, remained implicit in RCT: If two people have identical preferences, they constitute for theoretical purposes a single individual. In the current context of science, it is not preferences but observations that, when identical, constitute the logical "superperson."[11]

Matters are different, however, for other kinds of scientists. They are not philosophers, and they can, and clearly do, have substantive disagreements. For Reichenbach, this must mean that their observations are in disaccord. Thus, applying Reichenbach's observation about philosophers to empirical scientists would require a further qualification: Disagreements among such scientists are impossible if their opinions are clearly stated *and* if the relevant observations are identical for all of them. The establishment of scientific fact, "the cumbersome work of observational and experimental research," however much intuition and guesswork it may contain, is carried out to ensure that the resulting observations are the same for everybody. The "observational material" to which scientific reason is applied is thus not raw sensory experience, but has been subjected to scientific procedures. To that extent, it belongs to the context of justification, not that of discovery. It is not a given, but the result of scientific work.

For Arrow, the principle of consumer sovereignty was among the presuppositions that made it impossible to understand how agreement could be rationally reached on matters of social utility. Reichenbach's problem is that when we try to apply this to science, we run into the fact that the whole point of scientific work is to reach rational agreement among scientists. Reichenbach solves this by, in effect, reassigning observational sovereignty from the individual to the scientific "superperson." When scientific workers pool their intellectual strength to apply universal mathematical reasoning to a common set of scientific observations, both imposition and dictatorship are indeed excluded from science, as in RCT: the scientific superperson alone is responsible for its own observations. In this convoluted way, Reichenbach accepts a version of salient thesis (5) from chapter 3: Each (super)person is responsible for its own observations.

The scientific community, or superperson, thus adopts a dominance over the individual investigator akin to the kind it has for Kuhn. Two differences, however, are important here. One is that the scientific community, for Reichenbach, operates only with the analytical *a priori* of logic and mathematics; for Kuhn, the valuations and commitments conveyed in a paradigm are much more concrete. And those commitments, for Kuhn, influence the actual perceptions of individual scientists. For Reichenbach, as we will see, science begins with empirical reports that are independent of such influence. Experimental reports are built up from these by employing the universal procedures of science.

Reichenbach's account of scientific reason thus accords with RCT on the key exclusions of emotions, history, culture, imposition, and dictatorship. It makes, however, two significant alterations in RCT. First, the single procedure of globally ranking preferences in accordance with transitivity is expanded to include logical and mathematical procedures generally; second, sovereignty is relocated to the level of the community rather than the individual. These alterations allow the principles of RCT to apply to scientific work in general. Since reason for Reichenbach is scientific (indeed, mathematical), his view of it elevates principles of RCT into an overall view of the proper functioning of the human mind as such—into the kind of philosophy America needed to fight the intellectual Cold War.

RATIONAL CHOICE THEORY AND THE EPISTEMOLOGY OF SCIENTIFIC PHILOSOPHY

Methodological monism, we saw, requires that the many and varied aspects of human knowledge be sufficiently similar to each other that a single method can cover them all. Reichenbach agrees: "Knowledge is ultimately of the same nature whether it concerns concrete objects or constructs of scientific thought" (*RSP*, 177–78). It (all) divides into synthetic and analytic statements, and constitutes "a system of inductive posits based in immediate report sentences" (*RSP*, 276; see also 269). This rules out concrete epistemological approaches such as that of contemporary philosopher Michael Williams, which suggest that "knowledge" means different things in different contexts (Williams 1995) and so would permit alternative accounts of rationality.

The previous chapter settled on four types of knowledge needed to make a rational choice ("RCT knowledge"): (a) observational knowledge of current circumstances; (b) predictive knowledge of what sequence of events will follow on a given set of initial conditions; (c) knowledge of one's own preferences; and (d) knowledge of the relevant mathematical procedures. All these points are sustained in *RSP*.[12]

Observation occurs for Reichenbach when "our senses tell us what exists outside our bodies" (*RSP*, 176). It is "the source and ultimate test of knowledge" (*RSP*, 78; cf. 75, 176, 252) and is the "only admissible criterion of nonempty truth" (*RSP*, 252; see also 257). This restricts the objects of knowledge in two ways. First, since an observation is an event, it cannot tell us more than what we are experiencing at the moment it occurs, and so it cannot tell us whether what we observe will exist in the future. There are no eternal sensibles, and for Reichenbach we can attain no eternal truths (except the analytical, and therefore empty, ones of mathematics [*RSP*, 49, 170, 231]). Sensory observables, moreover, are for Reichenbach always public; though he mentions Hume's "inner sense" once, he never brings it up again, and his view that "our senses tell us what is outside our bodies" excludes knowledge of our own bodies from observation (*RSP*, 261–62).[13] What scientists observe, apparently, is other peoples' bodies—or their own taken as other (as when a radiologist looks at her own X-ray).

Though direct observation can verify at least some sentences (*RSP*, 257), Reichenbach never says that it is infallible. In particular, daily experience encounters difficulties at the level of "generalization," when we try to get at the underlying "mechanisms" of events by connecting individual observations together via cause and effect (*RSP*, 5, 10). To do that correctly, we need the "cumbersome work" of scientific experimentation: "Observable happenings are usually the result of so many factors that we cannot determine the contribution of each individual factor to the total result. The scientific experiment isolates the factors from each other; the interference of man creates conditions in which one factor is shown to be at work undisturbed by the others, thus revealing the mechanism of the complex occurrences that happen without man's interference" (*RSP*, 97–98; see also *RSP*, 9).

The reason we need to correlate causes with effects in the first place is that observation is restricted to knowledge of the present and past (the latter knowledge coming, presumably, via reports of observations: *RSP*, 91). It is, however, prediction that, as with RCT, is the inherent purpose of all knowledge (*RSP*, 252; salient thesis [6]). The reason for this is that knowledge's ulterior aim is the control of the future—"to shape future happenings according to a plan." Even Reichenbach's verificationism—the doctrine that a sentence has meaning only if it can be verified—is grounded on this (*RSP*, 246, 258). If knowledge is truly to be knowledge, then—and more than disconnected reports of past occurrences—it must be able to yield reliable predictions (*RSP*, 89).

Prediction, however, is at best probabilistic. In this it contrasts with generalization, which in turn is the same thing as explanation (*RSP*, 6): "That fire can be produced by rubbing wood in a certain way is a knowledge derived by generalization from individual experiences; the statement means that rubbing wood in this way will always produce fire" (*RSP*, 5). Such a generalization claims to give us knowledge of what states of affairs will ensue upon any action we may take: it is the origin of science and, we may say, of predictive knowledge in general (ibid.). Reichenbach's choice here of examples, however, points to its primitive nature. The "if-then-always" character of generalization (*RSP*, 5), which expresses what is often called a natural law, is in fact unwarranted, because it implies that we have empirical knowledge of something eternal—the unchanging law of nature itself ("if-then-*always*"). A probabilistic approach is more sophisticated: if an event of type *y* has followed an event of type *x* in 60 percent of the observed cases, then if an event of type *x* is an observed part of our current circumstances we can say that there is a 60 percent probability that one of type *y* is to follow (*RSP*, 236).[14]

Predictions of this sort cannot, however, claim truth. The best we can do is maximize our probabilities: an explanatory generalization that has held true in 60 percent of cases to date is better than one which has held true in 40 percent, and is what we are to "posit." When Reichenbach calls knowledge "a system of inductive posits" (*RSP*, 269), then, he is referring to devices for treating a statement as true when we do not have conclusive knowledge that it is. The point is to "posit" or "accept" (i.e., to choose), the theory or explanation that has the greatest probability of actually being the case (*RSP*, 240): "A set of observational facts will always fit more than one theory . . . The inductive inference is used to confer upon each of these theories a degree of probability, and the most probable theory is then accepted."[15]

Theory choice is then ubiquitous in science: all theories are rationally chosen. In such choice, the alternative explanations, or theories, are ranked transitively according to their probability, and the one with the highest rank is chosen. The overarching preference in scientific philosophy is for the highest probability, just as the overarching preference in RCT is for the highest utility. Mathematical reasoning now serves to establish probabilities for alternative explanations, and so performs a ranking of those probabilities. As in RCT, then, reason functions as a ranking procedure (salient thesis [1] from chapter 3), leading to rational choices (salient thesis [2]). Scientific reason—that is to say, reason itself—is now a preference ranking.[16]

As objects of a ranking procedure, scientific theories or explanations—unlike observations in scientific philosophy, but like preferences in RCT—are assumed as given; thus, Reichenbach eschews questions of how theories are formed and relegates that to the context of discovery. This means that he applies salient thesis (4) from chapter 3, that preferences are given, to theories rather than to preferences. Because a theory cannot change while it is being ranked, Reichenbach also accepts salient thesis (3).

Theory choice has long been recognized as an important dimension of science. Rudolf Carnap's 1934 *Logische Syntax der Sprache* (translated as Carnap 1937), provides a telling contrast with Reichenbach. Theory choice is discussed in many contexts there, one of which concerns the question of whether sentences stating laws of nature can be inductively established on the basis of direct observation reports ("protocol sentences")—that is, the question of how a string of observation reports can support a generalization. Choice enters in here, because if a set of reports cannot establish *a single* generalization, then either they support no generalization, in which case there is no issue, or they support more than one, and a choice must be made among them. In the latter case, the way is open for Carnap's "principle of tolerance."[17] In the case of induction, the tolerance is wide indeed, for induction "is not a matter of a regular method but only one of a practical procedure which can be investigated solely in relation to expedience and fruitfulness."[18] This is intentionally vague: fruitful and expedient for what? As Alan Richardson has noted, Carnap does not attempt even to spell this out pragmatically—for example, in terms of John Dewey's loose and flexible account of human nature, as discussed in chapter 2 (see Richardson 2007); he leaves them entirely open. Reichenbach, by contrast, presents a method for making at least some such inductive decisions—and, as we have seen, it is the RCT method of forming a preference ranking.

The sort of theory choice that Carnap discusses occurs, for Reichenbach, when posits cannot be ranked because they are equivalent. In Euclidean geometry, for example (*RSP*, 136), the angles of a triangle add up to two right angles. In non-Euclidean geometries, they can add up to more or less. Reichenbach invites us to consider a theory that holds that space is non-Euclidean, but that there are universal forces that distort all triangles into perfect Euclidean shapes. Both Euclidean and non-Euclidean theories make the same prediction—that for all triangles the sum of their angles is two right angles—so we cannot rank their "posits." The choice between them is not determined by either the facts or the probabilities: "Nature does not dictate to us one specific description. . . . Physical reality admits of a class of equivalent descriptions; we choose one for the sake of convenience, and this choice rests upon a convention only, that is, on an arbitrary decision" (*RSP*, 179–80; cf. 266–67).

Mathematics is entirely empty and must be, because it must be able to apply to all possible theories (as the ranking procedures in RCT applied to all preferences: salient thesis [8]). Hence the "disintegration" of the Kantian *a priori*, which went beyond mathematics and prescribed what geometrical theories we can adopt: it was wedded to Euclidean space. But "the geometry of physical space is an empirical question" (*RSP*, 134)—and as we have seen, observation will not settle it definitively. One result of this is that in order to apply geometry to the world, we must choose our units: we can measure length in feet or in meters, temperatures in Fahrenheit or Celsius; doing so yields different, but equivalent, descriptions (*RSP*, 179–80). Though what is measured is not arbitrary, the units of the measurement are.

That Reichenbach calls the decision among equivalent theories "arbitrary" is telling: the non-arbitrary, or the rational, is reserved for cases where probabilities can be established. When this is not the case, we do have a preference for "convenience," which, like probability, introduces order into our ranking of theories; the "arbitrary" decision involved here is not irrational in the sense that maintaining a contradiction is irrational. What makes it arbitrary is our second-order preference for convenience, which, like preferences in RCT, is simply given.[19] In this way, Reichenbach remains true to his libertarian creed: "Everybody has the right to do what he wants" (Kamlah 2013).

Equivalent descriptions are thus inherent in the nature of science; they are not merely occasional accidents. This, plus the need for posits, makes science itself—which means for Reichenbach all rationality—a series of rational choices that seek to maximize truth when possible (in the case of some direct observations), and otherwise to maximize high probability and convenience.

RCT AND SCIENTIFIC ONTOLOGY

If the job of ontology is to tell us what the most basic constituents of reality are, Reichenbach has a problem with it. Physical reality, as we have seen, is ambiguous, admitting of a variety of descriptions. So it would seem that what is ontologically basic for Reichenbach will be the most basic of ambiguous things. But what are these? Physics tells us that the world is composed of subatomic waves and particles; but these, for Reichenbach, are mere *illata*, theoretical constructs from ambiguous data; that is "the end of the story." So perhaps we can turn to the "observables," or *concreta*, from which we construct our worlds, both ordinary and subatomic (*RSP*, 186).

What we may call Reichenbach's hierarchy of knowables famously consists (at *RSP*, 263) of *concreta* ("observed things"), *illata* (things inferred from *concreta*, such as atoms and their components), and *abstracta* (conglomerations of *concreta* that are too comprehensive to be directly observed, such as universities). So are *concreta* ontologically basic?

They certainly do not seem very important to Reichenbach, who mentions them only on one page of *RSP* (263). Causality, however, is given much more space. It is the central theme of three chapters (9, 10, and 14) and returns sporadically through the rest of the book. Causality is basic enough to give rise to the order of time (*RSP*, 148–50), and it played a central role in the rise of scientific philosophy itself, for it was the construal of causality in probabilistic terms that spun philosophy out of modern rationalism (Kant, Leibniz, etc.) and made science—let alone philosophy—truly scientific (*RSP*, 164–65, 255). If *concreta* are what is ontologically basic in our experience, causality is clearly what is ontologically important. Indeed, when Reichenbach calls *concreta* "observable things," he identifies them as things that can enter into causal processes—for observation is a matter of the effects of outside bodies on our sensory organs (*RSP*, 262, 273). To be observable is thus to be able to stand in certain kinds of causal relation, and as Reichenbach's examples in the discussion of *concreta*, *illata*, and *abstracta* show, what is most basic for him is not objects, but objects *doing* things we can observe (or dream up: see *RSP*, 260).

What is ontologically basic for Reichenbach, and certainly what is ontologically most important, thus seems to be sequences of events beginning from a single earlier state of affairs ("cause") and ending in a single later one ("effect;" *RSP*, 148).[20] Reichenbach discusses two versions of such sequences. In one of these, which I call "causal sequences," cause and effect are, as we saw above, connected by a law of nature that does not allow exceptions: to say that event x is the "cause" of event y means, on Reichenbach's view, nothing more than that x has been found, without exception, to precede y. Causality is thus "exceptionless repetition" (*RSP*, 158). And that is all it need be. Once we have the concept of exceptionless repetition, there is no need for underlying mechanisms, such as forces, causal powers (*RSP*, 158), or causal mechanisms (cf. Somers 1998, 736).

But even this positivistically pared-down conception of causality is too strong for Reichenbach. As we saw in chapter 2, stratified nature got displaced onto the hierarchy of the sciences—that is, relocated to the operations of scientific mind. Exceptionless repetition is similarly displaced for Reichenbach: causality holds only for "ideal objects" (*RSP*, 164), and causal sequences are thus relocated to the mind. They are not part of our ordinary experience of the world, which as we have seen is vague and entangled, but usually have to be produced experimentally in order to be observed. Even when we achieve this, however, the integrity of a causal sequence, in the sense that all of the events along it can be explained by a single law of nature, cannot be guaranteed: as the foregoing example from geometry shows, some extraneous cause may always have entered in, only to have its effects canceled out subsequently.[21]

Rescuing science from "idealism" thus includes replacing the exceptionless causal structure of the world by a probability structure (*RSP*, 164). The probability, as Reichenbach argues in more detail elsewhere, is not merely subjective: it is not that we have defective knowledge of deterministic laws of nature. Rather, the laws themselves are probabilistic.[22] The result is that Reichenbach replaces the "if-then-only" causal sequences of primitive humans with what I call "probabilistic sequences" in which events follow one another, not always, but with some degree of probability. In a causal sequence, the probability would be 1, but we do not need a probability of 1 to make predictions. As we saw, if events of type y have followed those of type x in 60 percent of observed cases, we are justified in saying that there is a 60 percent probability, given an event of type x, that one of type y will follow. We cannot, to be sure, predict with certainty; but that is very far from saying that we cannot predict at all. And prediction, we saw, was the inherent purpose of knowledge. With the concept of the probabilistic sequence, the world is rich enough to be known scientifically, and the ontology of rational choice philosophy is complete.

The concept of the probabilistic sequence furnishes the model not only for prediction but for causal explanation: "Explanation in terms of causes means pointing out a previous event that is connected with the later event in terms of general laws" (*RSP*, 207). Explanation and prediction are thus two sides of the same coin. We explain a current or past state of affairs by pointing to a previous one to which it is connected by (probabilistic) laws of nature; we predict a future state of affairs by pointing to a past or current one and, again, invoking the appropriate (probabilistic) law of nature.

In order to decide for (or against) an alternative, the rational chooser needs to know its initial conditions and the probability of its outcome; there is no need to know the underlying mechanism that actually produces that outcome given that choice, and there is no need for exceptionless repetition. Reichenbach's two parings-down of causality—the elimination of underlying mechanisms and the introduction of probability-structures—thus preserve rational choice. The main difference between probabilistic sequences and alternatives in RCT is that an alternative begins with a choice; a probabilistic sequence can begin, not merely from a choice, but from any event whatsoever.

RATIONAL CHOICE ETHICS

The correspondences between RCT and scientific philosophy extend beyond these epistemological and ontological doctrines to hold for ethics as well. In RCT, as we saw, preferences are assumed as given; what Reichenbach calls "volitions" are, correspondingly, assumed. Preferences in RCT are given, and in accord with its doctrine of citizen's sovereignty, they cannot be criticized.

RCT thus has no ethical implications (unless we count that fact itself as an ethical implication). To be sure, ethical imperatives can be derived from RCT. If, for example, we take consumer sovereignty as a moral norm, we can say that everyone ought to make decisions independently of others' preference rankings and thus arrive at a vindication of individual autonomy somewhat like that of Kant or Socrates. This, as we saw in chapter 3, is how Arrow first introduces consumer sovereignty—as a desirable counterweight to imposition and dictatorship. But he then builds it into RCT, for which it serves as a presupposition: the theory applies specifically where dictatorship and imposition are not present. When RCT is elevated into a general theory of the human mind itself, this specificity is lost: we are each responsible for our own preferences. Thus, in scientific philosophy, as in RCT, individual preferences cannot be criticized, while the general principle that each person is responsible for her own preferences is not a norm but a fact. The result is that there are no ethical implications to reason itself: morality is not a matter of knowledge. Hence, Reichenbach's treatment of ethics in *RSP* does not present an ethical theory but instead argues that one is impossible. The two key concepts in this are those of the "volition" and the "imperative."

Reichenbach's discussion of volitions (at *RSP*, 282) parallels the view of preferences in RCT. A volitional decision, like a rational choice, is for a course of action leading to a desired outcome (Reichenbach refers to volitions as "desires" at *RSP*, 314). Just as preferences are assumed by rational choice theory as given (salient thesis [4] from chapter 3), so volitions are simply found in us; they appear as "products of our own" (*RSP*, 282). As with preferences, it is irrelevant where volitions come from (though Reichenbach hazards some conjectures); and, as with preferences in RCT (salient thesis [10]), it is impossible rationally to validate or criticize volitions (*RSP*, 280, 288, 315, 277). Substantive moral issues are therefore beyond the reach of philosophy: "There is no point in asking the philosopher to justify valuations. And he cannot supply a scale of valuational order distinguishing between higher and lower values. Such a scale is in itself valuational, not cognitive."[23]

It is tempting to contrast volitions with preferences in that, while preferences are rankings, volitions are not necessarily ranked. But this is not exactly the case. Ranking of volitions, Reichenbach goes on to say here, is possible and indeed "relevant," but it is not the province of the philosopher. Reichenbach does, however, classify volitions by their goals: some are more "primary" than others. The primary ones (which concern ends) are expressed in moral axioms, and the secondary ones (which concern means) follow from them. There is thus a logical ranking of ethical rules. A unified system of such rules is an axiomatic system, but it has no cognitive content, because the axioms themselves cannot be rationally validated (*RSP*, 279–80).

The expression of a volition to others with the aim of getting them to follow it is an "imperative" (*RSP*, 281). Such considerations were foreign to RCT, which aimed to explain behavior in the solitude of the voting booth or in the individualistic context of market choices, in which consumer sovereignty is a plausible assumption. But when these views must apply to all human behavior, it becomes necessary to discuss what, in chapter 3, I called "social polishing." Reichenbach renders social polishing compatible with individual (and "superpersonal") sovereignty by viewing it as a unidirectional process beginning from individual A's volition, for which A is the sole condition. This volition is then expressed to individual B as an imperative, and that is the end of the matter; if B expresses a volition to A, that is a completely different case.[24] Because social polishing is unidirectional, from one person to another, a moral imperative that applies to oneself is often seen as coming from outside—from a divine source (as with the Ten Commandments), or from one's higher self.[25] Though imperatives are probably, Reichenbach says, derived from the *mores* in force in one's society (*RSP*, 285), they actually take effect only as a result of an individual's volitions: "The fundamental ethical rules are not justifiable through knowledge, but are adhered to merely because humans want these rules and want other people to follow the same rules" (*RSP*, 304; also see 300).

A major restriction on the scope of RCT, I have noted, was its taking preferences as fixed, which barred such theory from application to the many cases where peoples' preferences are in flux. This restriction has some plausibility as to market and voting behavior; but when scientific philosophy extends the insights of RCT into all fields of human endeavor, it becomes unacceptable. Reichenbach therefore has a robust view of precisely what was ruled out of rational choice theory at its beginning in Condorcet's paradox: the changing of one person's preferences by other people, or "social polishing." Indeed, Reichenbach holds it as a merit of his subjectivist theory that it makes changing one's volitions easier: "If a person knows that moral rules are of a volitional nature, he will be ready to change his goals to some extent if he sees that otherwise he cannot get along with other persons. Adaptation of goals to those of other persons is the essence of social education" (*RSP*, 300).

The adaptation here is to the volitions of others, not to a divine or social moral order that exists independently of them. Expressed generally, this leads Reichenbach to what he calls the "principle of democracy:" "*Everyone is entitled to set up his own moral imperatives and to demand that everyone else follow these imperatives*" (*RSP*, 295; emphasis in original). Moral discourse is not a matter of integrating oneself into a single larger perspective, as the idealists and pragmatists thought, but of one individual seeking to impose her volitions, however whimsical or parochial, on other individuals.[26] The ancient project of edification is well and truly dead.

With its demise, we are very close to a major step that Reichenbach never takes, but which became enormously influential in the subsequent development of American society. Since ethical sentences are most basically imperatives, ethics is most fundamentally not a matter of behaving in certain ways but of getting other people to behave in accordance with one's own volitions; it is a matter of imposing one's own volitions on others. In democracy, the imposition is argumentative: the principle of democracy is "an invitation to take an active part in the struggle of opinions" (*RSP*, 296). So far, so good: we have an almost Habermasian picture of opinion-formation through rational dialogue. But as Reichenbach recognizes, the struggle of volitions goes well beyond argument. Power in all forms, including armed, also plays a leading role: "Yes, it is power that controls social relationships" (*RSP*, 201). Reichenbach's wistful tone here suggests that he does not approve of this; but he has no basis on which to condemn it other than his own personal volitions. There is then nothing in Reichenbach's formulation of scientific philosophy to block the following inference:

1. To act ethically is to impose one's volitions, whatever they are, on others.
2. Power is a means to doing this.
3. Therefore, one should accumulate as much power as possible.

Moreover, since wealth is a form of power, accumulation of wealth is also advised. A decision to pursue wealth and power thus has the ethical status of what Reichenbach calls an "entailed decision" (*RSP*, 288). The general principle of entailed decisions is that one who wills the ends also wills the means; in Reichenbach's example, not smoking is entailed by the goal of staying healthy. But the pursuit of wealth and power is unusual among entailed decisions, in that it is entailed by an extraordinarily broad range of goals. Whether I want to buy a personal jet, end world hunger, or obtain treatment for an illness, I will be better able to do so if I have wealth and power.

Rational choice ethics thus comes to have a central imperative not envisioned by Reichenbach: increase your wealth and power! So understood, it provides justification, of a sort, for capitalism's main imperative, and does so without the kind of appeal to social benefit found, for example, in Adam Smith's doctrine of the "invisible hand (Smith 2000 [1790], 264–65): I should increase my wealth and power irrespective of whether or not that benefits society at large. When Cold War philosophy became the operating philosophy of the United States, this was elevated into a new social gospel. Institutions that help individuals become powerful and wealthy (law schools, business schools) or stay that way (medical schools, hospitals) flourished; other public infrastructure, along with the environment, was left to rot. Many of the problems faced by the United States in the early twenty-first century are testimony to the power in it of Cold War philosophy's theory of mind.

CONCLUSION

There is something puzzling about Reichenbach's views on reason, epistemology, ontology, and ethics. Though they are presented in the context of a reflection on science—one that, as we saw in chapter 2, claims to begin with an empirically adequate account of it—they in fact attribute to science a number of features that are empirically foreign to it and have since come under heavy attack. Since even a partial bibliography of the attacks would be far too long, I mention only some particularly famous attacks; they include the following:

1. There is a single, unified scientific (and so rational) method (Feyerabend 1975).
2. Knowledge is predictive (Carr 1961).
3. The use of the mind divides into the contexts of discovery and of justification (Kuhn 1970).
4. Reason is empty and so analytic, as opposed to the "synthetic" truths yielded by observation (Quine 1953a).
5. History and culture are irrelevant to proper rational procedure (Fine 1986).
6. Emotions are irrelevant to rational consideration (Hull 1988).

Subsequent massive investigation has not supported any of these attributions. Scientists, we now know, work in culturally situated communities. They are emotionally bound together (and torn apart) by loyalty and the quest for personal advantage. They use many methods to achieve many goals. Sharp lines between discovery and justification, and between analytical and synthetic, have blurred into obscurity. Reichenbach thus attributes to science a whole string of characteristics that it simply doesn't have—while claiming, as we saw in chapter 2, that his account of science is empirically sound. The question arises: If the properties Reichenbach attributes to science are not empirically to be found in it, where did he get them?

We have seen all of them in RCT.

It is not that Reichenbach copied from Arrow; the chronology alone refutes this, for Reichenbach had long been working on his views of science when Arrow came to RAND. But to say that Reichenbach's philosophy derived exclusively from a reflection on physics is far too narrow. Whatever influences passed, and in which direction, between Arrow and Reichenbach in the corridors of the RAND Corporation, and whatever insights came to them from the many philosophers who have tried, from Socrates on, to dissociate reason from preferences (or "passions"), it is unlikely to be an accident that Reichenbach's "scientific philosophy" accorded, better than other approaches of the time, with the sociopolitical imperatives of the early Cold War.

RSP's agreement with RCT is not a convergence, which would be supportive of both RCT and scientific philosophy by showing similar views being arrived at in two different spheres, because the spheres have in fact very different status. This is because *RSP* takes its positions, not as parts of an empirically verifiable theory, but as components of an overall account of rationality. The result of this is a philosophy much more in tune with the Cold War spirit than were its main rivals, idealism and pragmatism.

The two aspects in which Reichenbach's account of scientific philosophy most sharply diverges from RCT can be seen as required for generalizing RCT from market and voting behavior to all human activities.[27] This means, first, that social polishing cannot simply be disregarded as outside the scope of the theory. Reichenbach, we saw, offers a robust account of it—but reduces it to the efforts of one individual to impose her volitions on others. The preferences of the members of a society may derive from the social structures and *mores* of that society, but, as we saw, they take effect only through the volitions of individuals.

One place where preferences are clearly not malleable for Reichenbach, however, is science itself, which is the other main area to which Reichenbach's thought extends principles of RCT. Science is governed by a fixed preference for truth—or, failing that, for the highest probability—or, failing that, for convenience. In Reichenbach's account of scientific theory choice, the differing theories purporting to account for some observed phenomenon are weighed against each other as to probability and convenience, but they are not ranked against all other theories: there is no "opportunity cost" to the scientist of pursuing truth in one area as opposed to other areas. Rather, each investigation is conceptually independent. The scientist "could find, for every problem, an answer in its own right. He was not concerned with the task of combining answers into a neat philosophical system. He did not mind whether his results were derivable from some general doctrine . . ." (*RSP*, 119).

Accepting one scientific theory does not raise the cost of adopting any other scientific theory (except, to be sure, those that contradict it); accepting the theory of evolution does not raise or lower the "cost" of accepting the theory of relativity. This is not the case in RCT. An overall utility function is needed, because in deciding what alternatives to pursue, the agent takes into account the costs of pursuing them, including the costs of alternatives foregone, given the agent's finite resources. The decision is taken, not independently for each alternative, but so as to maximize the chooser's *overall* utility: pursuing as many highly ranked alternatives as possible, given the costs and risks of obtaining them (see *SCIV*, 20). That is why any preference profile must be complete, ranking all my preferences against each other so as to achieve a general view of my overall welfare.

Each scientific question, on Reichenbach's model, is to be resolved "in its own right" (a feature he elsewhere calls the "autonomy of problems" [Reichenbach 1959b, 83]). Overall scientific utility, in other words, is relegated to the "context of discovery," where scientists must decide what problems to look at and must seek funding for some programs at the expense of others. The omission of the utility function is thus no mere oversight; it allows the expansion of RCT to cover scientific theory choice. That expansion led to a philosophical dispositive whose alliance with the bold and glamorous world of rational choice theory gave it a role in the global struggle of the early Cold War—and clear advantages over its pragmatic and continental competitors. But the rise of Cold War philosophy was not due merely to its usefulness in the global struggle against Communism or to the promise of its logical method. As we will see in the next two chapters, it was brutally enforced on academia by the domestic tumult of the early Cold War.

* Part 3 *

Purifying the Academy

CHAPTER 5

Organizing Academic Repression: The California Plan

Only scholars can judge scholars as such.

IMMANUEL KANT, *The Conflict of the Faculties*

The first two chapters of this book showed religious pressures on the UCLA philosophy department favoring the physics-based naturalism of the logical positivists to the detriment of the human-oriented naturalism of the pragmatists. The next two traced the intellectual alliance between Hans Reichenbach's "scientific philosophy'" and rational choice theory (RCT), which was fast acquiring enormous academic prestige, in part because of its own usefulness as an ideological weapon in the Cold War. On both sides of the subject-object divide, avoiding pragmatism (and continental philosophy) and converting to positivism were good tactics for the times.

This claim will seem bizarre, if not offensive, to many. The standard view among philosophers *now* is that the adoption of Cold War philosophy by philosophers *then* was itself a rational choice. The preceding chapters do not question this. What they have shown is that Cold War philosophy was rationally preferable, not purely for intellectual reasons, but because sociopolitical developments of the time favored it to the detriment of its alternatives. That is not the end of the story, however, for this chapter and the next show that adherence to Cold War philosophy was more than tactically advantageous. It was—and in California, was openly proclaimed to be—absolutely necessary in order to have a career in higher education. Individual philosophers were thus forced either to accept the main tenets of Cold War philosophy or to leave the field. This takes matters out of the realm of choice altogether, and moves them into what Foucault calls "subjectivation:" the creation, by sociopolitical forces, of investigators of a certain type. The main vehicle of this, to be examined in this chapter, was a set of exclusionary strategies called the "California Plan."

Imposed on all institutions of higher education in the state, the plan enforced Cold War philosophy at precisely the point where enforcement would have the most enduring effects: the hiring of junior faculty.

Though it was presented as a bulwark against campus Communism, the next chapter shows that the California Plan had, and depended upon, a rationale that was defined more widely: to target not only Communism but the competing philosophical paradigms we have discussed—idealism, pragmatism, and continental philosophy. This rationale, a form of knowledge called the "Allen Formula," rapidly gained the assent of many faculty members—and in so doing turned them, willing or not, into certain kinds of knowers.

PROBLEMS WITH COLD WAR PHILOSOPHY

Like any dispositive, Cold War philosophy had its weaknesses. Some of these were not only obvious, but lay close enough to its conceptual core that we cannot really understand it without understanding them. A rough tour of some of them reveals this.

The basic problem is that when we ask whether Cold War philosophy met its own "scientific" standards of rationality, we find at best a mixed record. We saw in chapter 4 that those standards, for Reichenbach, included empirical adequacy (as claimed for his opening account of science); dispassion (as claimed for his treatment of Hegel); and, more generally, clarity and logical consistency. Though *RSP*'s treatments of individual issues often exhibit these undoubted virtues, Cold War philosophy's overall approach lacks them in enough places to incite a general skepticism—or it should have.

The most famous problem at the time was perhaps that of the status of logical positivism's "principle of verification." This is, roughly, the claim that the meaning of a sentence lies in how we verify it, so that a sentence that cannot be verified has no meaning. A. J. Ayer had wielded this as a club against religion and art (Ayer 1936), and something like it seems to have motivated Arrow's rejection of cardinality for preferences (*SCIV*, 9). But its epistemic status was dubious, for it is hard to state precisely (what does "verify" mean? Or "lie in?"). Moreover, it was neither an observation report (people do not in fact use "meaning" that way) nor a clearly analytical truth—the only two kinds of knowledge it allowed for. But, as Hilary Putnam notes, "Strangely enough this criticism had very little impact on the logical positivists and did little to impede the growth of their movement." [1]

The principle of verification was thus neither clear nor clearly self-consistent, and we may presume that Hans Reichenbach was aware of this when he wrote

RSP, which both retains it and downplays it. Though, as we saw in chapter 4, Reichenbach clearly believes that only observation can determine the probability of theories, he does not explicitly advance this as a principle, and when he gets around to discussing verification, toward the end of *RSP* (256–59), it plays only a technical role concerning prediction. Beyond that, "The scientific philosopher is tolerant; he wants everyone to mean what he wants" (*RSP*, 258). This does not mean that Reichenbach has thrown down Ayer's club, however; he just wields it more selectively. "Everyone" here clearly does not include those adhering to "unscientific" philosophy, to which, as we have seen, it is now time to "put an end" (*RSP*, 302). Nor does it include those untrained in logical analysis, from whom truth is "screened off" by a "haze of vagueness" (*RSP*, ix).

Reichenbach's scientistic cudgeling is thus (unlike Ayer's) limited to philosophers. Even so, it attracted unfavorable attention from several early reviewers (e.g., Church 1956; Hess 1956; Withers 1952). In its treatment of Hegel especially, it is hardly dispassionate: "Hegel's System is the poor construction of a fanatic, who has seen one empirical truth and attempts to make it into a logical law within the most unscientific of all logics" (*RSP*, 67–72). Reichenbach's handling of Hegel, in fact, openly violates all the tenets of scientific philosophy listed above. It is not only passionate but, as we saw in chapter 2, inconsistent: it accuses Hegel both of being an idealist, and so wanting to escape the imperfections of reality to a fantasy world, and of wanting to provide concrete moral directives to that same reality. It is unclear (what does it mean to be "the most unscientific of all logics?") and, finally, empirically inadequate, for it fails to take note of countervailing evidence in the form of Hegel's famous and explicit claim, adduced in chapter 2, that philosophy is unable to issue moral instruction of any kind.

The problems with Cold War philosophy, to be sure, went deeper than these. I have presented such philosophy here as an amalgam of four components. It views the known object, nature, as allowing the sciences to be hierarchically structured, with physics at the bottom and chemistry, biology, psychology, and the social sciences layered in above it. And it views the knowing subject as an individual whose cognitive core is a set of mathematical ranking procedures. We thus have four basic components to the overall Cold War dispositive: on the side of the object, (1) stratification and (2) naturalism; and on that of the subject, (3) mathematicality and (4) individualism. Each of these components, except for stratification, was advanced by Reichenbach with careful scrutiny, but the scrutiny often raised more questions than it answered. The stratification of nature (1) is paired with the hierarchy of the sciences in ways mysterious enough to lead Oppenheim and Putnam, already in 1958, to reopen the entire question. Which comes first? If the stratification, we are on the doleful road to metaphysics; if the hierarchy, we head to idealism. When Oppenheim and Putnam seek passage beyond this Scylla and Charybdis, today's sciences become "largely, fictitious." Neither metaphysics nor fiction, of course, counts as "scientific."

Cold War philosophy's view of mathematics as a timeless, universally valid cognitive tool is at odds with its naturalism (2), and indeed with empiricism itself (see Richardson 1997, 422–23). Reichenbach's view that mathematics and logic are analytic, and so empty, mitigates this, but then runs into the "paradox of analysis" (see Bell 1999): if logic is too empty to constrain reality in any way, how does the logical analysis of a sentence improve upon its original formulation? Will not any unclarities and ambiguities in the terms of that sentence have to be imported into its formalization? If not, what—other than the philosopher's "volition—" makes *this* logical formula the restatement of *that* sentence?

The very care with which Cold War philosophy reflected on the nature of the human mind also led to problems, for it encouraged highly idealized accounts of both its mathematical (3) and individualistic (4) components. That people actually think mathematically and unemotionally, for example, was belied at the time by the vast body of literature and philosophy that Hans Meyerhoff adduced in his 1955 in *Time in Literature* (*TL*) to support his "subjectivist" view that art is a legitimate source of knowledge. That humans think individually—that is, that each individual is wholly responsible for her thoughts à la consumer sovereignty—is belied by the omnipresent phenomenon of social "polishing" that each of us undergoes in daily life. Once again: denying or omitting obvious facts of life is not part of a "scientific" attitude.

In addition, some of the conceptual bridges joining the four components of the overall dispositive are unstable. When individualism becomes mathematical, for instance, it ceases to be very individualistic.[2] It locates the stable core of each individual, not in something unique to her, but in a ranking procedure shared by all (rational) human beings; what differentiates one person from another is to be found only in the passing play of experiences.[3] This view, which, as we saw, culminated in Reichenbach's striking view of scientific work as conducted by a sort of "superperson" (his term), is in stark contrast to other, more traditional forms of individualism such as the "qualitative" individualism of Thomas Aquinas (each being has at its core a unique *actus essendi* [Aquinas 1963]), the dialectical and existential individualisms of Hegel and Sartre (individuals construct themselves as unique), and the expressive individualism of people like Ralph Waldo Emerson ("A foolish consistency is the hobgoblin of small minds" [Emerson 2007, 21]) and Walt Whitman ("Do I contradict myself? Very well then I contradict myself, I am large, I contain multitudes" [Whitman 1993, 113]). It is perhaps most like the sentimental individualism referred to by Tocqueville:

> I see an innumerable multitude of men, alike and equal, constantly circling around in pursuit of the petty and banal pleasures with which they glut their souls. Each of them withdrawn into himself, is almost unaware of the fate of the rest. Mankind, for him, consists in his children and his personal friends. As for the rest of his fellow citizens, they are near enough, but he does not notice them. He touches them but feels nothing. He exists in and for himself, and though he still may have a family, one can at least say that he has not got a fatherland. (Tocqueville 1969, 692)

But the Tocquevillian individual has, so to speak, only one level: that constituted by her unique circle of family and friends, in which "mankind" (including herself) "consists." She is missing the stable, logical level of the individual according to RCT and Cold War philosophy, who is not defined by any of her communities and has a more Kantian flavor. For Kant, each such individual is equipped with exactly the same type of human mind—to the extent that Kant can be plausibly accused of positing that there is really only a single human mind, in which each of us shares (Neujahr 1995, 11–44); Reichenbach's scientific "superperson" is a shadow of this Kantian supermind (which was shadowy enough already). The epilogue explains that this view of human individuality was not only a serious weakness of Cold War philosophy, but an explosive one.

Finally, Cold War philosophy's two core components—its view of the object as nature stratified through science, and of the subject as a rational chooser—do not seem to have much to do with one another. Does viewing the mind in terms of rational choice support the view that nature is stratified or the sciences hierarchized? Conversely, is there anything about the stratification and the hierarchy that even suggests that the human mind is primarily a utility-seeking decision device? If not, why did the two sides of Cold War philosophy gain prominence together? Both, to be sure, had a scientific orientation that brought them popularity in an age when the hard sciences, in Brand Blanshard's words, were "riding high" (Blanshard 1945, 8). But pragmatism, too, was in its own way science-oriented, and its emphasis on science as a means to better living was, if anything, more in accordance with utility-maximizing rationality than with the pure search for truth (or highest probability) portrayed by logical positivists.[4]

The point is not that these issues cannot be resolved; philosophers saw them early and attacked them often, sometimes successfully. But they do raise the question of whether the sudden triumph and subsequent endurance of Cold War philosophy can be explained entirely through conversion or well-chosen career tactics. We must dig deeper into the shifting political subsoil that underlay American philosophy during the early Cold War. And there we find a strategy of force that was not only compelling, but brutal: the California Plan.

ENFORCEMENT IN CALIFORNIA

The California Oath Controversy of 1949–1951, discussed briefly in chapter 1, saw the university's faculty caught up in a pitched battle with the Board of Regents and the state legislature over the infamous loyalty oath. The battle was extremely destructive. The university's faculty, for one thing, was thrown into utter disarray, which philosophy department chair Donald Piatt captured in a letter in March 1950: "As you may know, UCLA and Berkeley have been off base with the fight of our lives over the regents' requirement of a non-communist oath as a condition of continued employment. This fight has upset our routine and is responsible for the regrettable delay in my answering your letter of May Third."[5]

Not only were professors distracted from their jobs; hiring new ones became almost impossible. A faculty resolution of March 1, 1950, opposing the oath, stated that "Already, it is reported by some departmental chairmen, negotiations currently underway with some scholars in other institutions are in danger of being broken off because the regents' action has cast doubt on the desirability of coming to this University."[6] Hiring difficulties certainly affected the UCLA philosophy department on the senior level, where Rudolf Carnap, A. I. Melden, W. V. O. Quine, and possibly others turned down offers of its prestigious Flint Professorship because of the action of the regents.[7] Had the California Supreme Court not ruled against the regents in October 1952, it is hard to imagine that departing faculty would have been replaced with people of similar ability; requiring the oath thus amounted to a slow death sentence for the university. To stop further attacks, two things were needed: the university had to police itself, and it had to be *seen* to police itself.

This led to a system of triage for job candidates, put in place in the spring and summer of 1952. Any applicant for a position at the University of California would be politically scrutinized at three levels: first by the hiring department, then by the chancellor of the campus, and finally by the staff of CUAC. The two upper levels of this system, and they only, were publicly identified as the California Plan. They applied to all colleges and universities in the state, public and private, and governed their relations with CUAC. This arrangement was set up for Southern California in a meeting of the heads of all institutions of higher education in the area, which took place on March 24, 1952.[8] The lowest, departmental level was installed for the University of California by a memo from President G. Sproul to all "Chairmen of Departments and Other Administrative Officers," dated April 21, 1952—less than a month later. Since all three levels were clearly intended to work together at the University of California, I include them all in referring to the California Plan.

The stated aim of the Plan was to make sure that no subversives were hired to teach at any institution of higher education in the State of California. CUAC Council Richard E. Combs described it as follows: "The committee developed a procedure whereby applicants for positions are referred to us, their names are, and if we do have any documentation concerning their Communist activity over a long period of time, we make that available to the university as a guide to indicate whether or not the individual should be employed."[9] President Sproul provided a bit more precision and detail: "Contact men will only report on subversive activity in connection with faculty members and employees [i.e., they were not to report on students]. . . . Official channels to ferret out alleged Communists before they are hired will be provided by the contact man program."[10]

The stated core of the plan was that all applications for faculty jobs would be channeled to one person, usually the head of the institution, called the "contact man." He (they were all male) would then forward them to CUAC, which would consult its database of subversive individuals and organizations and provide "guidance." In fact, this word was highly misleading, for as Ellen Schrecker has pointed out, it would have been very difficult for any university to go against CUAC once it had declared that a given job candidate was a subversive. CUAC's policy was that if that ever happened, it would go public, issuing subpoenas and holding hearings (CUAC 7 [1953], 134). No college could hope to deal with such publicity, so the "guidance" was more like total control. As Schrecker concludes, "During the height of the McCarthy Era, the California Senate Un-American Activities Committee, and most probably the committee's staff of professional anti-Communists, exercised a veto over every single academic appointment in the state of California" (Schrecker 1986, 380).

The California Plan remained in place at UCLA from 1952 to, apparently, 1959, when (as we will see in chapter 6) the university's first chancellor, who had enthusiastically supported it, departed. Its existence, as the quotation from Schrecker shows, has long been known, but its workings have not. This is because the plan operated in the greatest secrecy. While its existence was and had to be public knowledge, its actual workings were, and had to be, confidential.

This was for a couple of reasons. One was that it was quicker and more efficient to end someone's career in secret; doing so in public required extensive justification, hearings, and due process. Moreover, as CUAC noted in its annual report for 1953, professors who were already on campus, even if untenured, had networks of friends and supporters. Efforts to remove them often provoked a loud backlash. In the view of the organizers of the California Plan, such backlashes were invariably orchestrated by the Communist Party. Carried out by dupes and fellow travelers, they seriously impeded what, as we will see, can only be called CUAC's "crusade" against subversion.[11]

Operating in secrecy was also, sometimes, more humane. Merely being publicly identified as a possible subversive usually meant the end of one's career. A department that offered a job to an openly suspicious candidate would also suffer. Questions would surely be raised about why she had become a candidate in the first place. Was someone already on the faculty pushing for the hire? Was the job advertisement written in such a way as to attract subversives? If so, by whom? Did some pinkish professorial cabal cough up a suspicious name? Secrecy was thus advisable, not only for the candidate herself, but for the department that tried to hire her. Indeed, it would benefit everybody. It would enable CUAC itself to operate freely, without the constraints brought on by publicity. It would allow administrators and faculty respite from damaging public outcries. And it would help the alleged Communists themselves—if anyone cared about them.

Though the three-level system was an exercise in political repression—indeed, it was a Kafkaesque Star Chamber in which job candidates were judged without an opportunity to defend themselves or even to know precisely what they had been charged with—it was actually in several ways significantly milder than what it replaced. First, the emphasis now was on preventing new hires, which reduced pressures on professors already employed. In particular, CUAC was no longer in the business of confronting suspect professors directly; everything would now be channeled through the contact man. Moreover, an outsider's suspicions about academic subversion could now be brought to CUAC or the contact man, rather than to newspapers and other public forums; letter-writing campaigns of the Max Otto variety would now be unnecessary. And finally, as the next chapter shows, the California Plan—unlike CUAC and other outside forces—was not arbitrary or hysterical, but was supported by a clear and persuasive rationale. This last was particularly important because, as a system of self-policing, the plan required the active cooperation of the faculty and administrators, many of whom were themselves members of the faculty.

The secrecy was successfully maintained at UCLA, enabling the administration to avoid provoking the newspapers, the public, the legislature, and the regents. For the plan's duration, no serious cases of subversion made the newspapers, and random attacks by outside forces became things of the past. In 1961, however, after the plan had ceased to function at UCLA, they resumed: anthropologist John Greenway was fired for maintaining that the Roman Catholic Mass exhibited traces of cannibalism (*TD*, 20–21). Three years after that, philosopher Patrick G. Wilson would, as we saw in chapter 1, be denounced by leading Los Angeles clergymen for the way he taught philosophy of religion. The seven years of silence while the California Plan was in effect are testimony to its success at tamping down controversy.

In terms of what was publicly stated to be its basic goal—actually stopping subversives from being hired—the plan was said to have functioned with great success. In 1953, after it had been operating for only ten months, CUAC happily reported that "the state university and all eight of its campuses are cooperating fully with the Committee," that "more than a hundred persons with documented records of Communist activities and affiliations have been removed from the educational institutions of California," and that all this had happened "without fanfare or publicity."[12] The counsel to the committee, Robert Combs (who admittedly had reason to exaggerate), went further and put the number of applicants whom CUAC prevented from being hired in California during those first ten months at several hundred—a rate of about one per day (Schrecker 1986, 280).

Because of the California Plan's secrecy (including the notable vagueness of such public statements as those quoted above), it is impossible to know the details of its functioning. Common sense, however, tells us that, as in all bureaucracies, lower levels wanted to look good to higher ones. Thus, no one wanted to be caught, either publicly or by higher levels of the vetting system, advancing a candidate who might be labeled as subversive. A department that repeatedly put forth such candidates would quickly acquire a dubious reputation, and if the contact man forwarded to CUAC too many names that it found unacceptable, he too would come under suspicion. Each level therefore had not only to judge the given candidate, but to guess how higher levels were likely to respond to her. Such guessing was not easy, and tended to displace power in the system upward, as each level tried to make decisions pleasing to the higher level, or levels.

My discussion of the three levels of the California Plan begins with the lowest level, that of individual departments and then moves to its highest level,

CUAC. I then discuss the overall role of the contact man, but only briefly, because that role was filled in very different ways on different campuses. At UCLA, the constraints were especially strong and so especially visible. I discuss them in the next chapter.

Departments

Departments were not formally part of the California Plan as originally announced, but were added to it at the University of California a few weeks later, in the memo mentioned above.[13] The memo directed departments to do what they could to make sure that prospective hires had no "commitments or obligations to an organization, Communist or other, which prejudices impartial scholarship and teaching and the free pursuit of truth."[14] Departments thus came to function in coordination with the California Plan as the first and lowest level of vetting for job candidates. The directive continues:

> Chairmen of departments and reviewing authorities . . . cannot be expected to initiate an exhaustive field investigation of an individual coming up for recommendation, but they should seek to obtain facts bearing upon the matter by clearly outlining the policies of the University in correspondence with candidates or with others from whom advice is being sought, as well as by *careful examination of the candidate's published writings*. It is important that *all* evidence which raises *any* doubt as to the qualifications of the individual be passed on to the reviewing authorities, and that special attention be called to it. The responsibility will then be passed to those who must share in it, including the President [emphasis added].

Political vetting is thus to begin at the department level, but all decisions are to be made by the higher administrators who constitute the "reviewing authorities." Though the memo expresses awareness that departments do not have time or resources for thorough investigations of job candidates, they are required among other things to "consult with others from whom advice is being sought" about political reliability and to examine a candidate's publications to see if they express "commitment" to subversive organizations. No candidate is to get the benefit of *any* doubt; even the least suspicions are to be shared with the administrators.

It is important not to be misled here by the reference to "organizations." It is, on the surface, in keeping with a desire to penalize Communist Party membership, rather than opinions and behavior. But it is opinions that the memo directs departments to scrutinize. How, indeed, would published scholarship indicate membership in an organization, Communist or not? Scholarly publications state and defend one's views, not one's political memberships. In fact, UCLA's Privilege and Tenure Committee, composed of faculty, was not above using professional activities and opinions as exonerating evidence against Communist allegiance (see chapter 1); now, departments were being required, if not openly ordered, to use such views to impute such allegiance (which amounts, of course, to censoring those views).

Suppose, then, that a candidate's dossier is in front of a departmental hiring committee. The committee has contacted what it believes to be a sufficient number of "others," and has received, perhaps, such coded messages as these: "I know nothing about him that would be prejudicial to his interests as a member of an academic community."[15] "My contact with him has been wholly on the academic side, but I know of no personal traits that would detract from the favorable picture I have formed of him."[16] Has the department done its job? It is hard to say, because the task assigned to departments is multiply open-ended. For one thing, departments have been instructed to supply *all* evidence that raises *any* doubt about the candidate. Where would that end? Given the McCarthyites' strong anti-Semitism, for example, would evidence of Jewishness have to be forwarded? For another, departments are told by the memo to seek advice from "others" about job candidates, but they are not told who or how many these others should be. This lack of specificity is, on the one hand, entirely reasonable: such matters would vary with the individual case. But it also plays into the vetting of lower levels by higher ones that I mentioned earlier. If a department forwarded the name of someone who was deemed unacceptable at either of the two higher levels, it could always be said that they had not contacted enough others, or the right others; the blame, in other words, could always be cast downward. This means, in turn, that a department's diligence in fulfilling the directive would be known mainly by its fruits, in two ways. A department would be doing enough to uncover subversives if, first, it did not forward unacceptable names to the higher levels; and if, second, it rejected a number of job candidates because of the discovery of subversive components in their background. In other words, a department was doing its job the more "subversive" candidates it could claim to have turned down, and the fewer it passed on to the contact man.

A third open-ended feature of the task imposed on departments comes from the vague specification of who is to come under scrutiny. The memo's reference to "an individual coming up for recommendation" is too vague even to make sense. "Candidate" presumably means "candidate for a job," but that can cover many things. It would have been absurd to view as a "job candidate" everyone whose name crossed some departmental transom, got mentioned over some departmental water cooler, or came up in some midnight phone call. Moreover, there were often, especially in the case of junior hires, too many applicants for a given position to make forwarding them all to the contact man feasible; he, as the head of the institution, had a lot of other things to do. "Job candidate" could not, then, be taken to mean just anyone who applied for a job. This meant that departments had discretion over whom they identified as "job candidates." This discretion was important, because forwarding a name that got rejected at a later stage could, as I pointed out above, hurt both the candidate and the department. This allowed some job candidacies—how many we will never know—to die silent deaths at the departmental level.

The Mind of CUAC

The highest level of the actual California Plan, and so its most feared, was CUAC. It was also the most unhinged. Like its federal exemplar HUAC, CUAC saw itself in a life-or-death struggle with Communist subversives. The ardor was undimmed as late as 1959, when after nineteen years of work, CUAC had still not uncovered a single seriously subversive professor at UCLA or elsewhere in California higher education: "If the co-operative efforts of the educational institutions and this committee can prevent one student from being . . . indoctrinated each year, then the effort is, in our view, more than justified for that reason alone" (CUAC X, [1959], 84). Beneath the crusading rhetoric, the bureaucratic self-interest is all too visible: as long as a single student was being "indoctrinated," CUAC had a reason to exist—and a claim on state funding.

CUAC's concern for its own survival became, we will see, increasingly strident as time went on, because the public record indicated that either CUAC was not catching the Communist conspirators on the faculty or that they were never there in the first place (the latter, as we saw in chapter 1, was the truth). [17] Hence, CUAC came to focus more of its anger on other groups: on job candidates, as we have seen, and on liberals, as we will see. But first: What was indoctrination, and who was doing it? Here, we see CUAC come up against the great question of McCarthyism: Who was a subversive?

There is no point here in rehashing the confused hysteria of the times, when neighbors suspected neighbors. [18] It has been well documented in many places. The problem was exacerbated because students could not be indoctrinated if they knew they were being indoctrinated; the whole point of being a "subversive" in the classroom was to operate undercover. That was why, as the leading academic Red hunter of the day, University of Washington President Raymond B. Allen, had pointed out, the party kept its membership records secret (*CAF*, 99–100). And these secret Communists sometimes went to great lengths, said CUAC, to conceal their views. Many of them, for example, took care to use only non-Communist texts in their classes: "An entire syllabus could be drawn up without one notably or openly Stalinite reference in it" (CUAC 8 [1955], 85). This level of subversive trickery was truly fiendish. If Communists did not even have Communist texts on their syllabi, subversion could only be detected by someone actually present in the classroom. But the only people who had time or occasion to be in classrooms were students—and they, by definition, did not know whether they were being indoctrinated or not. What to do?

The answer, according to CUAC, was to look at the long-term activities and affiliations of the professors: "The real and only infallible test to be applied is to determine by an individual's activities and affiliations over a long period of time whether or not he is under Communist Party discipline and is performing his duties in accordance with the current Party line" (CUAC 8 [1955], 50). This view of who was dangerous in the classroom thus begins with guilt by association. Membership in the Communist Party or in various front organizations was, so to speak, a red flag—and, contrary to CUAC's assertion here, affiliations did not have to be long-term: Rudolf Carnap, as I noted in chapter 1, was investigated by the FBI just for signing a couple of petitions (Reisch 2005, 271–79). But things got even more vague. CUAC was also checking for "activities" that were "in accordance with the current Party line." Publishing, of course, is an activity; departments were already scrutinizing that. But what does "in accordance with" mean?

The phrasing of the entire quotation above, though vague, is delicate. One thing it indicates, with its emphasis on activities and affiliations, is that CUAC was not taking into account a professor's personal intentions or moral convictions; they did not constitute part of the "real and only infallible test." Such things, of course, were difficult to determine; Communists, in CUAC's view, lied about them all the time. They were also irrelevant. A sincere dupe who taught students that capitalism was socially unjust, for example, could do just as much damage to an innocent student as a Kremlin-trained Communist.

Activities and affiliations were the stated objects of investigation, then. But how did one decide which of these "accorded" with the current party line? With respect to affiliations, CUAC cast a rather wide net. Membership in Consumers Union, for example, was openly stated to be a ground for suspicion—an issue for Rudolf Carnap, who had acknowledged his own membership in 1941 (Reisch 2005, 276). Consumer's Union was suspect because, as one witness against professors accused at the University of Washington explained, "Any organization concerned about the rights of the "public" against business was Communist, because the Communists hate capitalism."[19]

As the years dragged by without any actual Communists being uncovered, CUAC's targets increasingly came to include not only leftists and fellow travelers, but any professors who did not support CUAC's own cleansing efforts and who, by that very fact, were in CUAC's mind advancing the interests of the party. The 1959 report takes time to attack Berkeley law professor Edward Barrett, who had written a book critical of CUAC (Barrett 1951) and who is called "yet another sincere liberal whose lack of practical experience in the amorality of Communism led him to act as an innocent victim of a smear job" (CUAC 10 [1959], 49).

Another target was the Fund for the Republic, a Ford Foundation think tank that (according to CUAC) had found widespread support for a questionnaire on academic freedom, in contrast to the "storm of faculty protest" that greeted the committee itself in 1952 (CUAC 10 [1959], 58). And a third was a group of Berkeley professors, who announced their refusal to cooperate with FBI investigations of students: "What this situation actually amounts to is a defiant statement by employees of the State of California that they will flatly refuse to reveal their knowledge of subversive affiliations and activities on the part of their students to authorized representatives of the federal and state governments who are specifically charged with the gathering of precisely that type of information" (CUAC 10 [1959], 83).

In other words, opponents of CUAC's efforts were increasingly viewed as enemies of the state. Such enemies included people who wrote critically of the committee; those who independently gathered information about academic freedom; and professors who refused to inform on their students. In particular, it included liberals, for whom CUAC had open contempt—and *liberal* was defined broadly: "The inhuman tortures inflicted by the Soviet Secret Police are far more horrible than any ever employed by the Nazis; they covered a much longer period and affected more people by many millions. . . . [Those who do not see this] constitute a formidable obstacle to the effective protection of colleges and universities against subversive infiltration by members of the Communist Party or individuals under Communist discipline" (CUAC 10 [1959], 454–47).

Anyone who thought that the Nazis were worse than the Communists was thus a "formidable obstacle" to CUAC, which seems, like Sidney Hook, to have "regarded all intellectuals as foot soldiers in this ongoing, epic war between the freedom-hating Soviets and the freedom-loving West."[20]

CUAC's vagueness about who was a subversive is more than reminiscent of the outsiders who campaigned against Max Otto in 1947, and whose disruptive role CUAC had now assumed. The main differences are CUAC's angrier affect and its insincerity. The Southern Californians who protested Max Otto had nothing to gain personally from their protests, and the tone of their letters is concerned and regretful rather than angry. The regents also could hardly expect to profit personally from the oath or from the controversy it engendered. But CUAC, whatever the sincerity of some of its members, was in the end a bureaucratic career tool whose underlying concern was self-perpetuation. I noted above that this meant that CUAC had an incentive to uncover as many "subversives" as possible, and the record shows that it was not overly scrupulous in this regard. When it was finally disbanded in 1971, its files of "subversives" were found to contain the names of California legislators who had voted against committee appropriations and other bills that its chairmen had supported.[21] Long before then, its prevarications had been widely recognized: a doggerel of the time, referring to its chairman, State Senator Jack B. Tenney, ran as follows: "A Communist is any / Who disagrees with Tenney."[22]

The Role of the Contact Man

The most important part of the California Plan was the contact man. While there was only one CUAC, every college and university in California had its own contact man, normally its president or chancellor. The available descriptions of the contact man's actual role, however, are few, brief, and cryptic. They consist, in fact, of the two statements, by CUAC Counsel Richard Combs and by University of California President Robert Sproul, quoted above.[23] Both tell us only, in summary, that the contact man was to forward to CUAC the names he received of job candidates, and then wait for CUAC to tell him whether the candidate had any "subversive affiliations."

This meager evidence can be supplemented, to some extent, by two other kinds of consideration. One kind comprises the conclusions we can reach about the contact man's role from common sense and what we know about the overall structure of the California Plan. I present these conclusions in this section. Beyond them, we must turn to what facts can be gleaned from the behavior of specific contact men. Here, we confront the problem that different contact men performed the job very differently. As we will see shortly, UCLA's chancellor was an enthusiastic supporter of the plan, while Berkeley's refused the job altogether. This refusal at Berkeley means that any excavation of the activities of the contact man at the University of California must focus on UCLA, at that time the university's single other autonomous component. How far what we uncover there can be generalized to other institutions, public and private, in California and elsewhere, is a matter for other investigators; the present excavation can, perhaps, show them the kind of thing they should look for.

The statements available are too vague to tell us whether the contact man's activity was merely clerical or not. Was he obliged to forward *every* name he received from a department, or did he have some discretion about whether the name of a given job candidate should be forwarded to CUAC? Here, common sense suggests that he did have some discretion. As was the case with departments, forwarding a name that was likely to draw a negative reaction from CUAC would have been unwise, and for several reasons. First, if a candidate failed CUAC's vetting it could bring suspicion not only on the institution, but on the contact man himself; a group as prone to zealotry as CUAC would be quick to suspect negligence or worse. Second, it could also hurt the candidate himself (or, in rare cases, herself); no one wanted to be identified as having been denied a job because of political suspicions. Refusing to forward a name, conversely, would be advantageous to the contact man: CUAC, when informed of it (confidentially, to be sure), would be reassured that the contact man was doing his job and could add that unforwarded name to its list of "subversives" that the plan had kept from employment. The California Plan thus worked, at the level of the contact man, as did Sproul's memorandum to department chairs—to deny job candidates any benefit of doubt.

It is also true, finally, that a university the size of Berkeley, Stanford, UCLA, or USC produces a lot of job candidates. When we add to this the many other colleges and universities in California, all of which were under the California Plan, we see that forwarding every name to CUAC would have meant an enormous work load. As we have seen, CUAC bragged variously about a rejection rate of job candidates of about three per week, while its own counsel put the rate at around one per day; we do not know how many other candidates they passed, but if the ratio was even fifty-fifty, the burden was heavy at either rate. In addition, CUAC was also looking onto Hollywood and various other supposed foci of infiltration; its members also had to attend to other business in the state legislature; and, according to Clark Kerr, it had only one staff member (Richard Combs [Kerr 2003, 48–49]). The more candidates were eliminated at lower levels, the less work for CUAC, which could take credit for them anyway (as Combs did in my earlier quotation from him), because it held prime authority in the California Plan.

We may conclude that the conscientious performance of his duties would have required the contact man *not* to forward some names to CUAC if he thought that CUAC was not going to accept the candidate anyway. Not forwarding a name, of course, was no innocent act; it ended the candidacy of its bearer.

Since the automatic forwarding of every name was not a reasonable option, the contact man was required to decide, for every job candidate at the university, whether or not to forward that person's name to CUAC. This required, in every case, a judgment call. Judgment calls on job applicants are, in fact, a standard part of the job of any university administrator who reviews departmental hiring decisions. The whole point of such review, after all, is to catch departments that are collectively lazy, cronyistic, or overly wedded to a single approach to their fields, and such things are matters for experienced judgment. Nonetheless, the standard presumption in such administrative reviews is that any department that has decided to make an offer has done a thorough and diligent job of vetting its various candidates. Thus, it is a major principle of faculty governance that an administrator can overturn a department's hiring recommendation only if she or he can give compelling reason to do so. This arrangement serves as a check on the administrator—for administrators, too, can be lazy, cronyistic, or overly devoted to certain approaches. Since the operations of the California Plan were secret, however, these normal checks and balances did not apply. The contact man's decisions were not publicly announced, and the only place for a department to appeal them would have been to CUAC itself—hardly an inviting prospect.

In making such judgment calls, the contact man had to decide who would, and would not, be unacceptable to CUAC. On the basis of the evidence available at the time,[24] what could reasonably be concluded about CUAC was that it was composed of self-serving zealots who hated not only Communists but liberals, members of Consumers Union, people who despised Nazis more than Communists, and indeed "any/who disagrees with Tenney." CUAC also, as I have noted, had a strong bureaucratic interest in seeing people turned down, and was quite willing to designate even state legislators as subversive if it suited CUAC's interests.

Thus, while the contact man did not quite have carte blanche to end job candidacies, it was plausible for him to tell a department, with genuine or feigned regret, that he was not forwarding a candidate's name because in his view that candidate would be unacceptable to CUAC. Indeed, in the extreme, it would be possible for him to claim that he had obtained evidence independently that was unavailable to departments and that ruled out a given candidate. He could say this, moreover, either to the department or to the candidate, giving her a chance to withdraw her own name. If the contact man was willing to do this—and there is some evidence that the contact man at UCLA was[25]—his latitude to turn down job candidates without oversight or appeal was wide indeed.

That at least one contact man took an expansive view of his job is suggested by bizarre events at the University of California's senior campus, Berkeley. Though the contact man was usually the leader of the institution, Berkeley's chancellor, Clark Kerr, refused the job altogether, with the result that a security officer at the university named William Wadman took it over—unbeknownst to Kerr, who later stated that he "felt like [he] was being used by President Sproul."[26] Wadman's view of his job went well beyond the forwarding of the names of candidates for employment, and amounted to a general political policing of the faculty. According to a 1954 article in the Harvard *Crimson*, which relied on the testimony of Robert Combs, "If, after looking over charges against a professor and investigating them, Wadman thinks the man should be removed, he goes to the state Committee and discusses the case. If the Burns Committee agrees with him, the information is passed on to the president of the University [Sproul], who calls for the professor's resignation. Any professor in the college—not merely those in classified research—can be dealt with in this manner."[27]

The contact man thus had enormous power, if he was willing to use it. Kerr, the academic, was not. Wadman, the campus security officer, was. It is likely that Wadman was more zealous than the officially designated contact men across California: the *Crimson*'s account conflicts with other statements, some of them, as we saw, from CUAC itself, which limited the role of the contact man to preventing new hires rather than dealing with professors already on campus. But that Wadman was stopped only when his activities became public shows that there was room, at least, for a good deal of undercover zealotry.

The California Plan thus amounted to an organized and draconian cleansing operation, directed mainly against the young and vulnerable—candidates for jobs, most of which, then as now, were entry level. Though its specific actions were not known to the faculty, its existence and general orientation was. Nothing could be more antithetical to the academic freedom so dear to the professoriate. How could they have gone along with it?

CHAPTER 6

Rationalizing Academic Repression: The Allen Formula

It has not occurred to one of these philosophers to inquire into the connection of [American] philosophy with [American] reality, the relation of their critique to their own material surroundings.

— KARL MARX, *The German Ideology* (paraphrased)

In the 1947 Max Otto Affair, political surveillance of academic appointments had come from outsiders to academia, ordinary citizens motivated by honest concern. Four years later, after the brilliant formulation of rational choice theory by Kenneth Arrow discussed in chapter 3, prestigious figures within the American intellectual establishment began patriotically bending their disciplines to the urgent needs of the Cold War. And a year after that, in a crude parody of a Hegelian synthesis, external surveillance and internal prestige combined to produce—internal surveillance. As we saw in the previous chapter, the California Plan instituted a single apparatus of political vetting that reached from the head of each institution down to professors on hiring committees.

But there was one crucial problem with it: in order to function as a strategy of force, in Foucault's sense, it needed a very special "form of knowledge." This was because it required both active and passive support from the faculty: actively, individual departments had to perform their due diligence with regard to job candidates; passively, they had to acquiesce in the contact man's judgments on those candidates. Both types of cooperation required the faculty to accept the overall legitimacy of the California Plan. But the plan was, on its face, a massive intrusion of social and political forces into academic affairs, which was hardly something most professors were predisposed to support. It thus needed an extremely potent rationale if it was to function—a rationale at once strong enough to justify the immediate and permanent exclusion of any "subversive" from academia, and plausible enough to appeal to some of the most powerful and critical minds in America. It was a tall order, but the order was filled. The man who filled it was University of Washington President

Raymond B. Allen, America's leading academic Red hunter (see *TD*, 39–40; Schrecker 1986, 95–112), who, after leaving the University of Washington, became the first chancellor of UCLA.

The rationale he produced was commonly called the Allen Formula. Its core was an argument that Communists should be denied academic employment, not because they held undesirable opinions, but because their allegiance to Moscow had led them to abandon the scientific method—a method that Allen, though there is no evidence that he ever read Reichenbach, understood in unitary terms very similar to his. This means that the California Plan was in fact directed not only against Communists but against all "non-scientific" approaches, which in philosophy included pragmatism and existentialism.

This chapter proceeds in several stages. After first looking at Allen himself, I place his formula in the context both of his earlier writings and of its complex assortment of intended audiences. Then I look at how he argues for two things: that Communists should be excluded from teaching positions, and that administrators and regents are qualified to make these exclusions. I then turn to issues of how Allen's views on these issues would have influenced his own behavior as contact man at UCLA, before finally discussing faculty reaction both to the California Plan and to its rationale.

RAYMOND B. ALLEN AND HIS FORMULA

Allen is little remembered today at UCLA. Unlike other administrators and philosophy professors, such as Hans Meyerhoff, Ernest Moore, Franklin Murphy, and Charles Rieber (commemorated respectively in Meyerhoff Park, Moore Hall, Murphy Hall, and Rieber Hall), no facilities are named for him. Indeed, he is nowhere commemorated on the campus, having resigned very quickly in 1959 just ahead of a football scandal.[1] His early life was, however, exemplary in many respects.[2] Born in North Dakota, he began his career as a country doctor there. Eventually he held important administrative posts at several medical schools in the Midwest before serving as president of the University of Washington from 1946 to 1952. While at Washington, he gained a national reputation by dealing with a number of academic freedom cases. The most important of these concerned Herbert Phillips, a philosophy professor, who was not accused of any actual wrongdoing; the only charge against him was that he was a member of the Communist Party. His classroom practice was one of honest dissent, rather than subversion, for he was entirely open about his views. Indeed, he routinely told his classes that he was a Marxist and warned them to take that into account in assessing his lectures (Schrecker 1986, 44–45; Sanders 1979, 51).

As Schrecker has shown, the Phillips case and Allen's handling of it set the parameters and procedures for McCarthy Era academic freedom cases across the country (Schrecker 1986, 104). This was because, in order to fire Phillips, President Allen had to show that mere membership in the party provided sufficient grounds for dismissal. The rationale he articulated for this, the Allen Formula, quickly rose to national influence. Only at Reed College in Oregon did the professors refuse to go along with Allen's general rationale for firing Communists (Schrecker 1986, 240); everywhere else, in one way or another, openly or stealthily, they followed it. The formula quickly made its creator nationally known, in the words of the *Los Angeles Times*, as an "outstanding foe of Red influence on college campuses."[3]

We cannot understand the operations of the California Plan at UCLA, then, without taking into account the fact that the man who administered it there was also the nation's foremost rationalizer of academic repression. Because Allen produced that rationale, and because it bore his name, his commitment to it was particularly intense. This, as we will see, makes it relatively easy to understand how the Allen Formula governed his actions as contact man. It also, however makes it hard to generalize from UCLA to other institutions, where the administrators were not publicly identified with the Allen Formula the way Allen was. Nonetheless, it is clear that educators around the country supported the Allen Formula, though probably not as single-mindedly as Allen himself; and when push came to shove, they also acted in accordance with it.

Allen's qualifications for his position at UCLA were many, not least his background in medical education. But the hiring of America's leading academic Red hunter to lead the newly autonomous Los Angeles campus just after the California Oath controversy, at a time when CUAC, Congress, and the media were all serious threats, was clearly no accident. At this crucial moment, a proven anti-Communist at UCLA's helm was devoutly to be wished, and there is no question that Allen's anti-Communist credentials were an overwhelming plus, which, as the *Los Angeles Times* put it, "ought to reassure the most obdurate doubter."[4] The *UCLA Daily Bruin* reported that in recommending Allen to UCLA, University of California President Robert G. Sproul was emphatic: "Dr. Allen is a man of unquestionable devotion to American institutions, steadfast in combating Communism and all other subversive movements. The best proof of this statement, perhaps, is to be found in his dismissal a few years ago of three members of the faculty of the University of Washington who had been found to have Communist connections, and his brilliant and successful defense of his action both in the academic world and outside its walls."[5] The "brilliant and successful defense" to which Sproul refers was the Allen Formula, and the *Bruin* goes on to assert that it was his formula that had made Allen the "obvious choice" as Chancellor.[6]

It is impossible, to be sure, to determine to what extent the regents who hired Allen actually believed there was a serious Communist threat on campus, as opposed to merely wanting to prevent future uproars. Probably they wanted both; but whatever the relative weights of the two motivations, Allen was clearly brought to UCLA because his formula provided a persuasive rationale for doing what the outside world wanted UCLA to do: eliminate Communists and "subversives" from teaching positions.

Allen became an enthusiastic supporter of the California Plan. In a letter dated April 28, 1953, a year and a half after he took office, to Donald Anderson (an official at the University of Washington who had asked him for the minutes of the meeting at which the California Plan had been set up) he wrote, "So far, the arrangement is working to mutual advantage. The chief administrative officer of each campus is designated as the contact person, but he takes no action on information provided by the Committee without consulting with the President. The University, of course has other sources of information."[7] At the Chancellor's Administrative Council meeting the month before, Allen had been slightly more specific: "[The Chancellor] mentioned in particular our liaison with the Burns Committee [CUAC] which provides the presidents of major institutions in California with information germane to their institution. Such information goes to the principal administrative officer on each campus of the University, and all policy matters are decided with the President so that no campus can commit the University to any policy on its own initiative."[8]

Given their venues, these were not statements for public consumption. Still, we should not accept them at face value. That Allen was consulting with the president of the university confirms my hypothesis from chapter 5 that, at least in his case, the activities of the contact man were not merely clerical; clerks do not need to consult the presidents of their institutions. But his wording is delicate and seems designed to make the cooperation seem broader than it was. In the statement to Anderson, for example, Allen says he acts on information provided by CUAC to the university only in consultation with the president, but says nothing about the information going the other way: the information he was providing (or not providing) *to* CUAC in the form of the names of candidates for jobs at the university. In the statement to his own Administrative

Council, Allen characterizes the information received from CUAC only vaguely, as "germane" to the institution, while cooperation with the president is said to be restricted to "policy matters"; again, information that Allen provided to CUAC is not covered by this, since it concerned persons and not policies. Both statements, then, say that Allen acted on information coming *from* CUAC only in consultation with Sproul, but make no mention the fact that Allen was providing information (i.e., names) *to* CUAC and apparently (therefore) doing so without consulting with Sproul. In any case, Allen is being disingenuous. As we saw Schrecker point out, failure to act on CUAC's recommendations would bring public disaster to the university.

Giving to America's leading academic Red hunter the kind of leeway that the California Plan gave to the contact man may seem today to have been little short of suicidal; but at the time it proved to be a successful strategy, in that Allen did damp down the bad publicity. In May 1954, for example, the UCLA Office of Public Information learned that the *Los Angeles Examiner*, the Hearst newspaper that had earlier fomented the Max Otto Affair, was now preparing one or more articles on Communism at UCLA. On being informed of this, Allen scheduled an interview with a "Mr. Carrington—" apparently Richard A. Carrington, the paper's publisher. In preparation, he solicited advice from Andrew Hamilton of the information office. Hamilton's talking points for Allen included the following:

> As you know from my record at the University of Washington and my service with the Federal government, Communism is a problem with which I am very familiar. Public agencies, such as a state university, are in an exposed position. Communists frequently try to infiltrate the faculty and important positions of leadership in the student body. . . . During my two years at UCLA, however, I have found it to be one of the "cleanest" institutions of which I have had personal knowledge. . . . Through the cooperation of our police department, our faculty and our student body we have always defeated such attempts. We have done this quietly and without fanfare—but most effectively. I strongly feel that any article or expose at this time will hamper efforts we now have in progress, and will certainly make it more difficult to be as effective in the future.[9]

Allen thus used his personal credibility as an experienced Red hunter to persuade Carrington of two things: that Communism at UCLA was no longer much of a problem, and that what remained was best disposed of in quiet by the university itself rather than through the newspapers. His strategy worked.

In a note attached to the letter, in Allen's handwriting, are the jubilant words "All is OK—will tell you." Apparently Allen's personal authority had warded off the exposé.

THE ALLEN FORMULA 1:
STRATEGIES AND AUDIENCES

As a first step to understanding the Allen Formula, it is helpful to see that it is the product of an intellectual evolution that Allen had undergone in the years preceding its introduction at the University of Washington in 1949. In parts of his 1946 *Medical Education and the Changing Order* (hereafter, *MECO*), written while Allen was executive dean of the Colleges of Dentistry, Medicine, and Pharmacology at the University of Illinois, Chicago, he writes like a good pragmatist. He holds, for example, that "knowledge is wisdom only as it becomes useful through the teaching and actions of men." (*MECO*, 3, also see 32). Together with this emphasis on social usefulness goes a loosely pragmatic theory of truth, for the usefulness of knowledge is not a characteristic that is simply added to true theories; it actually constitutes their validity: "The test of any theory is: Does it work?" (*MECO*, 5). The final success of medicine thus lies, not in whether or not its scientific foundations correspond to reality in some way (or can be assigned a high probability, *à la* Reichenbach), but in whether or not it contributes to "healthful living." That, in turn, is a contextualized judgment: "Medical education, like medical science, is an experimental art dependent wholly for success on the learning, skills, imagination, resourcefulness, integrity, and courage of individuals" (*MECO*, 5).

As in Donald Piatt's 1939 essay on Dewey, discussed in chapters 2 and 4, Allen's pragmatism is tempered by a monolithic view of scientific method. Like Reichenbach, Allen believes that the scientific foundation of medicine operates everywhere by a single set of rules, and he does not hesitate to spell them out:

> Medicine, although it was to a large extent haphazardly empirical in its methods both before and after the dawn of Grecian learning, and although even to this day it includes valuable elements which are not susceptible to measurement, did not make significant advances until it began to employ the methods of exact science: observation, recording, comparison, measurement, rational thought, that is, the systematic application of the rules of inductive and deductive reasoning to a set of observed facts. To this the Greek mind added the equally important method of purposeful experiment. Progress in medical

science has come almost entirely from the application of the scientific and experimental methods (*MECO*, 35–37).

Just what components of science "are not susceptible to measurement" is a mystery. Apart from that, Allen's view differs from Reichenbach's account in *RSP* mainly in that it is slightly more detailed and in that Reichenbach believes the Greeks did not have the experimental method (*RSP*, 97–98). Allen, like Piatt in 1939, thus hovers between monolithic and concretized views of science.

When Allen articulates his formula in the 1949 *Communism and Academic Freedom* (*CAF*), a set of documents concerning the Herbert Phillips case, his primary concern is no longer with medical education. As befits his new position as a university president, he is now concerned with scholarly life in general—with the institutionalized operation of the human mind itself. In articulating this, Allen overcomes the tensions in his earlier views by moving unequivocally in the direction of Cold War philosophy.

The first thing to note about the Allen Formula itself is that it is an extremely complex intellectual construct, designed to serve several purposes at once. On the surface, it is a rationale for firing Communists even if they have done nothing wrong. This rationale, of course, was called forth by circumstances: by the fact that Allen, as president of a major university, was under heavy pressure precisely to fire a man who by common admission had done nothing wrong.

Underlying this anti-Communist level of the formula, however, are at least two more. On the more overt of these, the formula is also designed to tamp down anti-Communist furor, as we saw Allen do at UCLA with "Mr. Carrington." Allen, in fact, was not the kind of opportunistic Red hunter I portrayed in my *Time in the Ditch* (*TD*, 34, 39–42). In *MECO*, he had even said some good things about the Soviet Union (*MECO*, 1–2, 5), and Jane Sanders has shown that, at Washington, Allen was a strong believer in freedom of inquiry.[10] He saw himself as protecting the university from *all* outside influences—including not only the Moscow government, which he thought was ultimately behind American Communists, but also the Red-baiters in the press, the Board of Regents, and the public at large. Allen's task, as he saw it, was as much to deflect outside pressures on the university as to root out the "enemies within." But it was by doing the latter, and being seen to do it, that he would achieve the former.

Central to protecting the university was protecting its professors, and for Allen this had two sides: guaranteeing due process to accused professors, and saving individual departments from the pressures and distractions to which they would inevitably be subject if they became investigative bodies passing judgment on the political acceptability of their peers. To achieve his goal of protecting the university, its professors, and its departments from outside influences, Allen needed to keep academic freedom cases in his own hands; and his arguments for this constitute what we will see to be the third level of the Allen Formula.

Together with this complexity of levels and goals went a plurality of audiences. In order to do its various jobs, the Allen Formula had to be accepted by three very different groups: right wing Red hunters outside the university, who had to be persuaded that the university itself was effectively eliminating subversives; the administrators and regents, who were ultimately responsible for doing that job; and the faculty, who had to be convinced to go along with all this. The need to win over the faculty required Allen to incorporate in his formula, as its grounding, a general rationale for dealing with academic freedom cases. In order to be persuasive to such highly educated and intellectually critical people as university professors, this rationale had to be both self-consistent and consonant with their preexisting views and instincts. It also had to be absolutist, in that it had to justify the speedy and permanent exclusion of Communists from academic life, no matter what they had actually done. Rhetorical denunciations of Communism, however passionate, would not do; neither would the empirical accumulation of examples of Communist misbehavior in the classroom (of which, in any case, there were very few if any).

Allen's underlying rationale, as we will see, has every right to be called philosophical. It proves to be, in Foucault's phrase, a "form of knowledge" grounded not only in philosophical views of reason's nature, goal, and procedures, but in the actual historical conditions of the times. As such, it far surpasses the kind of ideology against which Marx protests in the epigraph to this chapter and constitutes one of the most influential pieces of philosophy ever produced by an American.

THE ALLEN FORMULA 2: STRICT OBJECTIVITY

Allen's innovative contribution, the one that gained widespread approval in academia and so made the formula work, lay in the rationales he used to establish the two overall rules that comprise its functional core: (1) Communists should not be allowed to teach in universities, and (2) any individual accused of being a Communist should only be fired after due process. Neither rule was particularly new or controversial in McCarthyite America. Without the consistency and comprehensiveness of the underlying rationale, however, rule 1 was vindictive, and rule 2 ad hoc. I discuss rule 1 and its underlying rationale in this section, reserving rule 2 and its (somewhat different) rationale for the next.

Allen's rationale for firing Communists was so successful because it solved a major intellectual problem of the early Cold War. The United States was, after all, a free country; it had no business censoring any kind of discourse, including academic. How, then, could it justify firing Communist professors merely for their views? This was the problem that the Herbert Phillips case had posed. Allen's answer was that purely by virtue of their membership in the party, Communists have forsaken the battle for objectivity that defines academia. They should not, therefore, be allowed within the university community—not as teachers, anyway.[11] Communist professors are professionally irresponsible and must be fired, not for being Communists, but for their incompetence. Firing them is thus not censorship—on the contrary, it is upholding one of the most sacred of Western and academic values, that of the search for truth.[12]

Allen's characterization of that search, though couched in impressionistic bombast, is familiar enough: "Unless [a scholar] can make his report so objective that it will withstand the fire of criticism from his colleagues, he should not offer a professional opinion. If he goes forth to battle the world armed only with half-formed judgments and prejudices, either those colleagues will expose him or someone in the tough, hard headed world of affairs will surely do so" (*CAF*, 93). Where, for Reichenbach, nonscientific philosophy contained only "intuitive guesses and unanalyzed conjectures" (*RSP*, 311), for Allen, the failure to pursue objectivity leaves one only with "half-formed judgments and prejudices." Truth itself, indeed intellectual life in general, is no longer for him a matter of whether or not a theory "works," or contributes to "healthful living," as it was in *MECO*, but whether it is "objective" enough to survive the "fire of criticism," not only from colleagues but from people in "the tough, hard-headed world of affairs." As in Reichenbach's account of ethical discourse, an adversarial style, here driven by fear of "exposure," becomes integral to science.[13]

By 1949, then, the pragmatism of Allen's earlier writing is gone. Science, and indeed intellectual life in general, are no longer subject to contextual evaluation. Instead, they now constitute a "timeless, selfless quest of truth":

If a University ever loses its dispassionate objectivity and incites or leads parades, it will have lost its integrity as an institution and abandoned the timeless, selfless quest of truth. . . . It is for this reason that a teacher has a special obligation to deal in a scholarly and scientific way with controversial questions. . . . Fortunately few faculty members make this mistake [of not being scholarly and scientific]. If they do make it, the institution from which they come will lose its academic standing, *as they will lose their security* (*CAF*, 90, 93; Allen's emphasis).

Allen's abandonment of contextualism thus serves the need to draw a sharp line between those who are worthy of academic employment and those who are not and must be permanently excluded from it. On his earlier, more pragmatic view, whether a given researcher is contributing to human progress can only be decided later—often, much later. On such a view, someone's exclusion from academia could come, if at all, only after time had shown their work to be valueless—which means that, at present, they should be allowed to continue with it. This is not good enough for Allen now, who needs to be able to fire Communists as soon as they are discovered; nothing less could satisfy the Red hunters. Fortunately, whether a researcher has achieved objectivity in their views can, according to Allen, be determined here and now by the local scientific community and the "hard-headed world of affairs."

In writing on medical education, Allen had specified that those who have wisdom—knowledge plus skill in its use—must be people of sterling "intelligence, character and fidelity" (*MECO*, 3, 5, 32). This survives in the later writings, and is expressed very clearly when Allen articulates his formula for handling Communists on campus: "Teachers in any field are also citizens and persons. . . . Because of the rigors of truth in their respective discipline, however, we expect them to be more objective toward society and politics than some who have not had their peculiar advantages" (*CAF*, 93). Because of their "peculiar advantages," scholars are duty-bound to seek the (objective) truth (*CAF*, 40). Sterling character is still a requirement; but now, along with professional competence, it is reduced to being "objective." Scholars who eschew this duty and do not pursue "objectivity" in Allen's sense are not merely trying something different, nor are they merely making a mistake. They are morally or psychologically flawed.

Allen's account of how the search for objective truth is to be conducted is simply a naive statement of what has been called the "experimental method" of science: "The scientist or artist makes his hypotheses and develops his insights. He makes observations. He creates conditions in which to test his observations, theories, and insights. He draws tentative conclusions from comparisons and experiments" (Allen 1953). The striking thing about Allen's view of the experimental method here—indeed, the only part of his views on it which is not standard issue for the time—is the breadth of its application. The experimental method is usually associated, or even identified, with science, as was the case in Allen's earlier writing. But in Allen's view in 1953, it goes far beyond science itself, to include not only artists but also "the realm of the moral and spiritual life" (ibid.); in other words, it has been almost comically expanded to cover the moral discoveries of people like the Buddha under the banyan tree, Moses on Sinai, and Jesus in the desert. More to the point, it now includes practically everything that anyone employed as faculty in a university ever does. Scientific method and objective truth are thus identified with rationality itself, and this makes them universal weapons that can be used to exclude people in any field from academic employment.

The single most basic difference between Allen's earlier writings and the Allen Formula, then, is that by the time of the formula, the pragmatic conception of truth is gone. The success of a theory is not a matter of the kind of contextualized, retrospective judgment of social or other worth that it is in pragmatism, but a matter of its "objectivity"—that is, its capacity to withstand critical fire from colleagues (and hard-headed folk from the "world of affairs"). This innovation in the nature of truth is what enables Allen to produce his formula, and it has two corollaries that are relevant here. First, appeals to the social context of intellectual life are subordinated to the more "objective" view of truth that Allen now advocates. The earlier calls for social relevance, along with the praise of the Soviet Union, are gone. Society is now relevant, not because it is a wider moral context from which the scholar comes and to which she must contribute, but only insofar as it can underwrite, via "tough, hard-headed" criticism, the "objectivity" of her theories. Reason is not only adversarial, but strictly adversarial.

Second, if intellectual life still requires, like medicine in *MECO*, "sterling character" from its practitioners, judgments of character themselves are now, like truth itself, decontextualized. They are, therefore, absolutized: intellectual life is governed everywhere by the same rules, and failure to observe these rules now means, not merely that any resulting theory will eventually be judged "unsuccessful," but that the theorist will be excluded from the academy altogether.

THE ALLEN FORMULA 3: WHO SHOULD ENFORCE ACADEMIC FREEDOM?

The strict definition of the scientific method and its extension to rationality itself were also required by part 2 of the Allen Formula, the view that any faculty member accused of being a Communist was entitled to due process.

The way this part of the Allen Formula worked is a bit complicated, in part because Allen needed to express it carefully; his views on the matter landed him in opposition to many academics, including W. V. O. Quine and, more troublingly, his old ally Sidney Hook, the pragmatist philosopher discussed in chapter 1. Hook by now had become not only a vehement anti-Communist but an extremely prominent one, and it would hardly have suited Allen for their disagreement to be noticed.[14] We can see the potential conflict by looking at an article Hook wrote for the *New York Times Magazine* in 1949, at the height of the University of Washington cases. Hook had written,

> The presumption is that university professors engaged in the search for truth are qualified by their professional competence. The judges of their competence can only be their intellectual peers or betters in their own fields. If this is denied, the university loses its *raison d'etre* as an institution, not only for free research but for critical teaching. . . . I am confident that if the execution of the policy were left to university faculties themselves, and not to administrators and trustees who are harried by outside groups, there would be little ground for complaint (Hook 1949).

Hook here remains true to his origins in the contextualized approach of pragmatism. On this view, which we saw represented at UCLA by Donald Piatt, different disciplines can be so fundamentally different that their ways of ascertaining truth cannot be judged by outsiders. Hence, professors caught up in academic freedom cases need to be judged by colleagues in "their own fields," rather than by college wide committees, administrators, trustees or regents, or outside groups.

Hook's view is compatible with Allen's earlier writings about medical education as an "experimental art." It is also true to the long, and occasionally honored, tradition that universities are places where, in Kant's phrase, "only scholars can judge scholars as such."[15] Most academics would subscribe to it today, when the idea of a single "experimental method" applying to all of intellectual life is little more than a joke. Hook's view is also, finally, compatible with part 1 of the Allen Formula, for the view of truth as strict objectivity, in and of itself, provides no reason to think that there is only one set of rules for discovering truth.

Allen's change of mind here comes from what he considered to be a fatal *practical* flaw in Hook's view. Allen was not, or not only, conducting a disinterested philosophical investigation. He was trying to get control of academic freedom cases for some of the same reasons that had led to the adoption of the

California Plan in the first place. One of these, of course, was to serve the goal of eliminating Communists from the university, because professors could not be trusted to do this. It was one thing, in, the abstract, to support the firing of Communists, as most professors did; it was another to vote a valued colleague down for tenure or promotion. A second reason was to guarantee due process to those accused, and a third was to free faculty from the distractions of dealing with academic freedom cases. A fourth, perhaps, was simply to increase the power of administrators such as Allen himself. In the perspective of *all* of these, Hook's view was simply inconsistent. If inquiry operates according to local principles and procedures, then there is no justification for the universal firing of Communists simply for being Communists; it would have to be shown that their allegiance to Moscow had led them to violate the rules of their own fields. If mass firing of Communists is justified, it can only be in terms of universal rules that apply to all inquiry—and so can be understood just as well by administrators and regents as by faculty. That Allen adopted this view for political rather than philosophical reasons is suggested by the fact that, when eight of the eleven members of the tenure committee at the University of Washington construed incompetence to mean "unfitness in a faculty member's field of scholarship and teaching," Allen simply, and without argument, overruled them (Sanders 1979, 48, 54; *CAF*, 89–90).[16]

We thus have here a political motivation for what Arthur Fine calls "truth-mongering" (Fine 1986, 137–42): setting up a wholesale account of truth, in Allen's case as "objectivity," rather than doing the detailed inquiries that would indicate what "truth" is in the context of a given inquiry. Mongering truth allows you to specify rules and methods for obtaining truth itself, as you have defined it, and to condemn those who do not follow your rules. Thus, for the Allen Formula, there could be just one set of rules for obtaining truth: the basic rules of the experimental method, by which half-formed judgments are made objective. These are common to all disciplines, so one need not be a member of any given discipline to gauge whether someone in that discipline is following them. In particular, academic administrators—and, indeed, regents—are perfectly qualified to be judges in the matter. The problem with this, of course, is that the universal rules in question, just because they are universal, do not apply only to Communists. As we will see below, when Allen's rationale for firing Communists is spelled out in such a way that administrators and regents can do the firing, it becomes incompatible with the view that only Communists should be fired.

The high-handed way in which Allen dismissed the views of a majority of the Promotion and Tenure Committee at the University of Washington shows that he was not prepared to argue for his own thesis that intellectual life—the use of reason itself—consists in using a single set of rules to uncover or approach objective truth. Two possible reasons for this reluctance come to mind. First, it is not clear how Allen *could* argue for his view. "Reason" clearly means very different things for Plato and for Kant; how can we know it will not change again—that, as Hugh Miller had suggested (see chapter 4), Pythagorean music theory will not be resurrected in future thought? How, moreover, can such an account be argued for without circularity? It would have to be accepted under the very rational lights it argues for, which means it would presuppose them.

Second, with whom would Allen argue? Since he thinks he has given a criterion for the use of reason itself, anyone who disagrees with him is not rational—indeed, is "incompetent." Irrational people, by definition, are people with whom you cannot argue, and incompetent ones are people with whom you need not argue. Allen's position cannot consistently be argued for, and so needs to be presented as a truism—as a truth so obvious that no one in the university seriously challenges it.

THE PHILOSOPHY OF RAYMOND B. ALLEN

The Allen Formula argues that Communists are incompetent because they violate the universal rules of science. This grounds the formula in a theory of intellectual life in general that is broad enough to be called philosophical. As presented in the previous sections, that theory has five main tenets; the Allen Formula in the narrower sense—its surface level—consists in the two rules we have seen for applying them. The five tenets follow:

1. Rational inquiry has a single goal: truth.
2. Truth is "objective validity" (i.e., the capacity of a theory, opinion, judgment, etc. to survive the fire of criticism from colleagues and hard-headed outsiders).
3. There is only one basic set of rules for achieving truth: the experimental method.
4. The exemplar of those rules is science.
5. Anyone who does not abide by those rules is not merely mistaken, but incompetent—rationally and/or morally—and so unfit for employment.

The rules of application, again, are these: (1) Any member of the Communist Party comes ipso facto under tenet 5, and so should be denied employment in universities. (2) In virtue of tenet 3, rule 1 can be applied, with due process, by administrators and regents. Except for tenets 2 and 5, the basic tenets of the Allen Formula were already present in Allen's writings from before the McCarthy Era. His introduction of tenet 2 seems to have been an attempt to reinforce tenet 5: to absolutize the concept of truth beyond the mere judgment that something "works," so that the failure to observe the rules for obtaining truth could be ipso facto grounds for speedy dismissal from the university.

All five tenets of the Allen Formula are easily visible in Reichenbach's formulation of "scientific philosophy," as discussed in chapter 4, with the exception that "objective truth" is to be replaced with "highest probability." None is present in the thought of pragmatists such as Hugh Miller and Donald Piatt, or in that of existentialists like Hans Meyerhoff. It was thus Cold War philosophy that was, in the last analysis, most vigorously enforced by the tri-level vetting system in place at UCLA. It was logical positivism, not pragmatism (and certainly not existentialism), that could provide a persuasive and consistent rationale for immediate and definitive exclusion of "incompetents" from academia.

Consider, for example, how the tri-level vetting system would have treated Hans Meyerhoff had he been a job candidate in 1952 or after, rather than in 1948. There is no evidence in Meyerhoff's life or writings of left-wing opinions or "subversive associations," so we may suppose that his candidacy would have passed the departmental screening. But at the next level, it would have encountered a contact man who, like many of the faculty and administrators at UCLA and elsewhere, was openly committed to the Allen Formula—all the more because he had invented it. And Meyerhoff's philosophy is decidedly— indeed, determinedly—unscientific. In particular, his understanding of truth as subjective "illumination" revealed through personal commitment cannot begin to meet Allen's criterion of ability to withstand "critical fire," as Meyerhoff openly admits: "If [subjective commitment] fails to be forthcoming [from others], these philosophies can only appeal to a renewed and more intensive search of one's own consciousness: they cannot, and do not, provide any objective criteria by which these truths could be tested and measured" (*TL*, 141).

According to the Allen Formula, Meyerhoff's philosophy of subjective illumination was unscientific, incapable of meeting objective criteria, therefore irrational, and therefore incompetent. And these were not merely Allen's private views. They were built into the Allen Formula itself. Even more than other American academic administrators and faculty, Allen was publicly committed to the formula that bore his name. And as a general and consistent rationale for the permanent exclusion of some people from the intellectual community, the formula had to be applied even-handedly. Whatever his private sentiments, Allen would have had to reject a Meyerhoff candidacy on pain of exposing his formula for what it was: not a rationale, but a cynical rationalization. As it was, he had leeway, as contact man, confidentially to decline to forward Meyerhoff's name to CUAC (perhaps, as noted in the previous chapter, obtaining CUAC's gratitude as a result). Finally, if the UCLA philosophy department was as astute as it showed itself to be on other occasions (e.g., in the matter of the non-naturalist hire of 1953, for which see chapter 1), they would foresee all this and save Meyerhoff the anguish of being rejected at higher levels by turning him down at theirs—or by telling him, confidentially of course, not to apply.

When the California Plan was coupled with the Allen Formula, the result took on a life of its own. Having justified their practice of excluding Communists by the general principle of defending a "scientific" vision of competence allied with Cold War philosophy, administrators and faculty members found themselves required to act in accord with that general principle.

THE SUBJECTIVATION OF THE FACULTY

We have seen how Allen's dual position as at once the UCLA contact man for the California Plan and the chief rationalizer of that plan affected his relationship to the highest level of that plan, CUAC. When we ask about how he related to its lowest level, (i.e., to departments engaged in hiring), we can begin by reminding ourselves of the commonsense point made in chapter 5: that the lower levels of the California Plan were in fear of the higher levels. What would a department fear when trying to decide whether to forward the name of a job candidate to Allen? What would a department in such a situation think it knew about the kind of person he wanted, or more important did not want, at the university?

Allen's statements on this were confusing (see Sanders 1979, 60). Communists, of course, were out of the question; even worse, in Allen's eyes, was being a member of the party and lying about it or failing to disclose it (*CAF*, 91–92, 94). Forwarding the name of such a person to him as contact man would, therefore, almost certainly be fatal: he would hardly send such a name on to CUAC. Allen was also, however, publicly committed to the view that the only ground on which employment in the university should be revoked was membership in the Communist Party. Thus, commenting on the case of Garland Ethel, an English professor at the University of Washington, Allen wrote, "Ethel, I believe, is a sincere intellectual Marxist. . . . Such philosophies [*sic*], honestly held and divorced from the dogmas of the Communist Party are something quite different from active and secret membership in the Party. I think it is necessary that we maintain a place in the University for the holding of such philosophies. . . . To close the University's doors to honest nonconformist thought would do violence to the principles of academic freedom that we must maintain at all costs" (*CAF*, 107).

Someone who openly held Marxist views, but without the activities and af-filiations that indicated party membership, was clearly acceptable to Allen—at Washington. That this applied at UCLA a couple of years later, however, was not so clear. The California Plan was now in place, and given the zealotry at CUAC, forwarding the name of a person like Ethel who, even if free of Com-munist "dogma," would presumably not support CUAC's crusading efforts, would be risky.[17] In any case, Ethel was not a job candidate at Washington; he was an already-tenured professor. While Allen refused to fire him, it is not clear that he would have supported hiring him in the first place. Ethel had been a member of the party until 1941, which in Allen's opinion showed "extremely bad judgment" (*CAF*, 107). Bad judgment is not a ground for revoking tenure, but it is an acceptable reason not to hire someone.

Allen's own tolerance of "honest nonconformist thought," in fact, was not overly consistent. In a 1948 speech to the faculty at the University of Wash-ington, he had warned about activities that "might embarrass" the university (Sanders 1979, 29); we have seen his concern about such embarrassment at UCLA. And in discussing junior faculty at Washington who, in the wake of the firings there, were concerned about thought control at the university, Allen re-sponded that he was interested in hiring, not just non-Communists, but "men of integrity. I think men of that kind would be encouraged to come here and be men. I am not inviting anybody to resign, but I am not going to be unhappy if some resign who were taken in by these attitudes."[18] By "men of integrity," Allen can only have meant men who were untroubled by McCarthyite efforts to control hiring at universities. In an echo of McCarthyism's virulent homo-phobia, such support was equated with masculinity itself: "be men."[19]

This all had implications for the hiring of *liberals*, a term whose elasticity I noted in chapter 5. While Allen eschewed the violently antiliberal rhetoric of CUAC, he did go so far as identify Communism as "parasitic on real lib-eralism": "It is commonly accepted that . . . Communism thrives best where there is a background of honest liberalism, and that Communism, generally speaking, has taken advantage of liberal thought and action to further its ends" (*CAF*, 13). If liberals were no help in fighting the Communists for whom they provided the soil, the same would be even truer of those who, unlike standard liberals, did not accept Allen's monolithically "objective" view of truth. They would be unable even to identify the real failing of academic Communism, its abandonment of objectivity, *as* a failing, since they themselves did the same thing.

Allied with "scientific philosophy" and, behind that, with the prestigious RCT, the Allen Formula was an immense success. As I noted above, it was adopted throughout the country and, in Schrecker's words, "provided a model which the rest of the academy, under growing pressure to do something about Communists, could imitate" (Schrecker 1986, 104–5). This was not merely a matter of external sticks or establishment carrots. In fact, the five basic tenets of the formula's wider rationale captured the views of many of the professoriate.[20] Not all faculty, by any means, supported rules 1 and 2 of the Allen Formula. But, as the *UCLA Daily Bruin* put it in an editorial, "Most educators contend that a Communist is shackled to a dogma and is therefore unable to conduct a true search for knowledge."[21] One example of this was Abraham Kaplan, the philosophy department chair at the time of the *Bruin*'s statement and no friend of McCarthyism, who in an interview with the *Bruin* said, "I don't see how a professor who is a Communist . . . can do what he is supposed to do as a Communist and at the same time what he is supposed to do as a professor."[22]

The view that Communists should be fired for incompetence was also upheld by the UCLA faculty at large, and in a revealing way. Before Raymond B. Allen even arrived at UCLA, but after his articulation of his formula at Washington, a UCLA faculty resolution of March 1, 1950, included the following points:

> 4. The faculty *has gone much further* [than the regents] in implementing the Regents' 1940 policy [barring employment to current members of the Communist Party]. It has, itself, through its own officers and committees, always undertaken to exclude all subversive and disloyal persons. Nowhere in the world, and educational leaders in other institutions familiar with the situation here will bear testimony to this, are the screening procedures for appointment and promotion more rigorous than are those which the faculty of the University of California has imposed on itself.
>
> 5. [The oath] is completely futile as a means of implementing *the Regents' narrow policy* of barring Communists or *the faculty's broader policy* of barring *anyone* who is disloyal *or who will not live up to the University's standards of impartial scholarship and teaching* (emphasis added).[23]

This is to say that *the regents did not go far enough because of their narrow focus on Communists.* The professors proclaim their commitment to excluding not only Communists and everyone else who is "subversive and disloyal," but anyone who will not "live up to the University's standards of impartial scholarship and teaching." The faculty resolution follows the Allen Formula in explicitly replacing the outside world's focus on Communism with the broader issue of "incompetence"; not only Communists but anyone who fails the test of impartiality is to be permanently excluded from the university.

The resolution was no exercise in philosophical stealth. It was sworn to, in writing, by philosophy department members Christopher Jackson (who was about to leave), Donald Kalish, Abraham Kaplan, Hans Meyerhoff, Donald Piatt, Hans Reichenbach, and Robert Yost. Reichenbach attested the signature of Hugh Miller, who was away; only J. Wesley Robson, who around that time became an associate dean, did not sign.[24] In this resolution, the engaged, edifying, and pluralistic community that had invited Max Otto to be Flint Professor proclaimed its own death; the victory of the Allen Formula—and of its ally, Cold War philosophy—was conclusive. The subjectivation of the current faculty was thus completed before the California Plan, directed mainly against the next generation, even began.

The Two Fates of Cold War Philosophy

Making values explicit . . . is an activity that has been devalued and corrupted. . . . . The questions we might want raised—What is really important? Can we live in a different and better way? If we wanted to change society, how would we do it?—are not thought to be questions of a "fruitful, empirical nature," and thus are brushed aside.

STUDENTS FOR A DEMOCRATIC SOCIETY, The Port Huron Statement

The triumph of Cold War philosophy at UCLA was both quick and definitive. Hans Reichenbach arrived in 1938, its first major representative there. By the time of Raymond B. Allen's departure from the chancellorship, in June 1959, the tenured professors following (at various distances) Reichenbach's "scientific" restriction of philosophical reason to logical analysis constituted, according to the department's listing in the UCLA *General Catalogue*, a group of six: Rudolph Carnap, Donald Kalish, Abraham Kaplan, Ernest Moody, Wesley Robson, and Robert Yost. Of the two remaining, the continental philosopher Hans Meyerhoff was unhappy in the department (Wilson 2000, 80), and Donald Piatt, now the last pragmatist at UCLA, was 61; he would retire in 1965.

The new standpoint also brought programmatic changes. In the UCLA *General Catalogue* for 1947-48, PhD requirements were few and informal (though stringent). Students had to attain reading knowledge of two languages from a list of four (Greek, Latin, French, and German). They also had to pass five examinations: four written ones from a list of six (history of philosophy, contemporary philosophy, logic, philosophy of science, theory of value and ethics, and social philosophy), and one oral examination in their field of specialization.[1] The 1959 landscape was very different. The language requirement had been loosened, allowing candidates to petition to replace one of the four with another language.[2] But students now had no leeway in choosing examination fields and had to pass examinations in logic, history of philosophy, theory of value, and metaphysics. Logic was now required of all students; no UCLA student would be "screened off from philosophical knowledge" by a "haze of vagueness" (*RSP*, ix). Social philosophy was off the list entirely, and philosophy of science was apparently taught across the curriculum (as Harvard philosopher W. V. O. Quine had said in 1953, "Philosophy of science is philosophy enough" [Quine 1953a, 446]).

Perhaps the positivistic victory was *too* speedy. Of the twenty-one years (1938–1959) that it took for Reichenbach's approach to establish itself as the dominant paradigm at UCLA,[3] four had been taken up with World War II and at least ten with the McCarthy Era—both times when American scholarly debate was severely curtailed. The earlier dispute between idealism and pragmatism, by contrast, had been more protracted. It can be said to have begun with the founding of Charles Sanders Peirce's Metaphysical Club in 1872 and ended, according to Richard Rorty, around 1932—60 years later.[4] Idealism, having been thoroughly discussed and discarded, is hardly to be found on American campuses today; its proponents, in David Hollinger's words, "have been shelved alongside early editions of Baedeker, guides only to the taste of a distant and charming era" (Hollinger 1975, 48). But pragmatism, at the time of Rorty's writing (in 1976), was on the verge of a major renewal, brought about in large part by his own writings. Continental philosophy too remains a vibrant paradigm, though not usually in philosophy departments themselves. The returns of these "repressed" suggest that the issues among these paradigms were never adequately hashed out.

By the mid-1980s, as the end of the Cold War approached, the changes in philosophy had proved to be both nationwide and lasting. If Rorty's efforts had begun to reawaken pragmatism, for example, it was only in philosophy departments. As David Hollinger put it in 1980, "Scrutiny of the ideas of Charles Peirce, William James, and John Dewey goes forward as industriously as ever, to be sure, but this scrutiny is increasingly the business of philosophers addressing other philosophers. What has all but disappeared is a particular sense of the significance of pragmatism: That the works of Pierce, James, and Dewey manifest an important episode not only in the development of Western philosophy but in American history, and that these thinkers were somehow representative of the life of the mind in the United States."[5] Rorty's new and improved version of pragmatism, which was just taking hold when Hollinger wrote the above passage,[6] abjured interaction with other fields and relegated philosophy to its own "speech community" (see McCumber 2000a, 56–60). But pragmatism left to philosophers is, as we saw in chapter 1, pragmatism transformed. Critical dialogue with other fields, such as politics and religion, was philosophically essential to Charles Sanders Peirce, William James, and John Dewey—and to Hugh Miller, Max Otto, and Donald Piatt.

It was not only pragmatism that fell into shadows. The situation with respect to continental philosophy was in some respects the reverse of that with pragmatism. While pragmatism retained some interest among philosophers, continental philosophy (with some notable exceptions, such as at Binghamton, Emory, Northwestern, Penn State, Stony Brook, California/Riverside and Vanderbilt), never established itself in major philosophy departments outside the Catholic universities. But it became a (even *the*) major force in literary and political theory.[7]

Even in philosophy departments, however, Cold War philosophy attracted critical scrutiny. The decades after its triumph saw philosophers, along with economists and political scientists, launch at it a series of criticisms that were incisive, but relatively ad hoc and unsystematic in nature. Outside these academic redoubts, as we will see, the story was more explosive. In particular, the triumph of Cold War philosophy's rational choice component provoked a thorough and angry rejection that permanently transformed American higher education. Both these stories are epic and complex, but their details, if not their overall shape, are too widely known to require extensive rehearsal. The brief sketch to be given here is keyed to what we have seen are the three main components of the Cold War dispositive: its theory of the known object as stratified nature; its theory of the knowing subject as a rational chooser; and its practice of subjectivation as the exclusion of alternatives, so that individuals who (in Kuhn's term) "converted" to it were required to denounce other approaches as (in Allen's term) "incompetent."

HOW STEALTH OUTLIVED STRATIFICATION

Early Cold War political pressures favored, we saw, a stealthy view of nature as stratified into layers paralleling the hierarchy of the sciences. This stratification made avowals of naturalism and so, in the public mind, of atheism happily postponable, but it was difficult to maintain, because it could not be stated in a nonmetaphysical way. Philosophers usually articulated their naturalism, therefore, as the thesis that the hierarchy of the sciences could in some sense or other be "reduced" to its lowest (and most mathematical) level, physics. The view that science exhibits such a neat hierarchical structure proved, as I noted in chapter 2, to be seriously oversimplified. Though making observations and mathematically analyzing their results are important parts of scientific work, they hardly constitute all of it; and when we look at the ways scientists actually perform even that part of their work, we find so much diversity that to bring them all under the heading of a single unitary "scientific method" is, as we saw Donald Piatt suggest, simply misleading. Many since have agreed with him,[8] and the "disunity of science" (see Galison and Stump 1996) came to replace its hierarchical organization. Reduction thus ceased to be an overall philosophical program or "working phypothesis," as people like Hempel, Oppenheim, and Putnam had it, and was instead pursued piecemeal in various scientific research agendas, as when neurologists attempt to correlate pain with various brain states.[9] This development ended the alliance between Cold War philosophy and the Allen Formula, because a disunified science cannot serve as the basis for exclusionary employment policies.

Stealthiness itself, however, did not disappear entirely from American philosophy, which continued to keep certain doctrines veiled from outsiders. So much, in any case, is indicated by four points Richard Rorty made in a 1986 essay, "Philosophy as Science, as Metaphor, and as Politics."[10] First, Rorty flagged the intellectual isolation that had by then overtaken mainstream American philosophy: "Analytic philosophy has little influence on other academic disciplines, and little interest either for the practitioners of those disciplines or for other intellectuals" (Rorty 1991b, 23). Philosophy was clearly, by 1986, no longer the theater of intellectual warfare that it had been in the early Cold War. One reason for this loss of centrality is clear to anyone who knows even a little about human psychology: by the time of the Nixon-Khrushchev Kitchen Debate in 1959 (see Salisbury 1959), it had become obvious that capitalism was able to supply workers with a material lifestyle far beyond the dreams of Marx and Engels. In contrast to the situation at the beginning of the fifties, when the idea that capitalism could provide shared prosperity only by means of warfare was still current, the stoves, refrigerators, and built-in washing machines displayed in Moscow established capitalism's superiority far more effectively than the logical formulas of Cold War philosophy could do. With happiness firmly defined in terms of the accumulation of such possessions, there was little for philosophy to do.

Second, Rorty's passage continues as follows: "But analytic philosophers are not distressed by this fact." The story of the early Cold War at UCLA shows us why not. For more than twenty years (from Max Otto in 1947 to Angela Davis in 1967–69), philosophy had attracted plenty of outside attention— and it had hardly been welcome. The travails of Davis, Max Otto, Bertrand

Russell, and many others less famous had rendered public obscurity something devoutly to be wished.

Third, two pages earlier, Rorty has said not only that philosophers are happy in their public obscurity, but that their isolation is their own doing: "Analytic philosophy has pretty much closed itself off from non-analytic philosophy and lives in its own world" (Rorty 1991b, 21). This is puzzling, for one would think that fear of outside pressures must have attenuated by 1986. The last major public outcry against philosophy (the Angela Davis affair) had been eighteen years before, and even in the tenured stability of academic departments, that is time enough for memories to fade. Moreover, though philosophy departments were still places where atheism could be taught, literature departments, and in particular those given over to deconstruction, had taken over as public targets; the famous "culture wars" at the millennium's end largely spared philosophy. So if the ire of religious conservatives had been diverted, why was philosophical stealth still alive?

It is possible that by the time of Rorty's writing, philosophy's exclusionary bent, so loudly trumpeted by Reichenbach, had settled into mere habit. But Rorty identifies, fourth, a stealthy component in it: a "metaphilosophical" doctrine that philosophers held behind the walls they had erected. "Even though analytic philosophy now [1986] describes itself as post-positivistic, the idea that philosophy 'analyzes' or 'describes' some ahistorical formal 'structures'—an idea common to Husserl, Russell, Carnap, and Ryle—persists. However, there is little explicit metaphilosophical defense or development of this claim" (Rorty 1991b, 21).

Philosophical stealth, we may say, was still practiced in 1986, and not only from habit. It had in fact been redirected. Outside pressures on academia had largely subsided, only to be replaced by challenges coming from other disciplines within the university. The unpopular philosophical doctrine that required protection no longer concerned naturalism, but the nature of philosophy itself: the belief, inherited from what Rorty calls "the logical positivism of thirty years ago," that philosophy possesses "a secure matrix of heuristic concepts—categories which permit it to classify, comprehend, and criticize the rest of culture" (Rorty 1982b, 221).

Such philosophical hegemony over culture was difficult to defend openly. We saw in chapter 6 that Raymond B. Allen could not argue for his basic philosophical premises because, having defined everyone who disagreed with them as irrational, he had no one to argue with. Plenty of people were still taking that kind of attitude as the millennium began to turn (see Sokal and Bricmont 1998). But Rorty's account suggests a second reason for the stealth. Cold War philosophy was, on the surface anyway, an empiricist idiom (*TD*, 68–69), but the only empirical way to establish that the structures philosophy analyzes really are ahistorical would be to investigate them historically. Philosophers thus found themselves unable to defend their ahistoricism without abandoning it, and they apparently found it best to relegate it to what Rorty calls a "tacit presupposition" (Rorty 1991b, 21). With the main enemies now internal to academia, the elaborate tactics of stealth directed against outsiders that we saw in chapter 1—hiring one's own graduate students, publishing in obscure places if at all, and pretending to make hires while actually delaying them—were no longer necessary. Simply ignoring professors outside one's own field and being ignored by them in return provided sufficient cover.

Philosophers themselves were, to be sure, largely unaware of their own isolation, and so of this stealthy orientation. Certainly I was. When, in 1992–1993, I served as a philosophy professor on the Humanities Council at Northwestern University, much of our job concerned inviting potential speakers. I was surprised and then disturbed to find that when the name of some humanistic scholar would be advanced as that of a potential invitee, there would be a general reaction from the other members of the council. Professors of English, History, Religion, and French would all know something about that person and their work—I alone had never heard of them. It was only when I left philosophy five years later (and moved into German) that I discovered the extent of my previous isolation from other academic disciplines. Philosophy's stealthiness was thus, by that time, consummate: it was hidden even from philosophers.

THE INCORPORATION OF RATIONAL CHOICE INTO PHILOSOPHY

Issues of stratified nature faded away as the sciences moved on from their mid-century hierarchy. Cold War philosophy's account of the rational mind had more staying power, which led it to two very different fates. Within philosophy, to be sure, components of it came under quick attack. The ink was hardly dry on *RSP* when W. V. O. Quine's "Two Dogmas of Empiricism" (Quine 1953b) challenged Reichenbach's self-assured deployment of the analytic-synthetic distinction. Once Thomas Kuhn had exposed science's historical dimension, theory choice became historically constrained; by 1972 Kuhn was questioning its impartiality altogether (*SSR*[PS] 200–204). The ethical neutrality of Cold War philosophy, incarnated in Reichenbach's doctrine that volitions cannot be criticized (discussed in chapter 4) was profoundly challenged by John Rawls'

A Theory of Justice (Rawls 1971), which maintained that there are ethical constraints on rational choice. Yet—and in spite of Rawls' later critique of components of the rational choice theory of mind (for which, see Dreben 2003, 322)—the centerpiece of Rawls' argument in *A Theory of Justice* is a thought experiment in which a person chooses freely among kinds of social structure; Rawls characterizes his work there as "a part, perhaps the most significant part, of a theory of rational choice" (Rawls 1971, 16).

Other philosophers have seemed to have no trouble incorporating various rational choice procedures into their own views. When Saul Kripke pictures reference as a sequence of events that begins from a "baptism" that can only be arbitrary (i.e., volitional) and is sustained by the intentions of later speakers to conform to that baptism—intentions that, like preferences in RCT, are assumed as given—he is, in effect, viewing reference as achieved through a series of individual choices under a preference for sameness of reference (Kripke 1972, 302). Even Rorty, one of Cold War philosophy's most gifted antagonists, phrased his proposals, as Robert Scharff has written, in the "self-confident, post-traditional language of *choice*" (Scharff 1995, 123). Of particular importance in this regard, if only because of their philosophical fruitfulness, are the views of Harvard philosopher W. V. O. Quine and two of his most influential students, Donald Davidson and David Lewis. While I can hardly do justice to them here, a few brief remarks can suggest the importance of conceptions of rational choice in post-positivistic philosophy.

The general picture is conveyed, with respect to Quine, by Stuart Kauffman:

> The point, first stressed by Quine (1961) is that any hypothesis confronts the world intertwined in a whole mesh of other hypotheses, laws, and statements of initial conditions. Given disconfirming evidence, consistency requires that some statement(s) of the premises be abandoned, but we are *free to choose* which premise we shall abandon and which we shall save. . . . Typically, we *choose* to save those hypotheses that are most central to our conceptual web and give up peripheral hypotheses or claims about initial conditions. But *that very choice* renders those central claims very hard to refute, indeed, almost true by definition. . . . One can consistently maintain that the world is flat despite almost enormous evidence to the contrary. (Kauffman 1993, 17; emphasis added)

In spite of his brilliant critique of Reichenbach, then, Quine follows him in making science a series of rational choices, under a preference (among others) for retaining "central" views. Rational choice is also central to linguistic comprehension for Quine: in what he calls "radical translation," the hearer of an utterance shares no linguistic or cultural presuppositions with the speaker (Quine 1960, 29), and so cannot impute intentions to her. An utterance in such a situation can always be understood (i.e., "translated") in more than one way (Quine 1960, 26, 72). Selecting a single translation from the various possible ones throws us, in the first instance, onto guesses and intuitive judgments (Quine 1960, 29–30). To get beyond these to a rational ranking of translations, we must measure the current utterance against the whole range of speech behavior observed in the speaker's language (Quine 1960, 78). A particular translation is thus preferred to its alternatives, not in view of how it captures the "meaning" of an isolated sentence,[11] but in view of how it will contribute to the larger project of translating (understanding) the speaker's entire language. Quine's holism thus reintroduces into philosophy something that Reichenbach, we saw, had dispensed with: an overall "utility function" in which alternatives are measured against one another, with overall translatability standing in for overall utility.

In his 1974 "Belief and the Basis of Meaning," Donald Davidson, whose early work on decision theory I noted in chapter 3, explicitly models interpretation on decision theory: the holding of a sentence as true is glossed as the preference that it, rather than another sentence, be true. Since preferences are evidenced by choices, and choices are in principle observable, preferences can be known in ways that things like beliefs and meanings cannot (Davidson 1984a, 146–48).[12] An utterance is thus produced via a rational choice among it and its alternatives, in the context of an overall preference for truth: "Actual choices in decision theory correspond to actual utterances in interpretation" (Davidson 1984a, 146). The preference for truth, in turn, is embodied in Davidson's famous "principle of charity." Since, as with Quine's radical translation, different interpretations of a speaker's utterances are possible, we should "choose a theory of translation which maximizes agreement":[13] we should assume that the speaker whose utterance we are trying to interpret generally holds as true the same sentences that we do. In consonance with Davidson's holism (see Davidson 1984a, 152), the agreement to be maximized is, like utility in RCT, overall, holding across beliefs as a whole. Davidson's holism, like Quine's, thus proffers a more complete incorporation of rational choice theory into philosophy than did Reichenbach's view that problems are to be solved individually.

Both Davidson and Quine, then, view linguistic understanding as akin to scientific theory choice for Reichenbach: determining the meaning of a sentence includes choosing from an array of possible meanings it may have. But RCT is of limited usefulness in philosophy of language, because it has a solipsistic dimension. According to consumer sovereignty, rational choices are made without respect to the preferences or intentions of others (unless taking them into account is a preference of the chooser). Thus, Kripke already departs from RCT in that a preference for sameness of reference makes little sense unless the sameness is interpersonal. RCT's more complex sibling, game theory, integrates interaction, and so is more promising—but what it integrates it *into* is basically rational choice. Each player in a game chooses one strategy from an array of possible ones: "A move [in a game] is the occasion of a choice between various alternatives . . . under conditions precisely described by the rules of the game. . . . Each player selects his strategy—i.e., the general principles underlying his choices—freely" (von Neumann and Morgenstern 1947, 49).

In his 1969 *Convention*, David Lewis undertakes to use game theory to explain the nature of linguistic conventions (Lewis 1969, 3). This means viewing linguistic understanding as akin to an equilibrium in game theory—a situation in which each participant has done as well as she could, given the actions of the others (Lewis 1969, 8). Attaining such equilibrium is then the same thing as solving a "coordination problem" in game theory. Such a problem, in turn, is a "situation of interdependent decisions by two or more agents in which coincidence of interest predominates and in which there are two or more proper coordination equilibria" (Lewis 1969, 24). The coordination problem is solved when, of the available strategies ("contingency plans"), those chosen by all participants lead to equilibrium (Lewis 1969, 122–47). Once again, linguistic understanding requires a rational choice among competing strategies, under a preference for equilibrium.

There is no doubt, of course, that the phenomena discussed by Davidson, Kripke, Lewis, and Quine occur; but there is room to ask whether they have the kind of centrality these philosophers attribute to them. Many or most of our linguistic choices may, like our other choices, be socially or even politically constrained, perhaps without our knowing it. These piecemeal apropriations of RCT, however, mask a deeper disagreement: Davidson, Lewis, and Quine clearly see RCT not as generalizable into a systematic account of reason *à la* Reichenbach, but merely as exploitable for solving various philosophical puzzles and generating important philosophical insights. Davidson, in particular, is careful throughout "Belief and the Basis of Meaning" (Davidson 1984a) to be clear about where components of RCT can be carried over into his philosophical semantics and where they cannot. But he, like the other two, does not examine RCT critically on its own ground, and on that level his importation of it, like theirs, goes unquestioned.[14] Thus, all three philosophers run the risk of over-idealizing language in the direction of logic, a complaint often made about RCT. And how the alternatives among which a choice is made come to be (how, for example, languages derive their semantic capacities and whether those semantic capacities are in fact adequate to overall goals of understanding)—the issues broached in the quotation from the Port Huron Statement that serves as epigraph to this epilogue (Dewey and Gould 1970, 370)—is not open to investigation. The alternatives are apparently, like the formation of preferences in RCT, relegated to something akin to Reichenbach's "context of discovery."[15]

The various criticisms of Cold War philosophy made by Davidson, Quine, Rawls, and others thus appear to be piecemeal. In accordance with Reichenbach's principle of the "autonomy of problems" discussed in chapter 4, each philosopher has criticized those aspects of the Cold War theory of mind that he finds problematic: for Davidson, its rejection of holism; for Quine, its distinction between analytic and synthetic truths; for Rawls, its volitional amoralism. But these different criticisms are piecemeal only in appearance, for they proceed from a single position: the rejection of Cold War philosophy's claim to provide a systematic account of reason. This claim is not attacked directly but is implicitly rejected by the very piecemeal approach of these philosophers. Subjected to that approach, RCT becomes a reservoir of insights rather than a set of interconnected doctrines. Rational choice becomes merely a tool for solving various philosophical problems, rather than an all-embracing worldview. As such a tool, however, it has remained an important part of many philosophical investigations.

This piecemeal use of RCT signaled American philosophy's liberation from service to the ideological imperatives of the Cold War: that task, along with vast resources, went to economics and political science departments. If this left philosophy something of a backwater in the Cold War intellectual economy, the price may have been worth it. But it also exempted Cold War philosophy's basic commitments from critical philosophical scrutiny. Thus, Erickson et al. argue that, by the 1980s, "notions of rationality began to fragment. . . . What looks from one point of view [like] irrational behavior might appear rational from another perspective (Erickson et al. 2013, 177–80).[16] My suggestion here is that post–Cold War philosophy underwent such fragmentation but never adequately reflected on it, so that when Erickson et al. come to comment on *The Oxford Handbook of Rationality* (Mele and Rawling 2004), they find it "at first glance surprising that [Cold War] rationality has become a specialty within the academic discipline of philosophy" (Erickson et al. 2013, 187).

Academia's critical confrontation with Cold War rationality as such came, then, outside philosophy.

REASON BEYOND RATIONAL CHOICE?

Important to understanding the fate of Cold War philosophy outside philosophy departments is realizing that there are other ways of construing reason than as a series of impartial, rational choices. One of them dates back at least to Aristotle's account of his (unhappily named, in the Cold War context) "dialectical" method.[17] That method begins not with observation and generalization, as with Reichenbach, but with a dispute. Such disputes are not due to contingent failures to make one's ideas clear; they lie in the intractably perspectival nature of human knowledge in general: "On the one hand, no one is able to attain the truth adequately; while, on the other hand, we do not collectively fail, but everyone says something true about the nature of things, and while individually we contribute little or nothing to the truth, by the union of all a considerable amount is amassed" (*Metaphysics* 2.1.993a31–b3).

For Aristotle, the individual mind is restricted to a particular standpoint and so can obtain "little or nothing" of the truth. As the "or nothing" indicates, this is not what I called in chapter 4 a mere "quantitative" failure: it is not as if I have correctly added up half of a column of numbers and am waiting for you to add up the other half. It is that my own results cannot be known to be correct until they have been confronted by yours; truth emerges from a clash of standpoints. This emergence (i.e., the "dialectical" resolution of a dispute) consists for Aristotle in the harmonization of the conflicting opinions. The harmonization is not always complete: sometimes an opinion must simply be thrown out as incompatible with the emerging solution. But we can only tell what is incompatible with a harmonization of opinions once that harmonization has begun to take shape. It is not something that can be tacitly presupposed at the outset, and it follows that no views, and no thinkers, can be permanently excluded from the conversation. We thus find in Aristotle a strong intellectual generosity: "It is [proper] that we should be grateful, not only to those with whose views we may agree, but also to those who have expressed more superficial views; for these also contributed something, by developing our skill [*hexis*]" (*Metaphysics* 2.1.993b12–14).

In addition to its non-exclusionary quality, which, as we saw, placed it at odds with the Allen Formula and with Reichenbach's formulation of rational choice philosophy, such clash-of-standpoints reason is in fundamental opposition to several other characteristics of reason as understood in rational choice philosophy. First, the clash of standpoints is likely to exhibit anything other than the dispassion attributed to reason under the rational choice model. People stating their own points of view, especially to others who are unlikely to share them, tend to become quite excited, and this is not an "externality" to the debate itself: the degree of an arguer's excitement serves as an indication, to others and to herself, of the debate's importance. What is the point of arguing if the argument is not passionate?

Second, the aim here is not to articulate a view that, in Raymond B. Allen's words, can withstand the "fire of criticism" from colleagues and others. Implicit in Aristotle's view of the perspectival nature of the human mind is that one's initial view is never or rarely able to withstand such criticism. The point is not to bring others to agreement with my own view but to formulate a new view that is usually not held by anyone at the beginning of the debate but emerges out of it. This view of reason thus violates RCT's doctrine of consumer sovereignty: no one is solely responsible for her final view. It also (therefore) violates Reichenbach's view of social polishing, discussed in chapter 4, for it makes such polishing inherently reciprocal: I cannot polish you dialectically without you polishing me. In the dialectical perspective, argument is not a matter of one person "imposing" her opinions on others, *à la* Reichenbachian volitions, but of mutual aid.

Third, such debate does not concern the proper analysis or description of ahistorical structures; unlike rational choice reason, it is not ahistorical. Indeed, it is best defined as the critical appropriation of an historical heritage: the heritage constituted by the opinions with which it begins. Just by being debated, these are placed at a distance and so become "historical."

Fourth, rules and procedures need not be specified in advance, beyond the simple requirement to keep talking; there is no "method" to this reason. This is because the differences in perspective between the participants cannot be specified in advance; they may go beyond the topic at hand to include, for example, very general beliefs about how clash-of-standpoint debates are to be conducted. One of the principle uses of such debate, in fact, is to uncover such deeper disagreements. To achieve this, even the "laws" of logic can be accorded only provisional status.

Fifth, the results of such debate do not possess any single property that can be called "truth" or be specified as a weakened version of truth (such as Reichenbach's preference for the highest probability). Dialectical harmonizations for Aristotle are theories that obtain their validity by mutually reconciling a particular set of opinions (*dokounta*; see *Topics* 100b21). What constitutes such reconciliation is, like everything else in such debate, susceptible to redefinition as the debate progresses. And the reconciliation is at best provisional, for new opinions on the matter would place it into doubt. Its validity, in other words, is only temporary and *quo ad nos*. This does not for Aristotle deprive such truth of scientific import: it is only dialectically that the principles underlying all science can be established (*Topics* 101a36–b4).[18]

Though philosophers hardly stopped arguing during the early Cold War—the Allen Formula virtually mandated them to argue all the time—the arguments they usually engaged in differed in kind from the clash-of-standpoint model. In Jonathan Wolff's incisive caricature, "At its worst, philosophy is something you do against an opponent. Your job is to take the most mean-minded interpretation you can of the other person's view and show its absurdity. And repeat until submission" (Wolff 2013). This adversarial view of philosophical argument hardly resembles the clash-of-standpoints model of Aristotle, but it does conform to the impose-your-volitions model of Reichenbach, discussed in chapter 4, in which one's own view—one's preference that certain sentences be held as true—is taken as fixed.

The clash-of-standpoints view of reason, however, did not die with Aristotle. The construction of a Thomistic "article," with objections and contrary opinions laid out before the resolving conclusion is stated, is a variant of it. Shaftesbury's version of "social polishing," which I noted in chapter 4, is another. Hegel, as usual, provides the supreme example, telling us that "the highest truth, the truth as such, is the resolution of the highest opposition and contradiction."[19] I spare the reader a discussion of Hegel here,[20] and turn briefly to a more accessible discussion of a kind of philosophy that is not composed only of choices among competing theories. It is to be found in the "doctrine of method" at the end of Kant's *Critique of Pure Reason*.

The will, which makes us good, is not most basically a faculty of empirical choice; deciding what to have for dinner, for example, is a matter of *Willkür* ("power of arbitrary choice"), not *Wille*. Our moral actions, by contrast, are based on the will, which is the power "of overcoming . . . the impressions made upon our sensible power of desire" (*CPR*, B, 830). The will thus cannot "choose" to act against the moral law—it is, precisely, the power of acting in accordance with it. And we cannot "choose" to act in accordance with the will, because will is what we most basically are; as with modern philosophy generally, the will for Kant is the inner core of the human mind (McCumber 2012, 70). Moral improvement is thus not a matter of choosing to be good, but of strengthening the capacity of the will to direct our actions. Philosophy aids in such strengthening, negatively, by showing the mind what it can and cannot do. This is what Kant calls the "polemical employment" of pure reason, which amounts to "the defense of its propositions against their dogmatic denials" (*CPR*, B, 767); for dogmatism, the claim to know things about non-sensible reality, is for Kant a transgression of the mind's cognitive limits. The polemical clash between critique and dogmatism thus arrives at a proper view of the mind's powers and ends its "internal disarray" (*CPR*, B, 771), thus strengthening the mind's capacity to follow the will. Such philosophy is the "completion of all culture of human reason" (*CPR*, B, 878). It "secures the general order and the concord, and indeed the prosperity of the scientific community, and keeps that community's daring and fertile works from deviating from the main purpose, viz.—the general happiness" (*CPR*, B, 879).

The delimitation and ordering of the mind's *a priori* cognitions, to be sure, include, for Kant, choices among competing theories. It includes, along with the provision of hopefully compelling proofs, a certain amount of introspective intuition and, as Hans Saner has shown, some surprisingly harsh rhetoric; but these are in the service of a clash of standpoints (see Saner 1973, 114–62). By establishing the mind's proper limits, philosophy serves to render those who pursue it good—that is, able to oppose their current inclinations in the service of the general happiness. We can hardly ask for a sharper account of enlightened "edification."

The clash-of-standpoint view of reason was thus opposed to the logic-based "scientific" philosophy on point after point. It was not entirely absent from the university during the early Cold War. In an editorial for March 16, 1953, the student-edited *UCLA Daily Bruin* made a plea for it precisely in the context most inimical to it: that of allowing Marxists to teach: "[We are at a university] to assimilate differing ideas and judge them for ourselves. If one professor is biased, another will offer a different orientation to the problem. In the heat engendered by their conflicting views the student may draw some light." The grown-ups, of course, didn't dare listen. In the 1960s, they were compelled to.

EXPLOSION: THE SIXTIES

The rejection of Cold War philosophy in the university at large in the sixties took the form, not of a variety of specific criticisms, as in philosophy itself, but of a transformative convulsion that reshaped much of American higher education. The story of this is well known, for the convulsion left hardly a campus untouched. From the point of view of Cold War philosophy, it was directed against an issue indicated in my account of Kant above: You cannot choose what you most fundamentally are (see Rawls 1985, 241–42). On Kant's approach, we cannot choose whether to follow the dictates of our will or not; what one most basically *is*, is one's will, which is defined as following the moral law. Not to act as the moral law requires is not to "act" at all, but to allow one's inclinations—the presence in one of the results of a causal chain that began somewhere in the past—to do the acting. It is, at the limit, to decay into an ad hoc congeries of psychological operations.

Kant's account of the will as constituting the fundamental identity of the human individual is admittedly tendentious, but his underlying point can be generalized: if I am to choose among alternatives, then none of those alternatives can be who I am; for if I were identified with one of them, then to choose any of the others would be to put an end to myself.[21] Alternatives are thus, as Kenneth Arrow put it, "presented to" the mind; they are not part of it. And if everything is a matter for rational choice, then everything is presented to the chooser, and nothing is part of her. A human individual can, therefore, have no identity at all: her core is a set of logico-mathematical algorithms, which do not distinguish her from other people and have to be as Reichenbach had them: wholly empty.[22]

What happened in the sixties, from this point of view, was that large numbers of people discovered in themselves identities that were far more concrete than the logico-mathematical reason proffered by the Cold War theory of mind. African Americans, women, Hispanics, Asians, and LGBT people realized in rapid succession that their specific identities went all the way to their cores: they thought, felt, and were treated differently than they would be if they had other identities, notably that of straight, white male. From the point of view of Cold War philosophy, this could only be viewed as a willful intrusion of concrete content into the properly empty algorithms of the rational chooser—a denial of logic itself that, inevitably, placed those making it behind a Reichenbachian "haze of vagueness." Dismissals of the whole approach, soon routinized but rarely published, proliferated in the corridors and men's rooms of philosophy departments.[23]

In academia generally, this all led to two separate transformations that joined to make a third. First, reason became passionate. Instead of an objective evaluation of competing theories, it became the articulation, often enraged, of one's own experiences and feelings. Second, those feelings went along with modes of thinking and insights that could not be shared from the outset by those with other identities: standpoint scholarship came onto the scene. Finally, when standpoints became passionate, the result was advocacy scholarship, which now demanded a place in the conversation.

The older, clash-of-standpoints model of reason could have accommodated this. Cold War philosophy, entrenched on campuses since the early Cold War, could not; it violated too many of such philosophy's "universal" rules. The mentality of the academic establishment is conveyed by Raymond B. Allen's successor as chancellor of UCLA from 1960 to 1968, Franklin D. Murphy:

> I had, and I still have, very grave questions as to these black studies programs, Indian study programs, Chicano studies programs. I think they're devoid of much intellectual content. I think it was psychotherapy rather than intellectual activity. But I'm not going to second-guess anybody, because maybe some psychotherapy was needed to quiet people down. I think it's a miscarriage of space and everything else, on a campus that's very short on space, to provide a sort of social meeting room for these people. . . . The history of the blacks in this country and the history of the Chicano in this country ought to be an integral part of history. And any department of history with integrity will put it in. And they'd even have a separate course. But to create these so-called centers is, I think, really quite absurd. (Murphy 1976, 249–50)

Murphy's dichotomy between "intellectual activity" and "psychotherapy" reflects not only Reichenbach's dichotomy between scientific and speculative philosophy and Allen's dichotomy between doing competent research and "leading parades," but also what Ellen Schrecker calls the dichotomy that infected literary studies in the wake of the McCarthy Era: literature was regarded either as a "storehouse of abstract ideals" (such as truth) or reduced "to psychoanalysis" (Schrecker 1998, 404–5). Murphy's complaint is not a racist one. He does not claim that African American or Chicano history is unworthy of study; indeed, he believes that any history department with integrity will study both. What really troubles him is the *kind* of scholarship being pursued. He does not see what the students at the *UCLA Daily Bruin* saw: that truth can emerge from a clash of committed standpoints, as well as from impartial discussion. Passionate standpoints for Murphy are the province of psychotherapy.

The lasting effects of all this on American universities are easy to see today. Consider the remarkable multiplication of departments, especially in the social sciences and humanities, that has come about in the last four decades. Traditional departments of literature now find themselves complemented by departments of comparative literature; musicology is doubled by ethnomusicology, studying primarily non-European musical traditions; anthropology, focused on what is measurable about humans (and so on their physical characteristics), is now supplemented by world culture; and so on. There has also been an enormous proliferation of programs, their names often ending in "studies" (as in African American, Asian, Hispanic, Islamic, Jewish, and Women's Studies), whose practitioners are usually members of the group studied and where passionate advocacy is not only not excluded, but actively encouraged.[24] In almost every field a line can be drawn between, on the one hand, one or more older departments structured along the lines of the Allen Formula to favor dispassionate investigation and, on the other hand, newer fields whose goals and methods, as well as their subject matter, qualify them as representing newer dispositives. The inability of older departments to accommodate these newer paradigms is not, I suggest, the result only of the personal hostility of some professors to certain groups or methods—a hostility that is always strenuously, and usually sincerely, denied. It reflects in part something we have had to work to see: the ongoing influence in American intellectual life of the Cold War, and of Cold War philosophy.

APPENDIX

Roster of UCLA Philosophy Department
from 1947–48 to 1959–60

Source: UCLA *General Catalogue*

1947-48

Full Professors

Hugh Miller
Donald A. Piatt (chair)
Hans Reichenbach

Full Professors Emeritus

John Elof Boodin
Ernest C. Moore
Charles Rieber

Assistant Professors

Abraham Kaplan
J. Wesley Robson

Hans Reichenbach

Full Professors Emeritus

John Elof Boodin
Ernest C. Moore

Associate Professor

J. Wesley Robson

Assistant Professor

Abraham Kaplan

Instructor

Robert M. Yost Jr.

1948-49

Full Professors

Hugh Miller
Ralph Barton Perry (Flint Professor)
Donald A. Piatt (chair)

1949-50

Full Professors

Hugh Miller
Donald A. Piatt (chair)
Hans Reichenbach

Full Professors Emeritus

John Elof Boodin
Ernest C. Moore

Associate Professor

J. Wesley Robson

Assistant Professors

Abraham Kaplan
Robert M. Yost Jr.

Visiting Assistant Professor

Hans Meyerhoff

Lecturer

Donald Kalish

1950–51

Full Professors

Hugh Miller
Donald A. Piatt (chair)
Hans Reichenbach

Full Professors Emeritus

John Elof Boodin
Ernest C. Moore

Associate Professors

Abraham Kaplan
J. Wesley Robson

Assistant Professors

Hans Meyerhoff

Robert M. Yost Jr.

Instructor

Donald Kalish

1951–52

Full Professors

Hugh Miller
Donald A. Piatt (chair)
Hans Reichenbach

Full Professors Emeritus

John Elof Boodin
Ernest C. Moore

Associate Professors

Abraham Kaplan
J. Wesley Robson

Assistant Professors

Donald Kalish
Hans Meyerhoff
Robert M. Yost Jr.

Instructors

Melvin E. Maron
Wesley C. Salmon

1952–53

Full Professors

Hugh Miller
Donald A. Piatt
Hans Reichenbach

Full Professor Emeritus

Ernest C. Moore

Associate Professors

Abraham Kaplan (chair)
J. Wesley Robson

Assistant Professors

Donald Kalish
Hans Meyerhoff
Robert M. Yost Jr.

Instructor

Norman M. Martin

1953-54

Full Professors

C. D. Broad (Flint Professor)
Hugh Miller
Donald A. Piatt

Full Professor Emeritus

Ernest C. Moore

Associate Professors

Abraham Kaplan (chair)
J. Wesley Robson

Assistant Professors

Donald Kalish
Hans Meyerhoff
Robert M. Yost Jr.

Visiting Assistant Professor

Nathaniel Lawrence

Instructor

Alexander Sesonske

1954-55

Full Professors

Rudolf Carnap
Hugh Miller
Donald A. Piatt
W. T. Stace (Flint Professor)

Full Professor Emeritus

Ernest C. Moore

Associate Professors

Abraham Kaplan (chair)
Hans Meyerhoff
J. Wesley Robson

Assistant Professors

Donald Kalish
Nathaniel Lawrence
Robert M. Yost Jr.

Instructor

Alexander Sesonske

1955-56

Full Professors

Rudolf Carnap

Abraham Kaplan (chair)
Hugh Miller
Donald A. Piatt

Associate Professors

Hans Meyerhoff
J. Wesley Robson
Robert M. Yost Jr.

Assistant Professors

Donald Kalish
Nathaniel Lawrence

Acting Instructor

Richard Montague

1956-57

Full Professors

Rudolf Carnap
Abraham Kaplan (chair)
Hugh Miller
Donald A. Piatt

Associate Professors

Donald Kalish
Hans Meyerhoff
J. Wesley Robson
Robert M. Yost Jr.

Instructor

Alexander Sesonske

Acting Instructor

Richard Montague

1957-58

Full Professors

William C. Barrett (Visiting Professor)
Rudolf Carnap
Abraham Kaplan
Hans Meyerhoff
Donald A. Piatt
J. Wesley Robson
John Wisdom (Flint Professor)

Full Professor Emeritus

Hugh Miller

Associate Professors

Donald Kalish
Robert M. Yost Jr. (Chair)

Assistant Professors

Richard Montague
Herbert Morris

Acting Instructors

Ruth Anna Mathers
Nelson Pike

1958-59

Full Professors

Joseph M. Bochenski, O. P. (Flint Professor)
Rudolf Carnap
Abraham Kaplan
Hans Meyerhoff
Ernest Moody
Donald A. Piatt
J. Wesley Robson

Full Professor Emeritus

Hugh Miller

Associate Professors

Donald Kalish
Robert M. Yost Jr. (Chair)

Assistant Professors

Richard Montague
Herbert Morris

Acting Instructors

Nelson Pike
Larry E. Travis

1959-60

Full Professors

Rudolf Carnap
Abraham Kaplan
Hans Meyerhoff

Ernest Moody
Donald A. Piatt
J. Wesley Robson

Full Professor Emeritus

Hugh Miller

Associate Professors

Donald Kalish
Robert M. Yost Jr. (chair)

Assistant Professors

Richard Montague
Herbert Morris

Instructor

Mary Stewart

ACKNOWLEDGMENTS

I am deeply grateful to my editor at Chicago, T. David Brent, and to the anonymous readers for the Press. Robert C. Scharff solved some major problems of organization for me, and a number of others have commented on parts of the manuscript: Dana Belu, Edward S. Casey, Robert Daseler, Ann Garry, Sandra Harding, Doug Kellner, Noelle McAfee, Heidi Ravven, Rob Sullivan, Julia Syshitska, and Mary Watkins. Among the many who have given me general encouragement for this project, Amy Allen, Judith Butler, Barbara Cassin, Daniel Dahlstrom, Karen Feldman, Nancy Fraser, Françoise Lionnet, Heidi Ravven, Dianna Taylor, Cynthia Willett, and Brenda Wirkus have been especially generous. And there are those who, in very different ways, started it all: Frank Cunningham, Danny Goldstick, Susan Harris, and Curtis Stokes.

I would also like to acknowledge the unknown hand that placed the letters protesting the appointment of Max Otto as Flint Professor at UCLA in the university archives rather than in the philosophy department records. The latter, I was told, seem to have been purged.

NOTES

PROLOGUE

1. *Los Angeles Examiner*, February 24, 1947, 3.

2. Sproul to Otto, February 24, 1947, MOA, series 1, box 7, folder 9.

3. Kruse 2015, 35–36; http://www.demographia.com/db-la-area.pdf (accessed June 10, 2015).

4. For Rolf McPherson's life, see his obituary in the *Los Angeles Times*, March 29, 2009.

5. For details, see Edwards 1967, 7:235, 238; also see Edwards's appendix to Russell 1957, 207–59.

6. Monk 2001, 239. As David Hollinger notes, this injustice to one of the world's most eminent philosophers is "not much remembered today, but it was a cause célèbre in the culture wars of the early 1940s" (Hollinger 1996c, 159).

7. Ralph E. Hammer, March 10; cf. Mr. and Mrs. E. C. Plies, March 11; Pauline J. Lindblad, March 13; L. Marsh, April 13; all from 1947, all to outgoing philosophy chair Hugh Miller. Unless otherwise noted, all letters cited in this prologue are in UCLAA series 410, box 3. Letters dated March 11, 1947, or before are in folder 2; letters dated 12 March 12, 1947, and after are in folder 3.

8. Stanley M. Thatcher to Hugh Miller, March 10, 1947 . The evidence in these letters requires me to retract one statement in my *Time in the Ditch*: "Philosophy was not knowingly singled out as a target by the vigilantes of the 1950s. The coalition of anti-intellectual forces that came together then was, almost by definition, too untutored, diverse, and confused to have any clearly defined targets" (*TD*, 25). I did not take into account that such a coalition could indeed strike specifically at philosophy departments—if, as seems to have been the case here, its members had been told to do so by religious leaders.

9. Miss M. McEwan to Hugh Miller, March 11, 1947.

10. See Otto to Donald Piatt (the new philosophy chair), August 15, 1947; MOA, series 1, box 7, folder 12.

INTRODUCTION

1. No wonder, then, that standard histories of twentieth-century philosophy should present it as a series of socially detached arguments, with the better ones (usually) prevailing: see Soames 2003; WIlliamson 2014.

2. Foucault's and Kuhn's intellectual affinities are indicated by their common concern with Emile Meyerson and their shared exposure to the social sciences, where debates about scientific approaches (according to Kuhn) go deeper than among physical scientists. For Kuhn's debt to Meyerson, see *SSR*, vi; for his exposure to social science, see *SSR*, viii. For Foucault's filiation from Meyerson via Bachelard and Canguilhem, see Gutting 2001, 85–86, 228, 260–61.

3. See Hegel's temporalized account of contradiction (Hegel 1977, 2): the bud "contradicts" the flower because they are respectively the beginning and ending of a single process.

4. Margaret Masterman famously accused Kuhn of using the term in no fewer than twenty-one different senses in the 173 pages of *SSR* (Masterman 1970).

5. For the personally isolated yet politically dependent lifestyle associated with the Manhattan Project, see Kelly 2007.

6. *SSR*, 69. This is in contrast to Kuhn's earlier book, *The Copernican Revolution*, which discussed the roles of religion in several places (Kuhn 1957, 106–12, 124–25, 195–99).

7. The quoted phrases are from Foucault 1979, 295, 204, and 201, respectively. The "closure" of the Panopticon's network follows from its nature as a prison, and that one enters by "conviction," rather than Kuhn's conversion, is—perhaps—a pun of my own. For Foucault's general description of the nature and functioning of the Panopticon, see Foucault 1979, 195–228; for his discussion of its paradigmatic status, see ibid., 293–308.

8. For illuminating remarks on microhistory, see Kracauer 1995, 104–38.

9. There are distinctions to be made between logical empiricism, the branch of science-oriented philosophy to which Hans Reichenbach belonged, and the logical positivism of the Vienna Circle. I flag them when necessary, but I generally use the more familiar expression.

10. Biographical information on Hook is available online at https://en.wikipedia.org/wiki/Sidney_Hook (accessed June 21, 2015).

11. See Soames 2003 for a purely "philosophical" account, and Kuklick 2001 for a more socially sensitive one.

12. In addition, my own status as one of UCLA's proud employees not only makes those archives easily available to me, but renders their institutional context more familiar and so more comprehensible.

13. Santa Barbara received autonomy in 1959, when campuses at Davis, Riverside, and San Diego were added to the system. Irvine and Santa Cruz followed in 1965, and Merced in 2005.

14. For a brief discussion of this, see chapter 1.

15. William L. Worden, "UCLA's Red Cell: Case History of College Communism," *Saturday Evening Post*, October 21, 1950, 42; quoted in Starr 2002, 324.

16. For the proliferation of these state committees, see Heale 1998, 8–12. For their mutual aid and coordination, in which the California committee played a leading role, see ibid., 17–18.

17. CUAC 6 (1951), 50–51, 54; see also CUAC 9 (1957), 5.

18. Heale 1998, 284. The epithet "little red schoolhouse in Westwood" is attributed to "eastern journals" by Paul A. Dodd (1985).

19. "California U Head Hits Red Charges," *New York Times,* June 10, 1951; http://www
.timesmachine.nytimes.com/timesmachine/1951/06/10/84851560.html? page number 32; retrieved April 9, 2016.

20. As it turned out, the German government was not even trying to develop the atom bomb,
but the Americans could not know that.

21. This they have remained. When Wills wrote an article for the *New York Times* in January
2007, saying that the president was not his "Commander in Chief," he received abusive emails
demanding that he leave the country (Wills 2007); for the reaction, see Wills 2010, 47–48.

22. See online at http://en.wikipedia.org/wiki/Interstate_Highway_System (retrieved September 6, 2012).

23. McMahon 2003, 28–29; quoted in Wills 2010, 73.

24. For Groucho, see "The Non-Communist Party of the First Part Was an Upstart," *New York
Times,* September 20, 1998, 7. The full story of Einstein's harassment is told in Sayer 1985, 249–66.

25. *UCLA Daily Bruin,* "Ethical Implications," editorial, March 16, 1953.

26. Also see Nash et al. 1990, 917. For the pivot among southern Red hunters from fighting
Communism to persecuting African Americans, see Heale 1998, 25–27.

27. Anti-atheism was so strong in America that seventeen years after the end of Communism
in Europe, a study conducted at the University of Minnesota found that atheists were still "less
acceptable than other marginalized groups" (Edgell et al. 2006, 212. On *God's Not Dead,* see
http://en.wikipedia.org/wiki/God%27s_Not_Dead_%28film%29 (retrieved March 12, 2015).

28. I return to this, briefly, in the epilogue.

29. *Boulder Daily Camera,* February 2, 2008 . Even Judd was refused recognition, on several
occasions to my personal knowledge, by the American Philosophical Association.

CHAPTER ONE

1. The only person whose behavior Monk thinks was mysterious was Jean Kay, the woman
who sued to keep Russell's appointment (Monk 2001, 235). This is in contrast to the case of Max
Otto, where we cannot be sure of anyone's real motivation.

2. Mr. and Mrs. Gus R. Swanson to Hugh Miller, March 10, 1947. Unless otherwise noted, all
letters cited in this chapter are in UCLAA, series 410, box 3. Letters dated through March 11 are
in folder 2; letters dated from March 12 on are in folder 3.

3. Mrs. H. Groom to "Dear Sir," March 26, 1947.

4. Lyle Baker to Miller, March 8, 1947.

5. Olive Perry to Miller, March 10 1947; see also the letters of A. J. Diderich of March 8; of
Charles A. Anderson and E. Smith, March 10; of Lyle Baker, March 12—all to Miller, all in 1947.

6. Otto to Piatt, August 15, 1947; MOA, series 1, box 7, folder 12.

7. Piatt's worries are referred to in Otto to Piatt, August 25, 1947, MOA, series 1, box 7,
folder 12, which I discuss below.

8. Overstreet to Otto, September 11, 1947; MOA, series 1, box 7, folder 12.

9. Lindeman to Otto, December 1, 1947; MOA, series 1, box 7, folder 12.

10. Sproul to Otto, February 24, 1947; MOA, series 1, box 7, folder 9.

11. Otto to Dykstra, January 18, 1947; Dykstra to Otto, January 21, 1947; Piatt to Otto, January 26, 1947; all in MOA, series 1, box 7, folder 9.

12. Dickinson to Otto, October 2, 1947; MOA, series 1, box, 7, folder 12; emphasis in original. For Miller's residence in Bostone, see Miller 1975, 25.

13. Sellery was dean of the College of Letters and Science at Wisconsin from 1919 to 192 (http://en.wikipedia.org/wiki/George_Sellery [accessed April 12, 2014]).

14. Sellery to Otto August 27, 1947; MOA, series 1, box 7, folder 12.

15. The last three lines of this quotation ring strangely sarcastic—not least because reason (2) is clearly specious: Otto knew what he was getting into when he accepted both the Flint professorship and the job teaching summer school. Was (1) sarcastic as well?

16. Otto to Piatt, August 25, 1947; MOA, series 1, box 7, folder 12.

17. They were still there on December 15, 1947, when Piatt wrote him there and expressed hopes of seeing them over the holidays. Piatt to Otto, December 15, 1947; MOA, series 1, box 7, folder 13.

18. Academic year 1967–68, I should note, is an exception to all this. In that year, the title "Flint Professor" is listed at the end of the listings for visiting professors that follow those of regular faculty, and next to it is a dash.

19. "Otto, Center of Atheist Row, to Teach at UCLA," *Los Angeles Examiner*, February 24, 1947, 3.

20. *Time*, March 22, 1943. Online at http://www.time.com/time/magazine/article /0,9171,796135-5,00.html#ixzz0cb1aumeL. For information on Otto's life, see http://www .harvardsquarelibrary.org/unitarians/otto.html (both accessed October 30, 2011).

21. Piatt to Hahn, February 2, 1953; UCLAA, series 411, box 3. The naturalistic turn in American philosophy seems, unlike the scientistic turn I am examining here, to have been a matter of the better set of arguments winning. I discuss it briefly in chapter 2.

22. For a general history of this tradition, see McCumber 2011.

23. Sartre's atheistic red flag was particularly visible: I remember walking down a street in Claremont, California, where I was attending college, and seeing in a vending box the banner headline of the early edition of the *Los Angeles Times* for October 21, 1964, screaming at me, "Atheist Declines Nobel Prize."

24. See the introduction to Kaufmann 1975, 46, first printed in the original edition of 1956.

25. Piatt to Mrs. J. G. Maccabee, June 2, 1952; UCLAA, series 411, box 7.

26. Meyerhoff 1942, 185. In general, the dissertation is a critical account of the basic premises used by Hume, Kant, Nietzsche, and Spinoza to account for "moral phenomena." While concluding that none of these philosophers succeeds in accounting for them, it proposes no account of its own, which is possibly why Reichenbach approved it.

27. For biographical information on Boodin, Meyerhoff, Montague, Moore, Piatt, Rieber, and Robson, see the entries at http://sunsite.berkeley.edu/uchistory/archives_exhibits/in _memoriam/nameindex/nameindex_a.html. For Donald Kalish, see http://en.wikipedia.org/wiki /Donald_Kalish. For Abraham Kaplan, see http://en.wikipedia.org/wiki/Abraham_Kaplan. For Richard Montague, see http://en.wikipedia.org/wiki/Donald_Kalish (retrieved May 5, 2012).

28. The UCLA *General Catalogue* first lists Meyerhoff as an associate professor in its edition of 1954–55.

29. For information on Bochenski, see http://en.wikipedia.org/wiki/J%C3%B3zef_Maria _Boche%C5%84ski (accessed May 16, 2015). That a priest should be free to teach the

philosophy of Marx when others were not illustrates an important dynamic of the history of continental philosophy in America. While secular universities, public and private, were regularly accused of propagating the doctrines of atheistic Communism, such an accusation was simply nonsensical in the case of Catholic universities. They were thus left free to hire scholars of, and indeed members of, the atheistic continental tradition. They often did. To this day, continental philosophy, in spite of its tendency to atheism, is largely supported in America by Catholic universities—a whole new dimension of academic "stealth."

30. For details, see Schrecker 1986, 115–25, and Gardner 1967. A summary of the complex history of the California Oath Controversy is available at http://www.fsm-a.org/stacks/AP_files /APLoyaltyOath.html (retrieved May 5, 2012).

31. See "California U Head Hits Red Charges," *New York Times*, June 10, 1961. President Robert G. Sproul is quoted as dating the regents' anti-Communist policy to October 11, 1940.

32. See Munger 1950. If the aim of the regents was to weaken Sproul, we have an early attempt to make use of anti-Communism for other goals, confirming Richard Hofstadter's observation that "in this crusade Communism was not the target but the weapon" (Hofstadter 1963, 41–42).

33. This is from a letter quoted in the University of California Interim Report of the Committee on Academic Freedom to the Academic Senate, Northern Section, of the University of California, February 1, 1951; its author is not identified. UCLAA, series 393, box 2.

34. Carnap to Reichenbach, October 12, 1950; UCLAA, series 411, box 3.

35. "Summary of Loyalty Oath Hearings," June 22, 1950; UCLAA, series 393, box 4. Kalish, for his part (and wisely, given that he was untenured), soon mended his ways; in July 1950, he received a letter from University President Robert G. Sproul congratulating him for signing his letter of appointment for the following year "in the form set by the Regents' resolution of April 21," which included the Oath. Sproul to Kalish, July 24, 1950; UCLAA, series 393, box 2.

36. Letter of UCLA Committee on Privilege and Tenure to President Robert G. Sproul, June 5, 1950, re: Kenneth Roose; UCLAA, series 393, box 2.

37. Letter of the Privilege and Tenure Committee to President Sproul re: Donald Kalish, May 26, 1950; UCLAA; series 393; box 2. This comment was important enough to be included not only in the committee's letters to the regents, but in its public "summaries" of its cases: series 393, box 2.

38. Reisch 2007, 62. For a brief summary of some of the issues concerning Marx's philosophy that are still open and promising today, see Fuller 1996, 186.

39. Kaplan to Dodd, October 6, 1952; Kaplan to Miller, January 12, 1953; UCLAA, series 411, box 4; the former letter is in the personal collection of the author.

40. Piatt to Hahn, February 2, 1953; UCLAA, series 411, box 3. This box also contains the letters referred to below from UCLA professors seeking recommendations from professors at other institutions.

41. Yost to Kaufmann, January 28 1953; UCLAA, series 411, box 3.

42. Kaplan to Miller, January 12, 1953; UCLAA, series 411, box 4.

43. See Piatt to Mrs. J. G. Maccabee, June 2. 1952; UCLAA, series 411, box 7.

44. "McCarthy Set to War on College Commies," *UCLA Daily Bruin*, January 5, 1953; for other stories see *UCLA Daily Bruin* January 8 and 9, 1953. The *Bruin* also published stories on

the upcoming hearings on November 28, 1952. The hearings were held in the spring of 1953; for an account, see Shrecker 1986, 194–218.

45. Yost to Kaufmann, July 1, 1953; UCLAA, series 411 box 4.

46. Wilson 2000, 77.

CHAPTER TWO

1. Dennes 1944, 289. This anthology was often called the "Columbia Manifesto," because many of its writers, including John Dewey, were associated with Columbia University.

2. Rorty 1979, 5–6, 365–72; Kim 1980, 593. For a statement and defense of idealist edification, see Harold Taylor 1952. For the contrast with later, more individualistic views, see p. 156: "The primary task of our colleges and universities is to transform the intellectual, moral, and social values of American youth so that the education they receive will be put to good use, not merely for private gain and individual success, but for the development of a free community here and abroad."

3. Donald A. Piatt et al., *John Elof Boodin: In Memoriam* (statement of University of California Academic Senate), 1950; available at http://texts.cdlib.org/view?docId=hb9g5008vb&doc .view=frames&chunk.id=div00001&toc.depth=1&toc.id= (retrieved September 11, 2012).

4. Hugh Miller et al. *Henry Rieber: In Memoriam* (statement of University of California Academic Senate) http://texts.cdlib.org/view?docId=hb9p300969&doc.view=frames&chunk .id=div00022&toc.depth=1&toc.id= (retrieved May 27, 2013).

5. Recommendation from UCLA chancellor regarding Regents Agenda Item re: Estate of John Elof Boodin; UCLAA, series 359, box 307. The recommendation was to compile a subscription list; if it attained seventy-five names, a limited edition would be printed and sold to the subscribers.

6. See Hollinger 1996c, 161; for general problems with American idealism, see Hollinger 1975, 47–48.

7. Dewey 1944, 3. For accounts of this development, see Kuklick 2001 and Menand 2001.

8. In his discussion of George Herbert Mead, Moore endorses Mead's view of supernaturalism as *mystification*: see Moore 1937, 54–55. For Moore's debt to Dewey, see Moore 1915, vi.

9. Quoted in F. J. Klingberg, E. A. Lee, and E. T. Moore, *Ernest Moore: In Memoriam*; online at http://texts.cdlib.org/view?docId=hb0w10035d&doc.view=frames&chunk.id =div00039&toc.depth=1&toc.id= (retrieved September 11, 2012).

10. On the vagueness of Dewey's view of science, see Hollinger 1996b, 105. Similarly loose characterization of the scientific method to which naturalists give allegiance can be found in Dennes 1944, 283; Krikorian 1944b, 242; and Lamprecht 1944, 18, 36, 40–41. Thelma Lavine gives an interestingly historicized version that refers to "the checks of intelligent experimental verification in accordance with contemporary criteria of objectivity" (Lavine 1944, 184). Issues of scientific and rational method will occupy us again in chapters 4 and 6.

11. The shift from "material" to "physical" may have to do with the uncertain status of "matter" within the probabilistic horizons of quantum physics.

12. For Neurath's complex views, see Cat et al., 1996; Creath 1996; Dupré 1996, 161; and Uebel 2007, 260–71. For Nietzsche, see (among many other passages) the end of his *The Will*

to Power: "This world: a monster of energy, without beginning without end, . . . a sea of forces flowing and rushing together, eternally changing, eternally flooding back, with tremendous years of recurrence with an ebb and a flood of its forms; out of the simplest forms striving toward the most complex, out of the stillest, most rigid, coldest forms toward the hottest, most turbulent, most self-contradictory; and then again returning to the simple out of this abundance, out of the play of contradictions back to the joy of concord" (Nietzsche 1967, §1076, 548–50).

13. We could say "logical empiricism"; I need not distinguish the two here, and I refer to them both as "logical positivism." For a concise statement of the main affinities and contrasts, see Milkov 2013.

14. The association was highlighted in Karl Popper's *The Open Society and Its Enemies* (1950), published in the United States the year before *RSP* appeared.

15. See Nietzsche's treatment of "ascetic ideals" (1994, 72–128).

16. Thomas Ryckman (2003, 168–78) has shown how Reichenbach began from a conventionally Kantian view that the mind constitutes objects of knowledge but later moved to a more standard realist position.

17. This problematic takeover was an important aspect of Reichenbach's philosophical move beyond Kant: see Friedman 2000, 85 and Ryckman 2003, 160.

18. Others, to be sure, have disagreed. Kant, who is Reichenbach's foil at *RSP*, 125, is, as I have noted, one of them. Hegel goes farther. Even the principle of noncontradiction, the bedrock of logic, makes in his view significant—indeed, significantly wrong—claims about our experience: "All things," he famously proclaimed, "are contradictory in themselves" (1976, 439; my translation). Heidegger, for his part, detects a more specific constraining claim implicit in science—namely, that "nature is a calculable coherence of forces" (1977, 21). Anything that cannot be treated mathematically is scientifically unknowable—and, for Heidegger, there are many such "things."

19. Reichenbach spells that method out in a bit more detail than the pragmatists, though still casually, as including observation, experiment, and logical and mathematical theory construction (*RSP*, 118).

20. Reichenbach's argument about the social sciences in *RSP* is that mathematical methods are applicable to those sciences, which do not concern issues of reduction (*RSP*, 309).

21. For similar moves, see Hempel 1966, 2, 14, 220, 24, as well as the more technical Hempel and Oppenheim 1948, 140, 141, 151.

22. For introductions to this literature, see Parrini et al. 2003; Richardson and Uebel 2007.

23. Indeed, the lines between physics and chemistry have already done so (see Hempel 1966, 104–5; Hempel and Oppenheim 1948, 146–47).

24. For Oppenheim and Reichenbach, see Ziche and Müller 2013, 268–70; for biographical information on Putnam, see http://en.wikipedia.org/wiki/Hilary_Putnam (retrieved Oct. 8, 2013).

25. Reichenbach himself is even stealthier. In *RSP*, he does not even discuss, much less advocate, reduction as a general program. Even when he "reduces" mind to body (*RSP*, 271–72)—long after most religious fundamentalists would likely have stopped reading—he does not openly advocate naturalism. True to the general view that reductionism is a matter of language and thought, he presents the issue as linguistic: "The question of the existence of mind

is a matter of the correct use of words, but not a question of facts" (*RSP*, 272). It so happens that "mind" refers to a certain set of bodily states; it is not necessary to posit an independently existing mind to account, scientifically, for human behavior. But it also does not, we may note, contradict physical, chemical, or biological laws to say that at the moment of death, an immortal soul leaves the person and goes to heaven or hell. Experiments may one day even establish that there is such a soul. Reichenbach's reduction of mind to body is thus, like the rest of the naturalism in *RSP*, stealthy. It is presented late in the book, and so—like Meyerhoff's dissertation—resides in a place difficult to access. And it is presented, not as a question of fact, but as a set of linguistic recommendations. In this respect, *RSP* presents a case of what Arthur Melzer, working in the tradition of Leo Strauss, calls "defensive esotericism": hiding your true beliefs for fear of persecution (Melzer 2014, 127-59).

CHAPTER THREE

1. I am generally indebted to Philip Mirowski's work on the American reception/transformation of logical positivism via the RAND Corporation. While Mirowski concentrates on issues of intellectual temperament, such as suspicion of democracy and recourse to a metaphor of gambling (game theory), my aim here is to uncover the philosophical *doctrines* implicit in RCT and, as such, promulgated by RAND (see Mirowski 2002; 2005).

2. Hargreaves Heap and Varoufakis 2004, 3-4, 18; Maki 2012, v ("Preface").

3. "God is the unchangeable," Augustine 1982, 8.14.53-55, and 11.10.142; quoted in Raven 2013, 149. Kuklick has argued that American philosophy has always been an other-worldly enterprise, which was only partially interrupted by the social engagements of the pragmatists (2001, 282-85). If this is the case, so that logical space now stands in for the divine order in keeping philosophers away from politics, those who accuse contemporary philosophy of "deifying" logic are righter than they know.

4. Abella 2008, 49-51; Amadae 2003, 85. For Arrow's account of this, see Arrow 1991, 3-4, quoted in Mirowski 2002, 305. For biographical information on Helmer, see Rescher 2006, 281.

5. For a particularly clear account of this problem, see Okasha 2011, 88-89.

6. See http://en.wikipedia.org/wiki/Demographics_of_the_Soviet_Union#cite_note-and-1 (consulted July 24, 2011).

7. Amadae 2003, 2; as noted in the introduction, Amadae discusses the philosophical concern with the Cold War in von Hayek, Popper, and Schumpeter; she also documents their pessimism (2003, 15-23).

8. Though Hayek maintains in the passage cited that the intellectual background of capitalism can be traced back to the individualism of ancient Athens, the same is true of Marxism: see McCarthy 1992.

9. Amadae 2003, 28. One of these figures, Robert S. McNamara, would in the 1960s pioneer the application of RCT to national defense and other areas. He was a strong believer in the wide applicability of RCT to organizations: "Running the Department of Defense," he is reported as saying, "is no different from running Ford Motor Company or the Catholic Church" (Shapley 1993, 515; quoted in Amadae 2003, 58).

10. Sent 2007, 464-66. Also see Abella 2008, 177-78.

11. Reisch 2005, 350. These are in addition to Abraham Kaplan, whom I discuss below.

12. See for example Davidson, McKinsey, and Suppes 1955; Helmer and Rescher, 1959; Hempel 1991. For Quine's and Davidson's philosophical incorporations of RCT, as well as for the later one of David Lewis, see the epilogue. The relationship of game theory and RCT in Cold War philosophy is discussed there and in chapter 4.

13. Mirowski n.d.; quoted in Reisch 2005, 350.

14. Letter of the Privilege and Tenure Committee to President Sproul re: Abraham Kaplan, May 25, 1950; UCLAA, series 393, box 2.

15. For the expression of values as preferences see *SCIV*, 7; for transitivity and completeness in the ordering relation see *SCIV*, 12–17; for the building up of the overall profile from binary comparisons see *SCIV*(A), 16, 20. Note that Arrow does not use "preference pattern" in this way, since the relation R is not a preference relation but a preference-or-indifference relation [*SCIV* (A), 15]. Just what "relevance" amounts to varies, apparently, with circumstances [ibid., 12]. At *SCIV* (A), 17 the preference ranking is said to extend to "all conceivable" social states; but at *SCIV* (A), 11 it is referred to as a "basic set of alternatives."

16. The most important divergence between RCT and its philosophical generalization, as Reichenbach presents it, is that the latter drops the overall ranking and considers each set of alternatives separately. This, as chapter 4 shows, enables rational choice procedures to cover theory choice in science.

17. See *SCIV*, 104: "If we substitute a new set of individual orderings, we have a new social welfare function."

18. This exclusion is echoed in the Reichenbachian "context of discovery," which is examined in the next chapter; reason, for RCT, operates only within what we might call the "context of ranking," which corresponds to Reichenbach's "context of justification."

19. For other positivistic traits, see *SCIV*, 9; 21, n. 18; *SCIV* (A), 109; 110.

20. Knight 1947, 69; quoted in *SCIV*, 8, n. 23; emphasis in original.

21. For a fully rational choice, she must also know that her knowledge of those sequences is complete.

22. For example, "In a generalized sense all methods of social choice are of the type of voting" (*SCIV*, 27–28).

23. It is because an alternative includes actions that it must, as we saw, make a difference in observable behavior: see *SCIV*(A), 110.

24. This is, of course, consonant with Arrow's general assignment, which was to begin with the preferences of individuals and move to those of an entire society: "All social choices are determined by individual desires" (*SCIV*, 29).

25. Vickery's concept of admissibility might furnish a basis for moral judgment in that it forbids alternatives that go against the "patent interests" of the individual (whatever those are); as stated above, however, it excludes them from the analysis of the individual's actions, not from the choices and actions themselves.

26. Quoted in Herman 2001, 63.

27. Amartya Sen (1979, 539, 543) puts this differently: the paradox of voting only becomes relevant when all information about the voter beyond that of her preference order is excluded from the account. Along with that, we may say, goes social polishing, or edification, understanding which requires all sorts of information about the chooser beyond her preferences.

28. Idealism, we may note, has the same structure for Arrow that, in chapter 2, we saw

Reichenbach attribute to it: it comprises an illusory appeal to an ideal order to ground moral directives valid for all humans.

29. Arrow et al. 1996, iii; quoted in Mirowski 2002, 296, n. 69.

CHAPTER FOUR

1. Piatt to Gordon S. Watkins, January 27, 1951; UCLAA, series 411, box 7.

2. Indeed, Piatt's 1939 view that thought "follows the lead of its subject matter" (Piatt [1939] 1951, 108, 109) is more akin to the phenomenological battle cry "to the things themselves," and particularly to Heidegger's reading of this (for which see McCumber 2011, 161–65), than to the methodological monism of RCT.

3. Miller's characterization of the "theoretical attitude" had broad-scale affinities to Kuhn's views, as discussed in the introduction. Like Kuhnian perception, Miller's epistemic bedrock is not pure sensation (or raw "sense-data") but the recognition of something as similar to, or different from, other things. Theoretical knowledge must be supplemented by knowledge of "large historical units," which sounds like Kuhnian paradigms or Foucaldian dispositives—except that, for Miller, these units are themselves merely phases of a single, still larger "unitary occurrence."

4. There are some remarks on "sociological science" at *RSP*, 309–10.

5. von Hayek 1983, 17–19, 235–36. Hayek describes there how small the intellectual circles in Vienna were: "It was only a short while ago, when somebody like you inquired about whom I knew among the famous people of Vienna, that I began to go through the list, and I found I knew almost every one of them personally. And with most of them I was somehow connected by friendship or family relations and so on."

6. For the two von Mises see http://go.galegroup.com/ps/retrieve.do?sgHitCountType=None& sort=RELEVANCE&inPS=true&prodId=GVRL&userGroupName=ucdavis&tabID=T003& searchId=R1&resultListType=RESULT_LIST&contentSegment=&searchType=Advanced SearchForm&currentPosition=1&contentSet=GALE|CX2830902986&&docId=GALE|CX 2830902986&docType=GALE. For the Mengers, see http://www.iit.edu/csl/am/about/menger /about.shtml#biography (both retrieved September 14, 2012).

7. As Erickson et al. (2013) have shown, that *Geist* was largely predicated on game theory, in which the reasoning person must take account of the intentions of other people. Reichenbach's scientific philosophy remains focused on the virtually solipsistic model of individual choice presented by Arrow; I discuss the reasons for this later in this chapter.

8. Miller offers a somewhat anxious acknowledgement of Reichenbach (Miller 1939, viii), while Meyerhoff prefaces his book with a virtual paean to Reichenbach, who had died eighteen months before the preface was written, as my "former colleague and friend" (*TL*, vii).

9. These two features may of course be connected: the more the method is spelled out, the less "universal" it will look.

10. The arguments run, for example, throughout Husserl 1960.

11. Since a community of mathematical philosophers effectively contains only one individual, there is no strategic interaction among philosophers: philosophy is not, for Reichenbach, a game in the sense of game theory. Though game theory is an important component of other versions of Cold War rationality (see Erickson et al. 2013), and would be appealed to by later American philosophers (see the epilogue), its insights do not apply to philosophy itself.

12. Deirdre McCloskey's account of the role of observation in what she calls "economic modernism" captures many of Reichenbach's views. Indeed, her whole account of economic modernism and its intellectual "poverty" can be compared with my account of Reichenbach in this chapter (see McCloskey 1998, 143–44; more generally, 139–55). McCloskey, however, concentrates on how economics was influenced by philosophy. I argue here that the influences also went, later on, in the other direction: while one approach in philosophy—that of "positivism" (McCloskey 1998, 141) contributed to the intellectual basis of modernist economics, the influence of such economics during the early Cold War rebounded to help establish the dominance of one philosophical approach—that of "logical positivism."

13. The emphasis on public observability is where W. H. Sheldon (1945), discussed in chapter 1, would say Reichenbach is smuggling materialism into his naturalism.

14. Strictly speaking, we cannot assign probabilities to single events in this way; the 60 percent tells us that of the cases so far observed, y has followed x in 60 percent of them. Probability thus applies strictly to sets of events, not to individual ones. Since Reichenbach regards the assigning of probabilities to individual events as "harmless" (*Rise*, 239), I pass over this matter here.

15. *RSP*, 232; see also 240. It is not clear what the relationship is among generalizations/explanations and theories in the context of scientific theory choice. Because the main similarities between scientific philosophy and RCT on theory choice as rational choice are clear, I ignore this issue here.

16. Samir Okasha has recently shown that a formal identity between rational choice and scientific theory choice can be established by construing a single criterion for theory choice (say the highest probability of being true) as an "individual" in RCT (Okasha 2011, 9), since a single criterion establishes a single preference order among the alternatives. This has the effect of absorbing the individual scientist entirely into the rational choice procedure, ignoring the rest of her individuality—along the lines of Reichenbach's statement that mathematical philosophers cannot disagree if their ideas are clear.

17. "Everyone is free . . . to build up his own logic, i.e., his own form of language, as he wishes"; see Carnap 1937, 51–52.

18. Carnap 1937, 317–18. For careful accounts of Carnap's views, see Friedman 1998, 249–51; and 2002, 175–76.

19. I thus agree with Alan Richardson (Richardson 2005, 746–47), as against Mirowski (Mirowski 2005, 171, n. 19) that volitions for Reichenbach exist inside science; reliance on volitions is not a criterion for distinguishing scientists from nonscientists. What muddies the waters here is Reichenbach's assertion, noted earlier, that mathematical logicians cannot disagree with one another if their terms are made clear, which suggests that they are not relying on volitions; but that has to do with scientific philosophy, not science itself.

20. See also McCloskey 1998, 144, no. 9.

21. See Cartwright 1983; Armistead 2014.

22. Reichenbach 1938; 1959a, 92–98; 1959c; 1959d; see *RSP*, 162–63.

23. *RSP*, 315. The tension, noted by Hollinger, between the "great production" Reichenbach makes of disavowing ethical implications and his actual "relentless arguing that most moral issues of the day were really empirical scientific ones" may constitute another example of philosophical stealth (Hollinger 1996c, 164; see also McCloskey 1998, 144, no. 10.

24. Thus, for Reichenbach, all imperatives are "token-reflexive": they contain a reference to the individual who is issuing them, so that "what is expressed is actually an attitude of the speaker" (*RSP*, 288–89).

25. As with Kant; see *RSP*, 284–85, which coincides with Arrow's discussion at *SCIV*, 81–88.

26. See Kamlah 2013. Piatt's comments on Reichenbach to the provost at Riverside, discussed in this chapter's n. 2, suggest that Reichenbach actually operated on this principle.

27. The third divergence, the extension of rational procedure from ranking by transitivity and completeness to mathematics and logic generally, is obviously for the same reasons.

CHAPTER FIVE

1. Putnam 1981, 105–6. As Richard Creath notes, the fact that "a great many different formulations of verificationist principles" mostly "came to a bad end rather quickly" is no reason to conclude that the principle is without merit (Creath 2011). But it is reason to suspect it.

2. For an account of how neoclassical economics' valorization of the individual and her freedom are "more or less a sham," see Mirowski 2002, 448–53. The corresponding individualism of rational choice philosophy is, on this view, merely another case of philosophical stealth. Also see Davis 2012.

3. Hence Reichenbach's startling claim, noted in chapter 4, that mathematical philosophers do not disagree with one another if they know the meaning of their terms.

4. The mutual unrelatedness of the two sides of Cold War philosophy can be explained, of course, by the fact that the sides were responses to very different political pressures—one coming from frightened religious conservatives far outside the university, and the other coming from the Cold War military and intellectual establishments.

5. Piatt to Edward J. Machle, March 17, 1950; UCLAA, series 411, box 3.

6. UCLAA, series 393, box 4; copy in author's personal collection.

7. The string of rejections was not, it turns out, entirely uncongenial to the department. As Piatt wrote to A. I. Melden after the latter's rejection, the refusals could be turned into weapons to fight the oath: "The Department was unhappy to lose you but at the same time very pleased with your reasons for your decision. . . . There comes a time when successive refusals, all on the same ground of the 'oath,' penetrate even the thickest of skulls. . . . But for our obligation to make the department operate as well as possible we would refuse to invite anyone else and would inform president Sproul that we have no reason to expect that any man qualified for the job would accept it" (Donald Piatt to A. I. Melden, April 30, 1951; UCLAA, series 411, box 7). The department, in fact, had already used the first two rejections to campaign against the oath, writing to University President Robert Gordon Sproul that "in the light of these two refusals [Carnap and Quine] our department is unwilling to invite anyone else to accept the Flint Chair of Philosophy so along as the Regents' 'oath' requirement is in force" (Piatt to Robert Gordon Sproul, Nov. 22, 1950; UCLAA, series 411, box 3). The department's astute use of the various rejections calls to mind what I suggested (in chapter 1) may have been its strategy with respect to the non-naturalist hire: in both cases, letters were stealthily turned to purposes very different from the obvious one.

8. "Senate: Report on Burns Committee," May 26, 1952; UCLAA, series 393, box 257; also see Schrecker 1986, 279.

9. Combs, testimony before the United States Senate Internal Security Subcommittee, quoted in Schrecker 1986, 279; also see CUAC 7 (1953), 134.

10. "Sproul Clarifies Contact Stand," *UCLA Daily Bruin*, February 9, 1953.

11. See CUAC 7 (1953), 209–10. UCLA philosophy's in-house hires, discussed in chapter 1, were thus virtually mandated by CUAC.

12. CUAC 7 (1953), 201, 209, 134.

13. Robert G, Sproul to Chairmen of Departments and Other Administrative Officers, April 21, 1952; UCLAA, series 393, box 2; copy in author's personal collection.

14. Note the loose phrasing: in the minds of many at the time, this wording included Catholics. See Blanshard 1949.

15. Julian N. Hartt, associate professor of theology at Yale, writing the philosophy department on behalf of Robert C. Whittemore, Dec. 11, 1951; from Whittemore's dossier, UCLAA, series 411, box 4.

16. Brand Blanshard, professor of philosophy at Yale, also writing on behalf of Whittemore, November 28, 1951; UCLAA, series 411, box 4.

17. Schrecker shows conclusively that what Communists there were in academia hardly constituted a conspiratorial force (Schrecker 1986).

18. I saw this myself as a child: I can remember kitchen table discussions in which my parents, who were grocers in a university town in central Illinois, discussed whether various professors were, in my mother's phrase, "anti-anti"—that is, anti-anti-Communist and therefore sympathetic to Communism.

19. Sanders 1979, 49, paraphrasing the testimony of Joseph Kornfelder; also see Schrecker 1986, 280.

20. The words are those of George Reisch (2005, 279).

21. Kerr 2003, 65; Heale 1998, 23.

22. Heale 1998, 15.

23. Richard E. Combs, testimony before the United States Senate Internal Security Subcommittee, quoted in Schrecker 1986, 279–80; also see CUAC 7 on Un-American Activities (1953), 134; "Sproul Clarifies Contact Stand," *UCLA Daily Bruin* February 9, 1953.

24. What was not available was the full extent of the dishonesty at CUAC—that it had listed its chair's enemies in the legislature as subversives, for example (see above). But there was plenty of other evidence at the time that CUAC was not entirely honest; its continual screaming about the danger of Communists in academia after many years of not finding any was one tip-off.

25. In 1952, Martha Deane, chairwoman of the Department of Physical Education at UCLA, was accused of engaging in "obscene activities" with another woman. Dean Paul A. Dodd, who the next year would offer the non-naturalist position to the philosophy department that I discussed in chapter 1, conducted what he called an "exhaustive investigation over many weeks," and concluded that the charges were proved. He presented his findings to the Committee on Privilege and Tenure, but the committee voted unanimously to exonerate Deane. The UCLA chancellor, who was also the contact man, then entered the picture. He called Deane, Dodd, and a friend of Deane's to his office and told them that he had carried out his own investigation privately, had obtained "privileged testimony" (i.e., testimony which no one else could see), and that she was fired anyway. No one ever saw this evidence. Either the chancellor did not have such testimony, or he did have it and had withheld it both from Dean Dodd and from the

Committee on Privilege and Tenure. Withholding the evidence would serve no purpose; more likely is that he simply made the evidence up on the spot, after the committee exonerated Deane. See Weiler 2007 for details.

26. "UC Official Called 'Thought Cop,'" *San Francisco Chronicle* July 6, 1954; Kerr 2003, 52.

27. Harvard *Crimson*, March 17, online at 1954.http://www.thecrimson.com/article/1954/6/17/california-contact-men-are-they-campus/ (accessed June 11, 2013).

CHAPTER SIX

1. "Allen, U. C. L A. Chancellor, Quits," *New York Times*, June 12, 1959.

2. Biographical information on Allen appears in Sanders 1979, 3–4, and online at http://www.pastleaders.ucla.edu/allen.html (accessed June 4, 2015).

3. "Dr. Allen Slated as Chancellor of UCLA," *Los Angeles Times*, Dec. 15, 1951.

4. "A Promising Chancellor For UCLA," *Los Angeles Times* editorial, December 16, 1951. The local newspaper of the time, the *Westwood Hills Press*, also chimed in and received a thank you letter from Allen, by then Chancellor, on December 31, 1952; UCLAA, series 359, box 256. The *New York Times* also noted the connection between Allen's appointment and his "opposition to Communist influences on campus"; see "Dr. Allen Is Named Head of U. C. L. A." *New York Times*, December 15, 1951.

5. "The Allen Formula," *UCLA Daily Bruin* November 14, 1952. The Allen Formula was also lauded in an editorial in the *Los Angeles Times* for December 16, 1951.

6. *UCLA Daily Bruin*, "The Allen Formula," November 14, 1952.

7. Allen to Donald K. Anderson, April 28, 1953; UCLAA, series 359, box 280.

8. Minutes of meeting of Chancellor's Administrative Council, March 3, 1953; UCLAA, series 359, box 259.

9. Andrew Hamilton to Raymond B. Allen, May 26, 1954; UCLAA, series 359, box 280.

10. Sanders 1979, 25; also see Schrecker 1986, 97.

11. Allen's claim that Communists did not have freedom of thought was challenged at the time by Alan Barth, who pointed out that "it is clear from the great numbers of ex-Communists that one may leave the Party at will—that is, whenever one ceases to subscribe to its doctrines" (Barth 1951, 221; see the entire discussion of Allen at 221–23). Allen's rejoinder would presumably have been that Communists were not forced to remain in the party but were subject to mind control, which made them want to do so. They were zombies, not slaves—and willing zombies at that.

12. This concern for "competence," it should be noted, differed from another loudly promulgated academic value of the early Cold War, that of "academic integrity." This, as David Hollinger has shown, meant not lying to your colleagues about your Communist or leftist associations: "*Integrity meant, above all, a willingness to tell one's colleagues exactly what one's politics were, and academic freedom did not extend to a right to refuse to do so*" (Hollinger 1996a, 131; italics in original). As late as 1953, "academic integrity" was appealed to in efforts to get rid of people who lied about their Communist affiliations (Hollinger 1996a, 129–32). Like the argument to competence, appeals to academic integrity had wide support within the professoriate, but, as Hollinger points out, they presupposed that one was already a faculty member. They therefore did not apply, as the California Plan did, to those who were merely under consideration.

13. Allen himself had experience with such fear. His early pragmatic praise for the Soviet Union would get him in trouble at the University of Washington in 1949, when one H. L. Moody, an investigator for the state auditor's office, claimed that Allen's public anti-Communism was a cover for more suspect activities (Sanders 1979, 83–84).

14. Neither Allen nor Hook called attention to the disparity in their opinions. For Hook and Allen's collaboration, see Sanders 1979, 82. For Quine's views, see Quine to Reichenbach, Nov, 1 1950; UCLAA, series 411, box 7.

15. Kant, *The Conflict of the Faculties*, in AA, 7:17.

16. Allen would later admit, on a national radio show, that "the fact is that these gentlemen could defend themselves as scholars in their particular fields, as in fact they were" (*Town Meeting* 14 (1949): 11.

17. What if he turned out to be a member of Consumers Union?

18. "University Invites Study of Ousters," *New York Times*, February 10, 1949.

19. On McCarthyite homophobia, which was intense, see Johnson 2004. In an interview with the *UCLA Alumni Magazine*, Allen stated his conviction about the relationship of Americanism with athletics: "You won't find any Communists going out for a sport that involves rugged team competition, which stamps athletics as an excellent breeding ground for good, solid, American citizens" (Jackson 1952, 8). Given that Allen's sudden resignation from UCLA in 1959 was provoked by his involvement in a football scandal, this rings ironic. See again http://www.past leaders.ucla.edu/allen.html (accessed June 4, 2105).

20. Perhaps this is why, when Allen left the University of Washington in November, 1951, two years after the Herbert Phillips affair, he was given a standing ovation at his last faculty meeting (Sanders 1979, 95).

21. "Social Ramifications," *UCLA Daily Bruin*, editorial, March 16, 1953.

22. *UCLA Daily Bruin* interview with Abraham Kaplan, March 4, 1953.

23. UCLAA, series 393, box 4, also in author's personal collection; emphasis added, except for "anyone," which is underlined in the original.

24. See http://texts.cdlib.org/view?docId=hb267nb0r3;NAAN=13030&doc.view =frames&chunk.id=div00056&toc.depth=1&toc.id=&brand=calisphere (accessed August 3, 2015).

EPILOGUE

1. The dissertation itself was mandated by the university regulations.

2. When I was a graduate student at the university of Toronto in the Seventies, logic was an acceptable replacement language.

3. Richard Rorty allots to the establishment of analytical philosophy, the more flexible genus, of which logical positivism was an early species, an even shorter time—1951–1960 (Rorty 1982b, 214).

4. For the Metaphysical Club, see Menand 2001. Rorty dates pragmatism's establishment to about 1923 (Rorty 1982b, 214), but he may understate the time span, for senior idealists remained in place, at least at UCLA, long after that: Charles Rieber in would retire in 1936 and Jon Elof Boodin in 1939, which would give the argument a full seventy years.

5. Hollinger 1985, 25. See Rayman 2010 for documentation of the ongoing interest among

philosophers; but whether papers and a conference devoted to early pragmatism as a purely "philosophical" phenomenon, which it was not in today's sense of that term, constitute a revival is open to doubt.

6. Rorty's breakthrough book, *Philosophy and the Mirror of Nature* (Rorty 1979), was published the year before Hollinger's essay.

7. Philosophy's long and honorable history was also largely forgotten (though not at UCLA), so that Bruce Wilshire could write, again in 1985, that "many [newly-minted philosophy PhDs] had never read cover to cover a major treatise in the history of philosophy" (Wilshire 1985, 257–58).

8. The *locus classicus* for this view is Feyerabend 1975. For a less tendentious and more up-to-date version that contextualizes whether a theory is scientific or not with reference to the community of its practitioners, see Thagard 1978.

9. See Erickson et al. 2013, 176–81, and chapter 2.

10. For the complex provenance of this essay, see Rorty 1991a, ix.

11. Quine's underlying argument here is, famously, that the whole notion of "meaning" can be done without.

12. These are notions that Davidson, like Quine, thinks are useless.

13. Davidson 1984c, 101; see also Davidson, 1984a, 152.

14. All three thus remain true to Kuhn's insight that solving problems within a paradigm requires exempting that paradigm itself from critical attention (*SSR*, 42).

15. "Do we have the right words in our language" is thus a crucial philosophical question, largely unasked by philosophers today.

16. Welcome to Heidegger!

17. For a thorough treatment of Aristotle's views on dialectic, see Evans 1977.

18. Aristotle's own most basic principle—that forms exist in matter, rather than separately—is thus introduced, at *Metaphysics* 1.9, not via generalization or inference, but out of critical dialogue with Plato; see *Metaphysics* 1.9.990a32–993a10.

19. Hegel 1975, 99–100. Such resolution of oppositions constitutes his main methodological gesture, the redoubtable *Aufhebung*.

20. I have carried on such discussions elsewhere; see McCumber 1993, 2004, and 2012.

21. This is an important point behind game theory. You can always walk away from a game, and this is part of the burden of the game metaphor itself, which has so dominated economic and political theory that one forgets it was originally a metaphor (Leonard 1995, 730–31, 733).

22. A paradigm of such personal emptiness is provided by Mitt Romney, educated at the Harvard business school, who, for purposes of securing the Republican nomination for president in 2012, happily chose to repudiate the signal achievement of his entire previous life: the provision of health care to the people of Massachusetts.

23. Academic philosophy's problems with women and minorities have become too intractable to need documentation, but see, for starters https://beingawomaninphilosophy.wordpress.com/, accessed August 25, 2015.

24. "Programs" usually differ from "departments" in not containing tenure lines; a professor in a program also belongs to a department, and it is the department that makes final decisions on that person's promotion and tenure.

REFERENCES

Abella, Alex. 2008. *Soldiers of Reason: The RAND Corporation and the Rise of the American Empire*, Orlando, FL: Mariner Books: Houghton Mifflin Harcourt.

Agamben, Giorgio. 2009. *What Is an Apparatus?* Stanford, CA: Stanford University Press.

Aikman, David. 2007. *Billy Graham: His Life and Influence*. Nashville, TN: Thomas Nelson.

Allen, Raymond B. 1946. *Medical Education and the Changing Order*. New York: The Commonwealth Fund (abbreviated *MECO*).

———. 1953. "Cross Section of Faculty and Students Attempt to Put on Paper Their Beliefs and Guiding Principles." *UCLA Daily Bruin*, March 13, 1953.

Amadae, S. M. 2003. *Rationalizing Capitalist Democracy: The Cold War Origins of Rational Choice Liberalism*, Chicago: University of Chicago Press.

———. 2005. "Arrow's Impossibility Theorem and the National Security State." Part A. *Studies in History and Philosophy of Science*. 36, no. 4:734–43.

Aquinas, Thomas. 1963. *On the Division and Method of the Sciences*. Edited by Armand Maurer. Toronto, ON: The Pontifical Institute of Mediaeval Studies.

Arendt, Hannah. 1958. *The Human Condition*. 2nd ed. Chicago: University of Chicago Press.

Ariely, Dan. 2009. "The End of Rational Economics." *Harvard Business Review*, July. Online at http://hbr.org/2009/07/the-end-of-rational-economics/ar/1 (accessed November 11, 2013).

Armistead, Timothy W. 2014. "Resurrecting the Third Variable: A Critique of Pearl's Causal Analysis of Simpson's Paradox." *American Statistician* 68, no. 1:1–7.

Arrow, Kenneth. 1963. *Social Choice and Individual Values*. 2nd ed. New York: John Wiley & Sons. First published 1951.

———. 1974. *Essays on the Theory of Risk Bearing*. Amsterdam: North Holland.

———. 1991. "The Origins of the Impossibility Theorem." In Lenstra, Kan, and Schrijver 1991, 1–4.

Arrow, Kenneth, E. Columbatto, M. Perlman, and C. Schnidt, eds. 1996. *The Rational Foundations of Economic Behavior*. London: St. Martin's Press.

Augustine. 1982. *The Literal Meaning of Genesis*. Translated and annotated by John Hammond Taylor. New York: Newman Press.

Ayer, A. J. 1936. *Language, Truth, and Logic*. London: Gollancz.

———. 1977. *Part of My Life*. London: Collins.

Barrett, Edward L. 1951. *The Tenney Committee: Legislative Investigation of Subversive Activities in California*. Ithaca, NY: Cornell University Press.

Barth, Alan. 1951. *The Loyalty of Free Men*. New York: Viking.

Bell, David. 1999. "The Revolution of Moor and Russell: A Very British Coup." In *German Philosophy Since Kant*, edited by Anthony O'Hear, 193–208. Cambridge: Cambridge University Press.

Bernhard, Nancy E. 1999. *U.S. Television News and Cold War Propaganda, 1947–1960*. Cambridge: Cambridge University Press.

Bernstein, Richard J. 1989. "Pragmatism, Pluralism, and the Healing of Wounds." *Proceedings and Addresses of the American Philosophical Association* 63, no. 3 (1989): 5–18.

Betz, Albrecht. 1982. *Hanns Eisler, Political Musician*. Cambridge: Cambridge University Press.

Blanshard, Brand, Curt J. Ducasse, Charles W. Hendel, Arthur E. Murphy, and Max C. Otto, eds. 1945. *Philosophy in American Education*. New York: Harper Brothers.

Blanshard, Paul. 1949. *American Freedom and Catholic Power*. Boston: Beacon Press.

Burkhardt, Frederick. 1952. *The Cleavage in Our Culture: Studies in Scientific Humanism in Honor of Max Otto*. Boston: Beacon Press.

"California 'Contact Men': Are They Campus Spies or Necessary Investigators?" 1954. *Harvard Crimson*, June 17. Online at http://www.thecrimson.com/article/1954/6/17/california-contact-men-are-they-campus/ (accessed June 11, 2013).

Carnap, Rudolf. 1937. *Logical Syntax of Language*. Translated by Amethe Smeaton (Countess von Zeppelin). London: Routledge & Kegan Paul. Originally published as *Logische Syntax der Sprache* (Wien: Springer, 1934).

———. 1971. "Logical Foundations of the Unity of Science." In Neurath, Carnap, and Morris 1971, 42–62.

———. 1995. *Philosophical Foundations of Physics*. Edited with a forward by Martin Gardner. New York: Dover. First published in 1966.

Caro, Adrian del. *See* del Caro, Adrian.

Carr, E. H. 1961. *What Is History?* New York: Random House.

Cartwright, Nancy. 1983. *How the Laws of Physics Lie*. Oxford: Oxford University Press.

Cat, Jordi, Nancy Cartwright, and Hasok Chang. 1996. "Otto Neurath: Politics and the Unity of Science." In Galison and Stump 1996, 348–69.

Caughey, John. 1950. "A University in Jeopardy." *Harper's Magazine*, November.

Caute, David. 1978. *The Great Fear: The Anti-Communist Purge under Truman and Eisenhower*. New York: Simon and Schuster.

Church, Alonzo. 1956. Review of Hans Reichenbach, *The Rise of Scientific Philosophy*. *Journal of Symbolic Logic* 21, no. 4:396.

Creath, Richard. 1996. "The Unity of Science: Carnap, Neurath, and Beyond." In Galison and Stump 1996, 158–69.

———. 2011. "Logical Empiricism." In *The Stanford Encyclopedia of Philosophy*. Online at http://plato.stanford.edu/entries/logical-empiricism/ (accessed June 1, 2015).

Crouse, Eric R. 2002. "Popular Cold Warriors: Protestants, Communism, and Culture in Early Cold War America." *Journal of Religion and Popular Culture* 2 (Fall 2002): 1–18, Online at http://www.usask.ca/relst/jrpc/article-popcoldwar.html (retrieved September 19, 2012).

Cusset, François. 2003. *French Theory*. Paris: Éditions la Découverte.

Davidson, Donald. 1984a. "Belief and the Basis of Meaning." In Davidson 1984b, 141–54. First published 1974.

———. 1984b. *Inquiries into Truth and Interpretation*. Oxford: Oxford University Press.

———. 1984c. "On Saying That." In Davidson 1984b, 93–108.

Davidson, Donald, C. J. McKinsey, and Patrick Suppes. 1955. "Outline of a Formal Theory of Value." *Philosophy of Science* 22, no. 2:140–60.

Davis, John B. 2012. "The Homo Economicus Conception of the Individual: An Ontological Approach." In Maki 2012, 459–82.

del Caro, Adrian. 1989. *Nietzsche contra Nietzsche: Creativity and the Anti-Romantic*. Baton Rouge, LA: Louisiana State University Press.

Demographia.com. "Los Angeles Community Areas Population and Density 1950–2010." Online at http://www.demographia.com/db-la-area.pdf (accessed June 10, 2015).

Dennes, William R. 1944. "The Categories of Naturalism." In Krikorian 1944a, 270–94.

Dewey, John. 1944. "Antinaturalisms in Extremis." In Krikorian 1944a, 1–16.

———. 1951. "Experience, Nature and Value: A Rejoinder." In Schilpp 1951, 517–608.

Dewey, Robert, and James A. Gould, eds. 1970. *Freedom: Its History, Nature and Varieties*. London: Collier-Macmillan.

Dreben, Burton. 2003. "On Rawls and Political Liberalism." In *The Cambridge Companion to Rawls*, edited by Samuel Freeman, 316–46. Cambridge: Cambridge University Press.

"Dr. Allen Is Named Head of U. C. L. A." 1951. *New York Times*, December 15.

Drumheller, Joseph. 1949. *Communism and Academic Freedom: The Record of the Tenure Cases at the University of Washington*. Seattle: University of Washington Press (abbreviated *CAF*).

Dupré John. 1996. "Metaphysical Disorder and Scientific Unity." In Galison and Stump, 1996, 101–17.

Edgell, Penny, Joseph Gerteis, and Douglas Hartmann. 2006. "Atheists as 'Other': Moral Boundaries and Cultural Membership in American Society." *American Sociological Review* 71, no. 2:211–34.

Edwards, Paul, ed. 1967. *The Encyclopedia of Philosophy*. 8 vols. New York: Macmillan.

Emerson, Ralph Waldo. 2007. "Self-Reliance." In Emerson, *Essays: First Series*. Stillwell, KS: Digireads, 17–30. First published 1841.

Erickson, Paul, Judy L. Klein, Lorraine Daston, et al. 2013. *How Reason Almost Lost Its Mind: The Strange Career of Cold War Rationality*. Chicago: University of Chicago Press.

Evans, John David Gemmill. 1977. *Aristotle's Concept of Dialectic*. Cambridge: Cambridge University Press.

Fackenheim, Emil. 1967. *The Religious Dimension in Hegel's Thought*. Boston: Beacon Press.

Feyerabend Paul. 1975. *Against Method*. London: New Left Books.

Fine, Arthur. 1986. *The Shaky Game*. Chicago: University of Chicago Press.

Foucault, Michel. 1972. *The Archeology of Knowledge*. Translated by A. M. Sheridan Smith. New York: Pantheon.

———. 1979. *Discipline and Punish*. Translated by Alan Sheridan. New York: Vintage.

———. 1980. "The Confession of the Flesh." In Foucault, *Power/Knowledge. Interviews and Other Writings, 1972–1977*, 194–228. New York: Pantheon.

———. 1990. *The History of Sexuality*. Vol. 1. *An Introduction*. Translated by Robert Hurley. New York: Vintage. First published in 1978.

Frank, Thomas. 2005. *What's the Matter with Kansas?* New York: Henry Holt.

Free Speech Movement Archives. "The Loyalty Oath at the University of California: A Report on Events, 1949–1958." Online at http://www.fsm-a.org/stacks/AP_files/APLoyalty Oath.html (retrieved September 10, 2015).

Friedman, Michael. 1998, "On the Sociology of Scientific Knowledge and Its Philosophical Agenda." *Studies in the History and Philosophy of Science* 29, no. 2:239–71.

———. 2000. "Philosophy as Dynamic Reason: The Idea of a Scientific Philosophy." In *What Philosophy Is*, edited by Havi Carel and David Gamez, 73–96. London: Continuum.

———. 2002. "Kant, Kuhn and the Rationality of Science." *Philosophy of Science* 69, no. 2:171–90.

Friedman, Michael, and Richard Creath, eds. 2007. *The Cambridge Companion to Carnap*. Cambridge: Cambridge University Press.

Fuller, Steve. 1996. "Talking Metaphysical Turkey: About Epistemological Chickens and the Poop on Pigeons." In Galison and Stump, 1996, 170–86.

Galison, Peter, and David Stump, eds. 1996. *The Disunity of Science: Boundaries, Contexts and Power* Stanford, CA: Stanford University Press.

Gardner, David P. 1967. *The California Oath Controversy*. Berkeley: University of California Press.

Green, Donald, and Ian Shapiro. 1994. *Pathologies of Rational Choice Theory: A Critique of Applications in Political Science*. New Haven, CT: Yale University Press.

Greider, William. 1997. *One World, Ready or Not: The Manic Logic of Global Capitalism*. New York: Simon and Schuster.

Gutting, Gary. 2001. *French Philosophy in the Twentieth Century*. Cambridge: Cambridge University Press.

Hacking, Ian. 1996. "The Disunities of the Sciences." In Galison and Stump 1996, 37–74.

Hamilton, Andrew, and John B. Jackson. 1969. *UCLA On the Move: During Fifty Golden Years, 1919–1969*. Los Angeles: War Ritchie Press.

Harding, Sandra. 2006. *Science and Social Inequality*. Urbana (Champaign): University of Illinois Press.

Hargreaves Heap, Shaun, and Yanis Varoufakis. 2004. *Game Theory: A Critical Text*. 2nd ed. London: Routledge.

Harvard Crimson. 1954. "California 'Contact Men': Are They Campus Spies or Necessary Investigators?" (March 17). Online at http://www.thecrimson.com/article/1954/6/17 /california-contact-men-are-they-campus/ (retrieved September 10, 2015).

Hayek, Friedrich A. von. 1983. *Friedrich von Hayek Nobel Prize Winning Economist Oral History Transcript* (interview with Earleen Craver et al.) Los Angeles: Regents of the University of California, UCLA Oral History program.

———. 1994. *The Road to Serfdom* Chicago: University of Chicago Press. First published 1944.

Heale, M. J. 1998. *McCarthy's Americans: Red Scare Politics in State and Nation, 1935–1965*. Athens: University of Georgia Press.

Hegel G. W. F. 1975. Aesthetics. Translated by T. M. Knox. 2 vols. (consecutive pagination). Oxford: Oxford University Press.

———. 1976. *Science of Logic*. Translated by A. V. Miller. New York: Humanities Press.

———. 1977. *Phenomenology of Spirit*. Translated by A. V. Miller. Oxford: Oxford University Press.

———. 1991. *Elements of the Philosophy of Right*. Edited by Allen W. Wood. Translated by H. B. Nisbet. Cambridge: Cambridge University Press.

Heidegger, Martin. 1977. "The Question Concerning Technology." In *The Question Concerning Technology and Other Essays*, translated by William Lovitt, 3–35. New York: Harper Torchbooks.

Helmer, Olaf, and Nicholas Rescher. 1959. "On the Epistemology of the Inexact Sciences." *Management Science* 6, no. 1:25–52.

Hempel, Carl G. 1966. *Philosophy of Natural Science*. Englewood Cliffs, NJ: Prentice-Hall.

———. 1991. "The Irrelevance of the Concept of Truth for the Critical Appraisal of Scientific Theories." In Hempel 2000, 75–84.

———. 2000. *Carl G. Hempel: Selected Philosophical Essays*. Edited by Richard Jeffrey. Cambridge: Cambridge University Press.

Hempel, Carl G., and Paul Oppenheim. 1948. "Studies in the Logic of Explanation" *Philosophy of Science* 15, no. 2:135–75.

Herbert, Bob. 2010. "Killing and Dying." *New York Times*, op-ed, November 12, 2010.

Herman, Arthur. 2001. *How the Scots Invented the Modern World*. New York: Random House.

Hess, Mary B. 1956. Review of *The Rise of Scientific Philosophy*. *Bulletin of the British Society for the History of Science* 2, no. 15:52–53.

Hofstadter, Richard. 1963. *Anti-Intellectualism in American Life*. New York: Vintage.

Hofstadter, Richard, and Walter P. Metzger. 1955. *The Development of Academic Freedom in the United States*. New York: Columbia University Press.

Hollinger, David A. 1975. *Morris R. Cohen and the Scientific Ideal*. Cambridge, MA: MIT Press.

———. 1985. "The Problem of Pragmatism in American History." In *In the American Province*. Bloomington: Indiana University Press, 1985. First published 1980.

———. 1996a. "Academic Culture at the University of Michigan, 1938–1988." In Hollinger 1996d, 121–54.

———. 1996b. "Free Enterprise and Free Inquiry: The Emergence of Laissez-Faire Communitarianism in the Ideology of Science in the United States." In Hollinger 1996d, 97–120.

———. 1996c. "Science as a Weapon in *Kulturkämpfe* in the United States during and after World War II." In Hollinger 1996d, 155–74.

———. 1996d. *Science, Jews, and Secular Culture: Studies in Mid-Twentieth-Century American Intellectual History*. Princeton, NJ: Princeton University Press.

Hook, Sidney. 1944. "Naturalism and Democracy." In Krikorian 1944a, 40–64.

———. 1949. "Should Communists Be Permitted to Teach?" *New York Times Magazine*, February 27, 1949.

Horwich, Paul. 2011. "Williamson's Philosophy of Philosophy" *Philosophy and Phenomenological Research* 82: 524–533.

Hull, David. 1988. *Science as a Process*. Chicago: University of Chicago Press.

Husserl, Edmund. 1960. *Cartesian Meditations*. Translated by Dorion Cairns. The Hague: Martinus Nijhoff.

Illinois Institute of Tehnology. "Karl Menger." http://science.iit.edu/applied-mathematics /about/about-karl-menger#biography (retrieved September 10, 2015).

Jackson, John B. 1952. "Chancellor States Views and Policies for His New Administration at UCLA," *UCLA Alumni Magazine* December 1952.

Johnson, David K. 2004. *The Lavender Scare: The Cold War Prosecution of Gays and Lesbians in the Federal Government*. Chicago: University of Chicago Press.

Kamlah, Andreas. 2013. "Everybody has the Right to Do What He Wants: Hans Reichenbach's Volitionism and Its Historical Roots." In Milkov and Peckhaus 2013, 151–75.

Kant, Immanuel. 1902–. *Gesammelte Schriften*. 29 vols. Berlin: Akademie-Ausgabe (abbreviated AA).

———. 1996. *Critique of Pure Reason*. Translated by Werner Pluhar. Indianapolis, IN: Hackett (cited from the "B" edition in AA, vol. 3; abbreviated *CPR*).

———. 1997. *Prolegomena to Any Future Metaphysics*. Edited and translated by Gary Hatfield. Cambridge: Cambridge University Press (cited from AA, vol. 4).

Kauffman, Stuart. 1993. *The Origins of Order*. Oxford: Oxford University Press.

Kaufmann, Walter. 1975. *Existentialism from Dostoyevsky to Sartre*. New York: New American Library, expanded edition (1st edition 1956).

Kelly, Cynthia C. 2007. *The Manhattan Project: The Birth of the Atomic Bomb in the Words of Its Creators, Eyewitnesses, and Historians*. New York: Black Dog & Leventhal.

Kennedy, Rev. Dr. Andrew C. 2005. *Max Otto: Founder of Contemporary Humanism*. Milwaukee, WI: First Unitarian Society of Milwaukee.

Kerr, Clark. 2003. *The Gold and the Blue: A Personal Memoir of the University of California, 1949–1967*. Vol. 2. *Political Turmoil*. Berkeley: University of California Press.

Kim, Jaegwon. 1980. "Rorty on the Possibility of Philosophy." *Journal of Philosophy* 77, no. 10:589–97.

Klingberg, F. J., E. A. Lee, and E. T. Moore. *Ernest Moore in Memoriam*. http://texts.cdlib .org/view?docId=hb0w10035d&doc.view=frames&chunk.id=div00039&toc.depth =1&toc.id=div00039&toc.depth=1 (retrieved September 11, 2012).

Knight, F. H. 1947. "Ethics and Economic Reform." In *Freedom and Reform*, 45–128. New York: Harper and Bros.

Kracauer, Sigmund. 1995 *History: The Last Things before the Last*. Completed after the author's death by Paul Oskar Kristeller. Princeton, NJ: Markus Wiener. First published in 1969.

Krikorian, Yervant, ed. 1944a. *Naturalism and the Human Spirit*. New York: Columbia University Press.

———. 1944b. "A Naturalisic View of Mind." In Krikorian 1944a, 242–69.

Kripke, Saul. 1972. "Naming and Necessity." In *Semantics of Natural Language*, 2nd ed., edited by Donald Davidson and Gilbert Harmon. Dordrecht: Reidel.

Kruse, Kevin M. 2015. *One Nation under God: How Corporate America Invented Christian America*. New York: Basic Books.

Kuhn, Thomas S. 1957. *The Copernican Revolution*. Cambridge, MA: Harvard University Press.

———. 1970. *The Structure of Scientific Revolutions*. 2nd ed., enlarged. Chicago: University of Chicago Press. First published 1962.

Kuklick, Bruce. 2001. *A History of Philosophy in America* Oxford: Clarendon Press.

Lakatos, Imre, and Alan Musgrave, eds. 1970. *Criticism and the Growth of Knowledge*. Cambridge: Cambridge University Press.

Lamprecht, Sterling P. 1944. "Naturalism and Religion." In Krikorian 1944a, 17–39.

Lavine, Thelma Z. 1944. "Naturalism and the Sociological Analysis of Knowledge." In Krikorian 1944a, 183–209.

Lenstra, J., A. Kan, and A. Schrijver, eds. 1991. *History of Mathematical Programming*. Amsterdam: North Holland.

Leonard, Robert. 1995. "From Parlor Games to Social Science: von Neumann, Morgenstern, and the Creation of Game Theory, 1928–1944." *Journal of Economic Literature* 33, no. 2:730–61.

Lewis, David, 1969. *Convention: A Philosophical Study*. Cambridge, MA: Harvard University Press.

Lewis, Lionel. 1988. *Cold War on Campus*. New Brunswick, NJ: Transaction Press.

Litvak, Joseph. 2009. *The Un-Americans: Jews, the Blacklist, and Stool-Pigeon Culture*. Durham, NC: Duke University Press.

Lyon, E. Wilson. 1977. *The History of Pomona College, 1887–1969*. Published by Pomona College.

Maki, Uskali, ed. 2012. *Philosophy of Economics*. Vol. 13 of *Handbook of the Philosophy of Science*. Amsterdam: North Holland.

Marx, Karl. 1906. *Capital*. Translated by Samuel Morse and Edward Aveling. New York: Modern Library.

———. 1947. *The German Ideology*. Edited by C. J. Arthur. New York: Progress Publishers.

———. 1988. *Economic and Philosophic Manuscripts of 1844 and the Communist Manifesto*. Translated by Martin Milligan. Amherst, NY: Prometheus Books.

Masterman, Margaret. 1970. "The Nature of a Paradigm." In Lakatos and Musgrave 1970, 59–89.

McCarthy, George E., ed. 1992. *Marx and Aristotle: Nineteenth-Century German Social Theory and Classical Antiquity*. London: Rowman and Littlefield.

McCloskey, Deirdre N. 1998. *The Rhetoric of Economics*. 2nd ed. Madison: University of Wisconsin Press.

McCumber, John. 1993. *The Company of Words: Hegel, Language, and Systematic Philosophy*. Evanston, IL: Northwestern University Press.

———. 1999. *Metaphysics and Oppression: Heidegger's Challenge to Western Philosophy*. Bloomington: Indiana University Press.

———. 2000a *Philosophy and Freedom: Derrida, Rorty, Habermas, Foucault*. Bloomington: Indiana University Press.

———. 2000b. *Time in the Ditch: American Philosophy and the McCarthy Era*. Evanston, IL: Northwestern University Press (abbreviated *TD*).

———. 2004. *Reshaping Reason: Toward a New Philosophy*. Bloomington: Indiana University Press.

———. 2011. *Time and Philosophy*. Durham, NC: Acumen.

———. 2012. *On Philosophy: Notes from a Crisis*. Stanford, CA: Stanford University Press.

———. 2014. *Understanding Hegel's Mature Critique of* Kant. Stanford, CA: Stanford University Press.

McLachlan, James. 2006. "George Holmes Howison: 'The City of God' and Personal Idealism." *Journal of Speculative Philosophy*, n.s., 20, no. 3:224–42.

McMahon, Robert. 2003. *The Cold War*. Oxford: Oxford University Press.

Mele, Alfred R., and Piers Rawling, eds. 2004. *The Oxford Handbook of Rationality*. Oxford: Oxford University Press.

Melzer, Arthur. 2014. *Philosophy Between the Lines: The Lost History of Esoteric Writing*. Chicago: University of Chicago Press.

Menand, Louis. 2001. *The Metaphysical Club: A Story of Ideas in America*. New York: Farrar, Straus, and Giroux.

Meyerhoff, Hans. 1942. *Types of Ethical Premises*. Ph D diss., Department of Philosophy, UCLA, June 1942.

———. 1955. *Time in Literature*. Berkeley: University of California Press (abbreviated *TL*).

Milkov, Nikolai. 2013. "The Berlin Group and the Vienna Circle: Affinities and Divergences." In Milkov and Peckhaus 2013, 3–32.

Milkov, Nikolay, and Volker Peckhaus. 2013. *The Berlin Group and the Philosophy of Logical Empiricism*. Dordrecht: Springer Science & Business Media.

Miller, Dickinson S. 1975. *Philosophical Analysis and Human Welfare*. Edited by Lloyd D. Easton. Dordrecht: Reidel.

Miller, Hugh. 1939. *History and Science: A Study of the Relation of Historical and Theoretical Knowledge*. Berkeley: University of California Press.

Miller, Hugh, et al. *Hugh Miller in Memoriam*. Online at http://texts.cdlib.org/view?docId =hb9p300969&doc.view=frames&chunk.id=div00022&toc.depth=1&toc.id= (retrieved May 27, 2013).

Mirowski, Philip. 2002. *Machine Dreams: Economics Becomes a Cyborg Science*. Cambridge: Cambridge University Press.

———. 2005. "How Positivism Made a Pact with the Postwar Social Sciences in the United States." In Steinmetz 2005, 142–72.

———. n.d. "The Social Dimensions of Social Knowledge and Their Distant Echoes in Twentieth-Century American Philosophy of Science." Unpublished MS.

Mises, Ludwig von. 2009. *Liberty and Property*. Auburn, AL: von Mises Institute. Originally published 1958. Online at http://mises.org/books/liberty_and_property.pdf (accessed November 16, 2011).

Monk, Ray. 2001. *Bertrand Russell: 1921–1970, The Ghost of Madness*. New York: Free Press.

Moore, Ernest C. 1915. *What Is Education?* Boston: Ginn.

————.1937. "The Record of a Famous Course." *Journal of Higher Education* 8, no. 1 (January 1937): 54–55.

Munger, Frank.1950. "Academic Freedom Goes on Trial." *Daily Northwestern*, October 26, 1950.

Murphy, Franklin D. 1976. *My UCLA Chancellorship: An Utterly Candid View.* (Interview with James V. Mink.) Berkeley: Regents of the University of California.

Nash, Gary B., Julie R. Jeffrey, John R. Howe, et al., eds. 1990. *The American People.* 2nd. ed. New York: Harper & Row.

Neujahr, Phillip J. 1995. *Kant's Idealism.* Macon, GA: Mercer University Press.

Neumann, John von, and Oscar Morgenstern. 1947. *Theory of Games and Economic Behavior.* 2nd ed. Princeton, NJ: Princeton University Press.

Neurath, Otto. 1971. "Unified Science as Encyclopedic Integration." In Neurath, Carnap, and Morris 1971, 1–27.

Neurath, Otto, Rudolf Carnap, and Charles Morris, eds. 1971. *Foundations of the Unity of Science: Toward an Encyclopedia of Unified Science.* 2 vols. Chicago: University of Chicago Press.

Nietzsche, Friedrich. 1967. *The Will to Power.* Walter Kaufmann, ed. London: Weidenfield and Nicholson.

————. 1994. *On the Genealogy of Morality.* Translated by Carol Diethe. Cambridge: Cambridge University Press.

O'Donnell, James J. 2008. *The Ruin of the Roman Empire.* New York: HarperCollins.

Okasha, Samir. 2011. "Theory Choice and Social Choice: Kuhn vs. Arrow." *Mind* 120, no. 447:83–115.

Oppenheim, Paul, and Carl G. Hempel. 1936. *Der Typus im Lichte der neueren Logik.* Leiden: A. W. Sijthoff.

Oppenheim, Paul A., and Hilary Putnam. 1958. "The Unity of Science as a Working Hypothesis." In *Minnesota Studies in the Philosophy of Science.* Vol. 2. Edited by H. Feigl, Michael Scriven, and Grover Maxwell. Minneapolis: Minnesota University Press (abbreviated *US*).

Parrini, Paolo, Wesley Salmon, and Merrilee Salmon, eds. 2003. *Logical Empiricism: Historical and Contemporary Perspectives.* Pittsburgh, PA: University of Pittsburgh Press.

Piatt, Donald A. (1939) 1951. "John Dewey's Logical Theory." In Schilpp 1951, 105–34.

Piatt, Donald A., Caolyn S. Fisher, and Waldemar Westergaard. 1950. "John Elof Boodin in Memoriam." Online at http://texts.cdlib.org/view?docId=hb9g5008vb&doc.view=frames&chunk.id=div00001&toc.depth=1&toc.id=&brand=calisphere (retrieved September 11, 2012).

Popper, Karl. 1950. *The Open Society and Its Enemies,* Princeton, NJ: Princeton University Press.

Putnam, Hilary. 1981. "Two Conceptions of Rationality." In *Reason Truth and History,* 103–26. Cambridge: Cambridge University Press.

Quine, W. V. O. 1953a. "Mr. Strawson on Logical Theory" *Mind* 62, no. 248:433–51.

————. 1953b. "Two Dogmas of Empiricism." In *From a Logical Point of View,* 20–46. New York: Harper Torchbooks.

————. 1960. *Word and Object.* Cambridge, MA: MIT Press.

————. 1969a. "Epistemology Naturalized." In Quine 1969b, 60–90.

———. 1969b. *Ontological Relativity and Other Essays*. New York: Columbia University Press.

———. 1969c. "Speaking of Objects." In Quine 1969b, 1–25.

Randall, John Herman, Jr. 1960. *Aristotle*. New York: Columbia University Press.

Ravven, Heidi . 2103. *The Self Beyond Itself*. New York: New Press.

Rawls, John. 1971. *A Theory of Justice*. Cambridge, MA: Belknap Press of Harvard University Press.

———. 1985. "Justice as Fairness: Political Not Metaphysical." *Philosophy and Public Affairs* 14, no. 3:223–51.

Rayman, Joshua. 2010. "Entrenched: A Genealogy of the Analytical-Continental Divide." *Radical Philosophy Review* 13, no. 2:107–34.

Reichenbach, Hans. 1938. *Experience and Prediction*. Chicago: University of Chicago Press.

———. 1951. *The Rise of Scientific Philosophy*. Berkeley: University of California Press (abbreviated *RSP*).

———. 1959a. "Aims and Methods of Modern Philosophy of Nature." In Reichenbach 1959c, 79–108. First published in 1931.

———. 1959b. "Causality and Probability." In Reichenbach 1959c, 67–78. First published in 1931.

———. 1959c. *Modern Philosophy of Science*. Translated and edited by Maria Reichenbach, 79–108. London: Routledge and Kegan Paul. First published in 1931.

———. 1959d. "The Principle of Causality and the Possibility of Its Empirical Confirmation." In Reichenbach 1959c, 109–34. First published in 1932.

Reisch, George. 2005. *How the Cold War Transformed Philosophy of Science: To the Icy Slopes of Logic*. Cambridge: Cambridge University Press.

———. 2007. "From the 'Life of the Present' to the 'Icy Slope of Logic': Logical Empiricism, the Unity of Science Movement, and the Cold War." In Richardson and Uebel 2007, 58–87.

Rescher, Nicholas. 2005a. *Collected Papers: Studies in Twentieth-Century Philosophy*. 4 vols. Berlin: de Gruyter.

———. 2005b. "Logicians at RAND." In Rescher 2005a, 181–207.

———. 2006. "The Berlin School of Logical Empiricism and Its Legacy." *Erkenntnis* 64, no. 3:281–304.

Richardson, Alan. 1997. "Toward a History of Scientific Philosophy." *Perspectives on Science* 5m no. 3:418–51.

———. 2005. "Reichenbach's Disease and Mirowski's Theory of Knowledge; or, Will to Power as Philosophy of Science." *Studies in the History and Philosophy of Science* 36 (December 2005) 744–53.

———. 2007. "Carnapian Pragmatism." In Friedman and Creath 2007, 295–315.

———. Richardson, Alan, and Thomas Uebel, eds. 2007. *The Cambridge Companion to Logical Empiricism*. Cambridge: Cambridge University Press.

———. Rorty, Richard. 1979. *Philosophy and the Mirror of Nature*. Princeton, NJ: Princeton University Press.

———. 1982a. *Consequences of Pragmatism*. Minneapolis: University of Minnesota Press.

———. 1982b. "Philosophy in America Today." In Rorty 1982a, 211–30.

———. 1982c. "Professionalized Philosophy and Transcendentalist Culture." In Rorty 1982a, 60–71.

———. 1991a. *Essays on Heidegger and Others*. Cambridge: Cambridge University Press.

———. 1991b. "Philosophy as Science, as Metaphor, and as Politics." In Rorty 1991a, 9–26. First published 1986.

Russell, Bertrand. 1957. *Why I Am Not a Christian*. New York: Simon and Schuster.

Ryckman, Thomas. 2003. "Two Roads from Kant: Carnap, Reichenbach, and General Relativity." In Parrini, W. Salmon, and M. Salmon 2003, 159–93.

Salisbury, Harrison E. 1959. "Nixon and Khrushchev Argue in Public as U. S. Exhibit Opens; Accuse Each Other of Threats" *New York Times*, July 24, 1959.

Sanders, Jane. 1979. *Cold War on the Campus: Academic Freedom at the University of Washington, 1946–62*. Seattle: University of Washington Press.

Saner, Hans. 1973. *Kant's Political Thought: Its Origins and Development*. Translated by E. B. Ashton. Chicago: University of Chicago Press.

Sartre, Jean-Paul. 2001. *Basic Writings*. Edited by Stephen Priest. London: Routledge.

Sayer, Jamie. 1985. *Einstein in America*. New York: Crown.

Scharff, Robert C. 1995. *Comte After Positivism*. Cambridge: Cambridge University Press.

Schilpp, Paul Arthur, ed. 1951. *The Philosophy of John Dewey*. New York: Tudor. First published 1939.

Schook, John R. 2005. *Directory of American Philosophers*. London: Thoemmes.

Schrecker, Ellen. 1986. *No Ivory Tower: McCarthyism and the Universities*. Oxford: Oxford University Press.

———. 1994. *The Age of McCarthyism: A Brief History with Documents*. Boston: Medford/St. Martin's.

———. 1998. *Many Are the Crimes*. Princeton, NJ: Princeton University Press.

Schulz, William F. 2002. *Making the Manifesto: The Birth of Religious Humanism*. Boston: Unitarian Universalist Association of Congregations.

Sen, Amartya. 1979. "Personal Utilities and Public Judgment; or, What's Wrong with Welfare Economics." *Economic Journal* 89, no. 355:537–58.

Sent, Esther Mirjam. 2007. "Some Like It Cold: Thomas Schelling as a Cold Warrior." *Journal of Economic Methodology* 14, no. 4:455–71.

Shapley, Deborah. 1993. *Promise and Power: The Life and Times of Robert McNamara*. Boston: Little, Brown.

Sheldon, W. H. 1945. "Critique of Naturalism." *Journal of Philosophy* 42, no. 10:253–70.

Smith, Adam. (1790) 2000. *The Theory of Moral Sentiments*. London, A. Miller.

Soames, Scott. 2003. *Philosophical Analysis in the Twentieth Century*. 2. vols. Princeton, NJ: Princeton University Press.

Sokal, Alan, and Jean Bricmont. 1998. *Fashionable Nonsense: Postmodern Intellectuals' Abuse of Science*. New York: Picador.

Somers, Margaret R. 1998. " 'We're No Angels': Realism, Rational Choice, and Relationality in Social Science." *American Journal of Sociology* 104:722–84.

Starr, Kevin. 2002. *Embattled Dreams: California in War and Peace, 1940–1950*. Oxford: Oxford University Press.

Steinmetz, George, ed. 2005. *The Politics of Method in the Social Sciences*. Durham, NC: Duke University Press.

Storrs, Landon R. F. Y. 2013. *The Second Red Scare and the Unmaking of the New Deal Left*. Princeton, NJ: Princeton University Press.

Students for a Democratic Society. 1970. "The Port Huron Statement." In Dewey and Gould 1970, 368–74.

Taylor, Harold. 1952. "The Education of Individuals." In Burkhardt 1952, 150–64.

Thagard, Paul. 1978. "Why Astrology Is a Pseudoscience." In *Philosophy of Science Association I*, edited by P. D. Asquith and I. Hacking, 223–34. East Lansing, MI: Philosophy of Science Association.

Tocqueville, Alexis de. 1969. *Democracy in America*. Edited by J. P. Mayer; translated by George Lawrence. New York: Doubleday Anchor.

Toulouse, Mark. 1993. "Christianity Today and American Public Life: A Case Study." *Journal of Church and State* 35, no. 2:241–84.

UCLA. "Past Leaders: Raymond Allen, 1952–1959." Online at http://www.pastleaders.ucla\.edu/allen.html (retrieved September 10, 2015).

Uebel, Thomas. 2007. "Philosophy of Social Science in Early Logical Positivism." In Richardson and Uebel 2007, 250–76.

University of California. "In Memoriam." Online at http://www.lib.berkeley.edu/uchistory/archives_exhibits/in_memoriam/nameindex/nameindex_a.html (retrieved September 10, 2015).

Vickery, William. 1960. "Utility, Strategy, and Social Decision Rules." *Quarterly Journal of Economics* 74, no. 4:507–35.

Wald, Kenneth D. 1994. "The Religious Dimension of American Anti-Communism." *Journal of Church and State* 36:483–506.

Weiler, Kathleen. 2007. "The Case of Martha Deane: Sexuality and Politics at Cold War UCLA." *History of Education Quarterly* 47:470–96.

"What Is It Like to Be a Woman in Philosophy?" Online at https://beingawomaninphilosophy.wordpress.com/ (accessed August 25, 2015).

Whitman, Walt. 1993. *Leaves of Grass*. New York: Modern Library. First published 1855.

Wieman, Henry, Douglas Clyde Mackintosh, and Max Carl Otto. 1932. *Is There a God?* Chicago: Willett Clark.

Williams, Michael. 1995. *Unnatural Doubts*. Princeton, NJ: Princeton University Press.

Williamson, Timothy. 2014. "How Did We Get Here from There? The Transformation of Analytical Philosophy." *Belgrade Philosophical Annual* 27:7–37. Online at http://www.f.bg.ac.rs/bpa/pdf/BPA-27-2014-Timothy-Williamson.pdf (accessed March 12, 2015).

Wills, Garry. 2007. "At Ease, Mr. President" *New York Times*, op-ed, January 27.

———. 2010. *Bomb Power*. New York: Penguin.

Wilshire, Bruce. 1985. "The Pluralist Rebellion in the American Philosophical Association: Eastern Division, 1978–1985." Unpublished MS.

Wilson, Patrick G. 2000. *Philosopher of Information: An Eclectic Imprint on Berkeley's School of Librarianship, 1965–1991*. Interviews conducted by Laura McCreery. Berkeley: Regents of the University of California, Berkeley oral history program.

Withers, R. F. J. 1952. Review of *The Rise of Scientific Philosophy*, by Hans Reichenbach. *British Journal for the Philosophy of Science* 2, no. 8:334–37.

Wittgenstein, Ludwig. 1958. *Philosophical Investigations*. Translated by G. E. M. Anscombe. 3rd ed. New York: Macmillan.

Wolff, Jonathan. 2013. "How Can We End the Male Domination of Philosophy?" *Guardian*, November 26, 2013. Online at http://www.theguardian.com/education/2013/nov/26/modern-philosophy-sexism-needs-more-women (accessed July 21, 2015).

Ziche, Paul, and Thomas Müller. 2013. "Paul Oppenheim on Order: The Career of a Philosophical Concept." In Milkov and Peckhaus 2013, 265–90.

INDEX

Abella, Alex, 73, 75
academic community, 169; attacks on, 16; Cold War effects on, 17; confidentiality, penchant for, 1–2; programs, proliferation of, 170
academic "stealth," 25–26, 31–32, 35–37, 47, 182n29, 185n25
Afghanistan, 76
Agamben, Giorgio, 8, 34
Alamogordo (New Mexico), 6
Allen, Raymond B., 129, 139–40, 143–45, 154, 156, 158, 165, 169, 192n4, 192n11, 193n13, 193n16, 193n19, 193n20; background of, 136–37; California Plan, supporter of, 138; as contact man, 136–37, 150; liberals, hiring of, 151
Allen Formula, 136–38, 140–41, 164, 166, 170; and California Plan, 150; Cold War philosophy, 150, 153, 157; Communists, and due process, 145–47, 149; Communists, firing of, 142–44, 150, 152; objectivity of, 142–45; rational choice theory (RCT), allied with, 152; scientific philosophy, allied with, 152; success of, 152–53; tenets of, 148–49, 152
alternatives, 82–83, 85; as feasible, 84; as fixed, 84; as mutually exclusive, 84; as objective, 84

Amadae, S. M., 12, 71, 73, 75–76, 82
American Philosophical Association, xi
American philosophy: as otherworldly, 186n3; as pluralistic, 9
analytical philosophy, 56–57, 158
Anderson, Donald, 138
anti-Communism hysteria, 16; targets of, 19–20, 22
anti-Semitism, 20
Aquinas, Thomas, 120, 166
Arendt, Hannah, 1, 34
Aristotle, 6, 59, 71, 194n18; clash-of-standpoints model of, 165–66; dialectical method of, 164; syllogism, definition of, 78–79
Arrow, Kenneth, 9, 72, 75–78, 81–82, 84–89, 94, 96, 113, 118, 135, 168, 187n15, 187n24, 188n7, 187n28; consumer sovereignty, 101, 109; imposition and dictatorship, 80, 100
atheism, xii, xiii, 11, 20, 44, 47, 56, 68, 181n27, 182n29; and "atheistic row," xi; as evil, 27; existentialism, association with, 34; fear of, 71; and naturalism, 33, 35; and philosophy, 26–27
Athens (Greece), 186n8
atomic bomb, 21, 181n20; Trinity Test, 17
Ayer, A. J., 57, 59, 68, 97, 118–19